J Hennessy 02 (signature)

W9-BZX-856

CHARLES PELLEGRINO
GHOSTS OF THE TITANIC

"Pellegrino is a spellbinding storyteller."
Los Angeles Times Book Review

"The *Titanic* is to the sea what the Civil War is to war:
a story of which we apparently cannot get our
fill . . . [Pellegrino] brings a fresh perspective to the
story, and it produces some interesting insights."
Washington Post Book Review

"Charles Pellegrino has raised the Titanic—
at least in my imagination."
Stephen King

"Pellegrino writes with . . . real authority . . . The
answers that Pellegrino proposes are in some cases
ingenious and in all cases interesting."
Chicago Sun-Times

"Splendid. Absolutely splendid."
William MacQuitty, Producer of *A Night to Remember*

"[His] fresh re-creation of the *Titanic*'s final
hours provides an eerie and astonishing adventure,
a time capsule gracefully wrapped in elegant prose,
deserving a place alongside Walter Lord's classic
A Night to Remember."
Publishers Weekly (*Starred Review*)

Also by Charles Pellegrino

TIME GATE
HER NAME, TITANIC
RETURN TO SODOM AND GOMORRAH
UNEARTHING ATLANTIS

FLYING TO VALHALLA (fiction)
THE KILLING STAR
with George Zebrowski (fiction)
DUST (fiction)

with Jesse Stoff
DARWINS UNIVERSE
CHRONIC FATIGUE SYNDROME

with Joshua Stoff
CHARIOTS FOR APOLLO

*with James Powell and
Isaac Asimov*
INTERSTELLAR TRAVEL AND
COMMUNICATION

CHARLES PELLEGRINO

GHOSTS
OF THE
TITANIC

AVON BOOKS

An Imprint of HarperCollinsPublishers

To Michel Navatril, Jr., Walter Lord, Bill MacQuitty,
Bob Ballard, George and Matt Tulloch,
and James Cameron—friends and explorers.
Each, in his own way, is remembering the *Titanic* tonight.
Each, in his own way, is laying the music to rest.

AVON BOOKS
An Imprint of HarperCollins*Publishers*
10 East 53rd Street
New York, New York 10022-5299

Copyright © 2000 by Charles Pellegrino
Illustrations by Charles Pellegrino
ISBN: 0-380-72472-3
www.avonbooks.com

First Avon Books paperback printing: July 2001
First William Morrow hardcover printing: July 2000

Avon Trademark Reg. U.S. Pat. Off. and in Other Countries, Marca
Registrada, Hecho en U.S.A.
HarperCollins ® is a registered trademark of HarperCollins Publishers
Inc.

Printed in the U.S.A.

10 9 8 7 6 5 4 3 2 1

Contents

• Foreword •

It was sad when the great ship went down, as the folk song says, and in the eighty-eight years since, the sinking of *Titanic* has continued to fascinate the human mind and tug the heart like few other events in history.

In those eighty-eight years, the human race has increased by over four billion souls, and profound changes to the fundamental rules of our existence have been wrought by advances in technology. The harnessing of nuclear energy has brought us to the brink of a precipice from which we may yet not escape, and the revolution in information technology has changed our world forever. From our current vantage point at the end of this remarkable century, we can view the *Titanic* disaster as a kind of Cassandran prophecy, a foreshadowing of the perils to come that would result from our collective hubris and blind faith in technology.

Some people connected with the story of *Titanic* on a purely human level, fascinated by the individuals on board and their ultimate fates as survivors or victims. But most surely relate to the event as a kind of parable, a cautionary tale, even a kind of morality play. Reams and reams of profound analysis have been written about this event, and it has become a kind of lens through which almost any social, political, moral, or psychological issue can be viewed, and through which all manner of viewpoints and theories can be projected.

I have heard it said that the *Titanic* story ranks third on the list of events about which the most has been written, behind the life of Christ and the death of JFK. If this is true, and it seems likely as I gaze over the rows of shelves stuffed full with my own research materials, then what is there to say that hasn't been said?

Plenty. And this book is the proof. The thing that continues to amaze me about *Titanic* is that her story grows constantly more complex and fascinating as new details emerge. Like a fractal, the *Titanic* reveals pattern upon pattern in an infinite regression as you move deeper and deeper into the story. What Charlie Pellegrino has managed to do once again is to create connections and reveal patterns which have eluded other eyes. His journey is a journey of the mind, which can travel instantaneously through time and space, from the night of the sinking to the wreck as she lies now on the sea floor, from the rusticle colonies inside *Titanic*'s disintegrating corridors back through time to the dawn of life and outward to Jupiter's moon Europa and the possibility of hydrothermal vent communities there. He cross-pollinates in flourishes of lateral thinking among the sciences of archaeology, biology, and geology.

But his journey is also a journey of the heart, and of the human spirit, as he follows a number of individuals on their paths through that hellish night, and puts us behind their eyes as witnesses to the disaster. For all its power as a metaphor and a parable, the *Titanic* disaster is ultimately the story of people. People who died that night, and people who lived on with memories and emotions difficult to convey to those of us who have never experienced cataclysm.

A true forensic study of the final hours of *Titanic* has been needed for some time, as theories have abounded and many have been accepted as fact throughout the years. Recent evidence and observations, carefully cross-referenced with a new look at old testimony and correspondence, is yielding some surprising insights into what really happened and in exactly what sequence. With the precision of an archaeological dig, the onion of *Titanic*'s mystery can be peeled back carefully to reveal the truth, or at least a better and more complete approximation of truth than has ever existed before.

But forensic precision can yield only a certain kind of truth, because archaeology is about people . . . what they built, how they lived and died, their hopes and dreams and all the complex pageantry of their lives. Let this book be your archaeological window on the historical event, a window which reveals not only much about the times but about the individuals who lived and breathed that history.

—James Cameron
April, 2000

                    . . . on the sand,
Half sunk, a shattered visage lies . . .
And on the pedestal these words appear:
"My name is Ozymandias, king of kings:
"Look on my works, ye Mighty, and despair!"
Nothing beside remains. Round the decay
Of that colossal wreck, boundless and bare
The lone and level sands stretch far away.
                        —*Shelley,* OZYMANDIAS

1

•

Thoughts for a Countdown

•

If you haven't found something strange during the day, it
hasn't been much of a day.

—JOHN ARCHIBALD WHEELER

AND YOU MAY ask me, why do I not believe in psychic events?

How can I not believe? you may ask, given what I have
seen, what I have learned.

And it occurs to me that I cannot provide an adequate
answer, because I do not believe the proper words exist for
me to explain my agnosticism. You cannot know, therefore,
and neither, it seems, can I.

What I do know is that odd coincidence, or synchronicity—call it what you will—has always surrounded the *Titanic*. And it has surrounded me, too, ever since the *Titanic*.

In the summer of 1985, I was a space scientist and paleontologist (or, as paleontologist Stephen Jay Gould once put
it, "an astronomer who occasionally looks down"). At that
time, no one in the world could have seemed farther from
the *Titanic*. In fact, most of my work was out of this world—
way out of it, way past Mars. I had, with my childhood
friend and fellow astrobiologist Jesse Stoff, proposed models for ice world interiors that were leading to the discovery
of new oceans beneath the crusts of Jupiter's moons
Ganymede and Europa, and Saturn's moons Titan and Ence-

ladus. The *Voyager II* spacecraft was supporting our models, and was flying on past Titan and Enceladus toward an encounter with the cryovolcanoes of Triton, but it saddened me that Jesse could not be with me at the Jet Propulsion Laboratory. About three years earlier, he had abandoned our ice world studies, literally in midstride, so that he could fly away to London and try to figure out how the human immune system evolved. Along the way, he focused attention on a rare genetic disorder. By coincidence, I was tracing this same genetic marker back through the origins of all the modern human races, following a trail of aberrant DNA as if it were a trail of footprints (and all the genetic roads were leading back to Africa, about 120,000 years ago). By coincidence, this same genetic trail—the entire gene complex—had turned up in my own blood, and was waiting to hatch out. And by sheer coincidence, Jesse had discovered treatments for this same genetic condition, even as I bemoaned his departure from the space program and into medicine, and said as much in the preface to a report titled, "Extraterrestrial Life: New Hope in our Own Solar System."

The words *ankylosing spondylitis* describe a condition in which the immune system becomes overly active, attacking cells that belong to "self" with as much vigor as those that belong to "non-self." It is similar in its effects to the graft-versus-host disease commonly seen as a result of bone marrow transplants, and when kept under control (or even when deliberately induced, and controlled via the emerging technology of immunogenetics), the disease becomes a powerful ally against other diseases, particularly cancer. When out of control, however, it can trigger a biological chain reaction that maims, and occasionally kills.

In July 1985, the disease aimed to kill me. My doctor in New York told me I should put my affairs in order. To judge from the rate of deterioration he was witnessing, he predicted that I would have "a short autumn."

Then Jesse showed up at my door—the only person I know of who, at that time, just happened to have a magic bullet sitting in his lab.

I got better.

My doctor died.

And then I received a call from Bob Ballard. By coincidence, he had been reading a book by Jesse and me in which we discussed the possibility of oceans inside ice worlds, and described the sorts of robots that might one day be sent to probe them. By yet another emerging coincidence, Bob had been building deep-ocean robots directly ancestral to the ones Jesse and I had described. One of them had just found the *Titanic*, and Bob had his next expedition already in mind. He wanted to know if I would be interested in joining him.

"Oooh, this can't be happening," my father said, when I told him of the call. It was just as I had said it would be, two months earlier, when I was so sick and dog tired that I lived what I was coming to call "koala bear days"— twenty-hour naps, almost comatose. And during those koala days I did a very strange thing, when Dad and I look back upon it now and come to consider that in July 1985 I had never even read the Walter Lord classic, *A Night to Remember*. During my few waking hours I somehow managed to construct a little white model of the *Titanic*, properly ballasted with some of its watertight compartments built in. I shut off the filter and pumps in my parents' swimming pool and sprinkled the water with the same red dust I had used in the laboratory to reveal patterns of circulation around the siphons of clams and octopi.

Each time I sank the ship, I watched very carefully the slipstream of dust that trailed behind it. After the model came to a sudden stop on the bottom, the dust spread out over a radius at least as large as the ship's length, in great cauliflower billows.

"Downblast," I had called it.

"Why are you doing this?" my father had asked. Of the very few hours I could remain awake, I spent an inordinate number sinking a toy boat in a swimming pool, and the water at one end was beginning to resemble blood. It was inexplicable to Dad and I was scaring the neighbors.

"Why this?" he demanded.

My father got his answer, which on first hearing, at that time, answered nothing. Yet when regarded from time present, it produces an illusion (albeit a stubborn one) of having answered all.

"They're out there, right now," I said absently. "They're searching for the *Titanic*. And I'm going to be part of that."

At that moment, the French research vessel *Le Suroit* was criss-crossing the *Titanic*'s last known coordinates with a new deep-search sonar. An American vessel, the *Knorr*, was steaming toward *Le Suroit* with Bob Ballard, Tom Dettweiler, and a new deep-sea robot named *Argo*. I had no way of knowing any of this. The expedition, which included a detailed robot reconnaissance of the sunken nuclear submarine *Scorpion*, was classified. "Top Secret." The whole mission.

THE FIRST THING Bob Ballard noticed, when he reached the *Titanic*'s stern, was that the hull appeared to have been simultaneously stamped flat, ripped open, and scattered in pieces along a radius exceeding its length, as though a mighty fist had pounded down from above, as though someone had exploded a small atomic bomb over the very center of the stern.

One of the last things Bob Ballard said to me, as we stood with the robot *Argo* on the fantail of the *Melville*, was that a curse went along with the *Titanic*, and with all who would touch her, from that day on.

I thought he was joking, of course. (I'm sorry for that now.)

"Sometimes she makes you very sad," he warned me. "She touches something in you, and you've begun to touch back."

That was late December, 1985, and *still* I had not read *A Night to Remember*. Yet Bob told me, even before it became a possibility, that I was going to write a book about "that ship." He handed me two small pieces of metal from *Argo*—souvenirs from the robot's collision with the *Titanic* three months before. "These are your touchstones," he said. "For your book."

And he warned me that the *Titanic* would soon sink as deep into my life as it had into the bed of the Atlantic. He told me I would be married to her, and that there would be no divorcing her, ever.

No, I don't believe in premonition, but if there is any one human being I have known who has been gifted and cursed with that kind of magic, it is Bob Ballard.

When I arrived home, just ahead of New Year's Day, 1986, my microscope revealed a tiny piece of *Titanic* herself embedded in one of the *Argo* fragments Bob had dropped into my palm. I put the *Argo-Titanic* sample in an envelope I had seen placed aboard a space shuttle during the summer of 1983. At the time, the envelope seemed a proper place for the sample, for no reason that I can recall today; to this day, it remains in that same envelope.[1]

---

[1] I had pointed out to Bob Ballard that international salvage law required only that he recover a piece of the wreck in order to claim site ownership, with absolutely no specification on how large that piece ought to be. He agreed that by the letter of the law, I could argue that he had indeed made the very first recovery of *Titanic* metal, and that even a microscopic fragment gave him (and the Woods Hole Oceanographic Institute) exclusive ownership of the wreck site (this would have required, however, that he return to the site at regular intervals; otherwise it would revert to "abandoned" status). "Only you and I know about this [micro-fragment]," he said. "Now, forget about it." And thus did Bob Ballard become the only person I have ever known who said he would never go back to *Titanic*, and who actually followed through.

Bob Ballard knew, at that time, that I was not satisfied merely to design space probes and see them flung into the far sky. He knew I hoped to actually go out there myself. He knew that Grumman President George Skurla and *Apollo 13* astronaut Fred Haise had recommended me for a seat on the shuttle, and he knew precisely which ship I hoped to fly in—the one I had watched being assembled in her cradle; the one that had carried the envelope and brought me to my knees in tears the night she was launched, the night the mist and the clouds—which had threatened to halt the launch—parted just long enough to reveal the moon, and the ship crossing directly in front of it, as if to signal to us in the present a vivid flash of the world yet to come.

I knew that ship, every inch of her, in and out: the pumping pressures, the exhaust velocities, the power and the beauty of her. I thought I knew exactly what I would see and feel, long before I watched her fly. But the mere act of knowing did not prepare me. When I returned to my room, I wrote:

Watching that great ship fly up, and up, and up against the night was an awakening, a vivid flash of something like God, something more powerful than nature itself. And it is us.

And we know. We who have seen.

Those were the words Bob Ballard called to my attention, while we were still out at sea, before I returned home and placed pieces of *Argo* and *Titanic* in an envelope from the rocketship *Challenger*—which would soon have more in common with the *Titanic* than the mere fact that no ship would ever again bear her name. Bob said that the words I had written during the *Challenger* flight were, to him, an echo from the past: "Not even God himself could sink this ship." He saw in my words the same fatal arrogance, "this time infecting the space program," that had made men believe they could run the *Titanic* at full steam through the dark into an ice field they knew lay directly ahead. He saw a generation of "young Turks" who did not remember the *Titanic*, and who were beginning to push nature too far. And nature, he saw, was about to push back.

He told me I was going to see a *Titanic* in space, far sooner than anyone believed possible. "And the reason it's going to happen," he warned, "is that none of you believe it will."

The *Challenger*. Only four weeks later, she was gone.

Two weeks after that, I began writing a book about the *Titanic*, just as Bob had said I would, part penance (for my arrogance), part exorcism (for my ignorance). And when I finished, I vowed in the last sentence of my preface[2] that I would never come back to this subject. Ever again.

49° 56' 49" west longitude, 41° 43' 57" north latitude; research vessel *Ocean Voyager*, August 13, 1996, 11:30 A.M.

Moth to the flame. That's what you can call me.

How else did I get here—again?

We have just arrived on site and the captain is blowing the ship's siren to signal that we are in a place of lost souls and I've had to find a place on the B deck where I can stand alone and unseen yet at the same time face the open sea. Tears. Damned tears, again.

At the moment of rendezvous, it is instinct that chooses my words for me, and I whisper them automatically, unable to understand why there seems nothing else to say:

"Hello, old friend."

---

[2]Owing to an unexpected visit from my friends Karen and Patrick Lagudi, completion of the last paragraph was pushed back more than two hours, to 2:20 A.M., April 15, 1987, exactly 75 years to the minute from the time the *Titanic*'s stern disappeared.

The thought catches me off guard. *Old friend.*

It's not a grave this time. This time, I won't find only death out here. This time, it's going to be different.

Right, Charlie. Convince yourself of that, as you try to rouse yourself, senses sharpened, and gaze out across one of the most haunting and haunted bodies of water on Earth. Convince yourself that two and one-half miles below, the "gray lady" is just another archaeological site, just another expedition.

(". . . Just another Belfast trip." So had one of the surviving stewards spoken to his friends after the first rumblings from the iceberg. "It's just a ride back to the H&W Shipyard for repairs—and plenty of free time for us all ashore." If history serves me correctly, Steward James Johnson's friends are still permanent residents of RMS *Titanic*.)

No, I've known too many of the *Titanic*'s survivors to be convinced that this is just another archaeological site. To the generation of explorers who will come after me, the bridge and the crew quarters and stateroom C-86 will no longer exist in that gray area between oral history and archaeology. But for me it is impossible to think of the shattered stern as an ancient Theran graveyard of forgotten rooms whose people have turned to dust.

Because I became acquainted with people who still remembered those rooms, after I sailed with Bob Ballard, *Titanic*'s rusticle-shrouded corridors remain part of a vibrant civilization whose dining saloon chairs still have people in them, whose architect still sits at his work table in stateroom A-36, whose passengers still have names and faces, just a few steps away in the past.

Eva . . . Marjorie . . . Louise . . . Frank . . . old friends, all. And all gone, now. They were here, that night—here on this very spot, in the lifeboats.

They come again, unexpected words bubbling up from

the subconscious: *Take care of Mommy. Be a good girl and stay close to Mommy. You'll be back aboard before breakfast* . . . the same words that went through eight-year-old Eva's mind, over and over in the lifeboat, after the stern had vanished, taking her father with it, leaving her with the only lie he ever told her.

A part of me feels as if I have just been given a shining glimpse into the soul of a little girl, though she was a retired magistrate by the time I met her. A part of me feels, at the same moment, like an intruder into her life, and this is a power that no other wreck site—no buried Minoan port, no Egyptian tomb—has over me. On the volcanic isle of Martinique in 1902, a city of thirty thousand people died with the steamship *Roraima*; with the buried city of Thera, in the autumn of 1628 B.C., an entire civilization passed into legend. Those places were awe and wonder and a sense of mystery to me (in other words, the substance of archaeology). The *Titanic* is all of these, too, but there is something else here, something that sneaks up and grabs you when you turn your back.

At this instant, it's Eva's teddy bear. She told me how she used to play with it on the deck with her father. The bear was taller than she was, and I know that it cannot possibly be resting where she last saw it, on her bed in a stateroom on E deck aft, because that region of the stern is so violently torn up that the bear, if it exists at all, must be little more than out-jetted shreds of fabric. It was a beautiful bear, by Eva's account. She never had another one. She never wanted another one.

And it comes again, that ghostly feeling of being unstuck in time; and the brain actually is a time machine, of sorts. A three-pound time machine. We are the only species that can touch a piece of fabric and share, with its owner, vivid recollections of what was happening almost a week ago today, or almost a century ago. Louise Pope once enclosed with a letter a strand of wool from the mouse-chewed blanket she wore that night. When I stand here, thinking of Louise, I imagine the lights of my own ship, the *Ocean Voyager*, gone, and nothing except starlight by which to see. Louise told me that she was only four years old in 1912. She should have been too young to remember, but to her dying day she was unable to look even at a mere painting of a star-lit sea (much less the star-lit Atlantic itself) without recalling the profound loneliness of April 15 and bursting immediately into tears. She said there was a feeling of childlike serenity and companionship, even in the midst of adult fear and jostling, that the brightly lit *Titanic* gave and which no lifeboat could reproduce. And so it is the lifeboats that my mind travels back to, the moment I arrive on site. Always the lifeboats, and the swimmers, with the *Titanic* gone.

And from their conversations, their letters, and their diaries, it is possible to know what they were thinking out here, out amongst the lifeboats.

There was much to think about. For Second Officer Charles Lightoller, as he hauled himself onto the keel of an overturned raft, there was the sudden realization, "None of this is going to look good for my career." The possibility that he might soon freeze to death had not yet occurred to him.

First-class passenger William Carter, a notorious playboy, had the disquieting knowledge that he had been caught in the act of ushering his mistress onto a lifeboat— by Mrs. Carter. He expected that if the entire triangle survived the night, he was due for some "really interesting times" when he reached New York.

Fireman George Kemish, as he swam an olympic mile toward the ghostly white outline of boat number eleven, glanced back to where the *Titanic* had been and wondered what became of the kindly stowaways living near William Carter's Renault town car and amongst crates of ostrich feathers in the forward cargo hold—which had flooded the moment the hull met the ice. He knew little about them, except that they were "world-wanderers"—young, penniless adventurers who were always welcomed by men like Kemish because in return for keeping their presence a secret, they kept the lower-ranking crews' quarters clean. The fireman was certain that the "bow people" had become the *Titanic*'s very first casualties, and he regretted that no one would ever know who they were.

Assistant Purser Frank Prentice had just set the world record for the high dive, dropping more than 120 feet in an adrenaline-driven attempt to save his friend, Ricks. He did not feel like a gold medalist, however. Leaping from a wooden sign that warned, in bold black letters, STAY CLEAR OF PROPELLERS, he had narrowly missed two blades on the way down. He struck the water with a bang that kicked every cubic inch of air out of his lungs and cracked his vocal cords. Ricks was not so lucky; he had pounded down on a floating slab of wood and was only semiconscious by the time Frank found him. Now, with the ship gone, and with something akin to distant cannon shots reverberating up from the sea floor and rattling his ribs (and also rattling the floorboards of boat number four), hundreds of people swam and wailed, and sobbed, and moaned, and prayed. Someone was shouting, "Stay together. We have more chance of being picked up if we stay together." But the shouter's calls soon weakened and died. Then Ricks died. Then the purser began to wonder what had become of poor Mrs. Ada Clark, who was refusing to leave her husband the last time he saw her. Was she in a boat, and saved? Or was she amongst the swimmers, and dying?

Mrs. John Jacob Astor thought she heard her husband

calling to her and stood up to holler that boat number four was "coming back as fast as hell!" But the passengers in the boat, among them Mrs. William Carter, overruled her, and ordered her to sit down and be quiet, lest she "attract a hundred swimmers and sink us all." Mrs. Washington Dodge became so embittered by the refusal of her fellow castaways to row in the direction of the wails and the sobs, the prayers for deliverance and the pleas for help, that she swore to Mrs. Carter and to everyone else aboard that if another lifeboat happened by, she intended to leave them all in midocean. As if on cue, number seven approached, and she decided to make good her promise.

In boat number two, Mrs. Walter Douglas had just become heir apparent to the Quaker Oats fortune, but she would gladly have cast all of her husband's wealth into the sea if only she could create magic and know that one of the boats would find him, and pull him out alive. She sat on the stern, maintaining her composure, tending the rudder for Officer Boxhall as she listened to the lap of water at the feet of several large icebergs nearby. But the ice itself could not be seen, even when Boxhall lit his green flares, which he did at regular intervals. The bergs revealed themselves only by the eclipse of stars on the horizon. She tried to push the icebergs and the memories out of her mind.

"Walter, you must come with me," she had begged. "Why do you have to stay behind?"

"Because," her husband replied, giving her a gentle kiss on the lips and stepping back from the boat, "the only honorable thing to do is to stay behind with the men."

"Then you must stay close to Colonel Gracie and Major Butt," she had commanded, as if laying down a final bit of wifely law. "They are big, strong fellows and will surely make it."

Had they? She had no way of knowing.

Then, as a dozen stars winked out in the north, eclipsed by approaching ice, the blue-white streamers of the aurora borealis blazed to life. They became a backdrop—a mere backdrop—for the meteors. Mrs. Douglas had never before seen an aurora, or so many meteors, or the stars like flecks of ice and dust. *Of course, there is no God*, she told herself. *All of this is just coincidence*. And she recalled a myth her mother had told her: that every time a shooting star appeared, it signaled the return of a soul to heaven.

Did Walter make it? she wondered.

Small details could become strangely magnified at a time like this, drawing inordinate attention, while the unbelievable was reduced to commonplace. Chief Baker Charles Joughin found himself swimming through a netherworld of lifejackets and curled flesh that must once have been a dozen swimmers in the path of a falling smokestack, but the thing that caught his attention, and kept it, was the dog he discovered paddling alongside him. *Now, isn't* that *unusual?* he thought, and decided to follow the dog—which soon outpaced him, "going nowhere fast."

Tennis star Richard Norris Williams II could not understand how he came to be in the water. He had been traveling with his father, who was aboard the Guion liner *Arizona* when it steamed head-on into an iceberg in November 1879, crumpling her bow plates back thirty feet. Like the *Titanic*, she was equipped with watertight compartments which, in theory, rendered her "virtually unsinkable." The *Arizona* had floated, flooding only the first two compartments, and she was even able to reach St. Johns, Newfoundland, under her own power. "The *Titanic* is built even better than the *Arizona*," Father had assured. "No need to worry this time."

Looking down from the rail with his father, Richard had

noticed a man in a departing lifeboat wearing a silken hat and woman's shawl. Somehow, this seemed perfectly natural to him. Another man—Major Arthur Peuchen—paused to ask Richard how long he thought the ship might last.

"A long while," Richard's father answered for him.

The man shook his head and said, "No, I think she's gone," and then, drawing his wallet from his pocket, concluded, "I might as well preserve at least this," leaving Richard to wonder whatever in the world the major had meant, as he flung the wallet overboard. Somehow, this too seemed perfectly natural. And then a gurgling noise drew him indoors for a moment, where he discovered water and wicker chairs rising two decks below, swirling up the Grand Stairway. He had mentioned to his father that the sea must soon reach their stateroom. Again, all seemed perfectly natural . . . right up to the moment the whole forward quarter of the starboard side left him, taking the boat called collapsible A down in a tangle of ropes and the crackle of gunfire. He heard shouts from his father but never did see him again, and then, as a miracle, collapsible A bobbed up to the surface, less than a hundred feet away. In his journal, Richard would later report, "many [people] fighting and scrambling to get in [the raft] . . . finally succeeded with about fourteen others . . . and slowly paddled out of the area."

Another of the collapsible A survivors, George Rheims, would write in a letter, "At first, they did not let me get on [the flooded collapsible known as 'A'], but I succeeded nevertheless . . . We had to push back about a dozen fellows who wanted to get on the raft; we were loaded to the limit. I will spare you the details, which were horrible." *(Which meant they had to kill people* filmmaker James Cameron would observe when he read this passage eighty-five years later.)

At 2:40 A.M., barely more than twenty minutes after the

ship disappeared and the hands on Richard's watch froze, the temperature of the sea had dropped to 28 degrees Fahrenheit, and many of the people in the water were already unconscious from cold-shock. The canvas sides of collapsible A were so torn that they leaked as much water out as in, and nothing except the buoyancy of the wood was keeping the survivors afloat. A man asked if he could put his arm around Richard's neck to support himself. "Sure," Richard said, and he felt the man's grip tighten and relax, tighten and relax, then relax completely as the stranger slid overboard and drifted off.

An unnatural succession of thoughts followed: Were the Marconi operators able to summon a rescue ship? How deep is the ocean here? Are there any other sunken ships lying in this spot, with the *Titanic*? How long will I last in this cold? My, those grapes tasted good at supper!

Finally, he noticed a man sitting in front of him, apparently dozing off and in danger of slipping into the water. It was the man's derby hat that seized Richard's attention.

Richard tapped him on the shoulder: "Do you realize your derby is dented?"

The man did not reply, but Richard refused to give up. He tried German, French, Italian—but the man continued to show no interest. *Damn!* The tennis player was overtaken by what became to him a personal and desperate mission to make the man understand that his derby hat was dented, but even after the hat was knocked overboard and began sinking toward the bottom, Richard did not succeed in getting a reaction.

Nearby, Rosa Abbott swam—bewildered, calling for her two sons, who had been barred from entering the lifeboats because at age nine, any third-class boy reaching the port side, under rules established by Second Officer Lightoller (who had misinterpreted the captain's order "women and children first" as meaning "women and children only"), was old enough to be a "man." Some deep, instinctive connection to her children seemed to have broken, telling her that they were gone already, although she continued to shout their names. Each cry, each kick of her feet, was accompanied by unbearable flashes of memory: Rossmore playing with his wooden blocks, Eugene with his sled that he used to enjoy more than anything else in the world. *I think I shall lose my reason*, she thought, and then thought that she would be with them soon enough, safe in God's keeping. *And if not*, she told herself, *I only trust they are better off out of this world . . .*

About 2:45 A.M., a woman in boat number six suddenly remembered, and began wailing for, the string of pearls she had confided to the care of Purser McElroy. When Helen Churchill Candee edged forward to explain that the purser had refused a seat in the lifeboat and, from everything she knew, gone down with the *Titanic* and did not deserve to be reviled for robbing her, the explanation seemed only to increase the woman's rage.

For Helen Candee, as she shifted to another part of the boat, there was remembrance of her early morning climbs onto the rail at the point bow. Usually she had made the excursion with Hugh Woolner, but on the Sunday of April 14, 1912, she had tricked Hugh by sneaking out early—just minutes ahead of the last sunrise the *Titanic* would ever see. Not quite twenty hours ago, Helen had stood on the prow, feeling as if she owned the ship, feeling as if the ship owned the sea, feeling as if together they were as . . . as God . . . God moving over the face of the waters in the First Book of Genesis. A sacrilegious thought, perhaps, but the machine had seemed actually to be alive and to have a soul, then. It impressed upon her its . . . *her* personality, as Helen leaned into the west wind and allowed herself to feel the touch of *Titanic*'s spirit. Glancing straight down, where tons of water were being thrown right and left, she remembered feeling as if the bow were cutting through the waves with light-hearted, playful intent, utterly indifferent to mankind. Self-absorbed. It was only at the bow that Helen was able to appreciate the ship's pride in her own size. She was certain that the ship liked its name. It suited her. *Titanic*.

And the dawn came on like a thunderbolt.

"And God commanded, 'Let there be light,' " she said, and laughed.

And an instant later she was stricken, as if by lightning, with an overwhelming sense of dread. She felt as if shadows were suddenly leering out at her from odd corners, and she turned and scurried back into the warmer recesses of the machine, wanting to be surrounded by electric lights and ankle-deep carpets and electric heaters, wanting to drive back the shadows. But they stayed with her, in her mind, and she had stayed in her room the rest of the morning, with her back to the wall, shivering.

By 3:00 A.M., the sound of the swimmers had diminished from a crowd's roar to a continuous moan, like the whisper of locusts on a midsummer night. It was a surreal, supernatural moan, and one witness would report hearing that same sound again, years later, when he reached the Buchenwald death camp.

Gone, now—gone so utterly that the last spark of light from the kerosene lantern on her stern was already flying beyond the orbit of Mars, the *Titanic* remained, for Helen Churchill Candee, the most seductive machine God had ever allowed man to create . . . or allowed the devil to create.

Jim Farrell must have wondered how he came to be on that machine at all. He was a milk truck driver who, after having a fight with his boss, had decided on the spur of the moment to take the very next ship to New York. Sixteen-year-old Katherine Gilnagh had taken a liking to Jim, but by now she had accepted the fact that she would never see him again. This was her first voyage, and she was able to convince herself that the tearful good-byes, the ship tearing itself in two, and that horrible moan were among the usual difficulties of crossing the Atlantic.

In boat number five, Karl Behr was rubbing his wife's feet, trying to warm them with his hands, when someone (whom Karl would describe by daylight as a normal, "attractive-looking middle-aged man") nudged him in the side. The man, apparently unaware that by aid of the new wireless telegraph, ships no longer disappeared without word of their demise, still believed that castaways were doomed to drift aimlessly until they died of thirst and starvation—he still regarded lifeboats as a means of committing suicide slowly to avoid being drowned.

He showed Karl a nickel-plated revolver and whispered in his ear, "Should the worst come to worst, you can use my gun on your wife, after my wife and I have finished with it."

"Thank you," acknowledged Karl, with curious detachment. In later years, it would appear strange to him, how natural the "gun man's" courtesy had seemed at a time like this.

Some curious things are done at a time like this, Charles Joughin concluded, as he threw away the heavy keys to the ship's bakery. He wondered what had possessed him to lock the bakery doors on a ship he knew was going under and then stuff the keys into his pocket. Out of all the items he could have chosen to keep with him at the hour of his death—including his mother's picture—he chose the bakery and pantry keys and two large cakes of now waterlogged tobacco. *Must have been the whiskey thinking*, he guessed. *God made the Irish perfect, and then he gave us whiskey.*

About 3:15 A.M., Hugh Woolner discovered a half-squashed tin of cookies on the floor of collapsible D, and began feeding them, one at a time, to the Navatril children, while in boat number ten a small riot broke out when a group of first-class women attempted to throw a Japanese passenger overboard. Elsewhere, the women of number fourteen mutinied against an officer who, upon approaching a floating stateroom door, and realizing that the man clinging to it was Chinese, commanded his crew to row away because, "there's others better worth saving." In boat seven, Olive Earnshaw asked Baron von Drachstedt of Cologne (who was really Alfred Nourney of New Jersey) how he had managed to get past the "women and children first" rule. He brandished a revolver and said, "I would have liked to see someone try stopping me."

Nearly a century later, it is impossible for me to be where they were that night—49° 56' 49" w, 41° 43' 57" n—and not hear their voices, not touch the water with my fingers and not feel them rising again in my imagination, rising like summoned spirits, acting and reacting. And the gnawing, inescapable question about that night is, *What would I have done*? I remember the arrogance of Helen Candee on the bow and the humanity of Mrs. Washington Dodge in boat four. I remember the bravery of Walter Douglas and the cowardice of "Baron von Drachstedt." And while it is true that these people belonged to an Edwardian civilization, as far removed from us today as a lost continent, it is also true that these people were us.

Maybe the Babylonian scribes and Old Testament prophets were right, more than 2,500 years ago. Long before the invention of iron boiler casings and rocket engines, before telegraph and computer, they had predicted that human civilization would never really change over time; it would merely become more fully what the human animal was.

"So much learning," one of my Jesuit teachers has said, "so little wisdom." To put it another way, a civilization does become more technologically skilled and more learned about science, and perhaps even a little smarter as well, when it is permitted to grow for hundreds of years and spread itself from pole to pole; but we also have more time and more tools to turn out as badly as our ancestors said we might.

2

•

The Hammer of God

•

As meteorites are a poor man's space program, archaeology is a pauper's time machine. But—oh, the places we go, the people we meet!

—C.R. PELLEGRINO
(the Fermilab lectures, November 1998)

Why meet we on the bridge of Time to exchange one greeting and then to part?

—THE KASIDAH OF HAJI ABDU EL-YEZDI

SOMETIMES THE TECHNOLOGY still seems brute force and primitive to me. William Beebe's hollow steel ball dangling from a string has not really evolved very far over the decades. It is now a hollow titanium ball equipped with batteries and motors, and it is built for three people: two "pilots," one "observer." The "bathysphere" has become a "submersible," and it has become all the rage these days, for observers to proclaim their machismo by emphasizing for *National Geographic* and the Discovery Channel how, at a depth of two and one-half miles, three tons of water pressure squeeze down on every square inch of the titanium hull—"If the seals give, there is no time to call, 'Houston, we have a problem.' You are dead even before you know you are about to die."

21

While it is true that six thousand pounds per square inch is equivalent to the force generated by a space shuttle's engines at liftoff, and that a crack in the hull would send water jetting in with a power sufficient to immediately separate one's body into individual cells, the actual structural demands on the submersible leave the crew in no greater danger, behind their thick titanium shell, than are the passengers of a jet airplane, behind their astonishingly thinner but equally well-designed aluminum membrane. What the submersible lacks are the creature comforts of the airplane. One does not eat before descent, for there is no bathroom, no toilet, no wash basin; nothing except a bottle for urine.[1] The mini-sub is really more of a garment than a vehicle. Like the old Mercury and Gemini space capsules, you do not so much crawl into the machine as put it on, like a suit.

It takes an hour and one-half to descend two and one-half miles in our three-man suit. Down there, the temperature is barely above freezing on most days, and the titanium ball, as it cools, condenses your sweat and your breath on its curved walls. After seven hours, you can no longer sit upright on the bench, and put your feet on the floor, because six to eight inches of water are sloshing around underfoot—water distilled from your own bad breath, and from the exhalations of your two companions. But it does not matter. Even if you happen to be germ phobic, the trip is worth every inch of that icy distillate—worth every inch, for I have seen, and held in my hands, an assemblage of contradictions:

---

[1] I once made the very bad mistake, before my first practice dive, of eating baked beans, garlic bread, and bananas (and washing the whole damned mess down with a chocolate egg cream). This produced emissions of "noxious fumes" so intense that one U.S. Navy pilot, after testing his oxygen mask three times and gagging between tests, brought us out of the sub early and vowed to his commanding officer that he would never get into a submersible with me again, even under threat of court martial.

Near the stern, an inch-thick piece of steel plate from the *Titanic*'s hull has collapsed into a pile of iron-oxide dust and bacterial "pudding" while, only a few yards away, bed springs remain untouched, and only a few dozen yards beyond that, another slab of hull plate has retained its original metallic luster. No answers, yet, as to why this is happening. No cause for despair, either. Archaeologists revel in contradictions, revel in a feeling that something should not be and might even be impossible, but somehow is. We all love a good mystery. It's what keeps us in the field. It's what keeps the field honest.

I have felt the weight of time in the heft of a steel shard from one of the *Titanic*'s boiler casings. Today it is lighter than a block of Styrofoam. Had the conservators aboard the research vessel *Nadir* not dipped it in shellac the moment they brought it to the surface, it would no longer exist. Designed to contain and harness steam pressures sufficient to rupture a modern-day scuba tank, the casing could now be crushed in my bare hands and chewed down to powder with my teeth; a curious bacterial assault has sucked all the iron out of it, leaving behind only the microscopic carbon seams that once resided between the iron crystals. All that remains is a carbon and lacquer fossil in the shape of a boiler plate.

And so it goes: Here and there, the steel simply vanishes, sometimes leaving behind formless piles of red dust on the sea floor. A comparison of photos taken since the very first Ballard expedition in 1985 shows it happening year by year before our very eyes: steel evaporating into the sea. And yet those same cameras once revealed paper lying in a bundle on a plain of grayish-white mud. My old friend Bill MacQuitty (who produced the film version of *A Night to Remember*) was with me when the bundle was raised. It turned out to be a pile of newspapers, dated April 10, 1912. It had turned almost entirely to pulp and decay—

almost, except for one little scrap preserving the date, and some words about the unsinkable *Titanic*'s maiden voyage. When Bill considered the odds of all but that one little scrap being reduced to bacteria-ravaged pulp, it put a chill through him.

"It makes you think of fate," he said.

I have seen a leather tool packet brought to the surface so perfectly intact that it apparently prevented even a single oxygen-loving (i.e., wood- and paper-eating) bacterium from establishing a foothold within. The conservators kept the packet immersed in water when they opened it for the first time. Inside, the wooden handles of awls and chisels seemed only to have aged a week or two during the better part of a century, but the metal tool bits looked shadowy and strange and they dissolved suddenly from view, like phantoms, leaving us with only the wooden handles. As near as microbiologist Roy Cullimore and I can tell, reducing bacteria (which thrive in the absence of oxygen) had penetrated the packet decades ago and, in much the same manner as the bacteria encrusting the ultra-light boiler plate, they devoured anything that was not carbon-based, including all trace of iron. Thus would the phantom tool bits have been precisely that: phantoms, carbon shadows of their former selves. It's the best explanation we have, for the moment. But, of course, it's only a guess.

I have seen multiple decks of hull plating peeled from the severed stern and reshaped as if they were sheets of tinfoil splayed out by the spreading shock front of a tremendous explosion. The long, spindly arms of two brass chandeliers, found near a rupture in the stern's starboard side, seemed to have become as flexible (during what must have been only one part of a second) as blades of grass swept by a gale-force wind that somehow froze them in midsway. The thin metal of a serving tray from Charles Joughin's part of the ship—the stern's kitchen area—resembles a flag rippling in

Twisted agony.
A chandelier was water-jetted from the stern by downblast. It reminds me of a storm at sea — — fossilized. —cRp.

that same gale-force wind, a wind that ceased abruptly, leaving behind a metal "flag," that had preserved, as if by a process of three-dimensional flash photography, a fossil impression of the wind—which is, perhaps, exactly what has occurred.

If you travel into the Arizona desert, to a high, sandy ridge about ten miles outside of Tombstone, and if you dig where lightning bolts have struck the ridge, melting every grain of sand through which they passed, it is possible to unearth impressions of actual lightning rendered in glass. We call these fossilized lightning bolts *fulgurites*, and that is precisely what the serving tray and the chandeliers have begun to resemble: the *Titanic*'s fulgurites.

Like grains of Arizona sand, thin leaves of metal are capable of capturing, or fossilizing, extraordinarily powerful events. With such grace does the *Titanic* become mathematical to me—fractal, with every new mystery opening the door to yet another new mystery. Open the first door, and you might be embarking on an infinite diverging regression, taking you far from the door you first opened. Hold a deformed chandelier or platter in your hand, and you might realize that you had seen this sort of thing before: metal rippling strangely and then freezing. I've seen it on film, actually. During the fission bomb tests of the 1940s and 1950s, generally at a distance of a half mile, the pressure wave, as it passed over vacant ships and planes, had diminished to seventy-five pounds per square inch, or five atmospheres. In other words, the densities and motions of air and water were, very briefly, indistinguishable. During an interval measured in hundredths of a second, sheet metal on airplanes rippled—resembling the skin of a dolphin moving at high speed through water—then froze, "fossilizing" the ripples, as the shockwave passed. Similar ripple patterns were etched into objects hurled from the decks of ships overwashed by waves created by underwater atomic blasts.

During the test known as "Baker,"[2] the aircraft carrier *Saratoga* was lifted forty-three feet out of the sea by a 100-foot-tall wave of water droplets mixed with air, which struck the starboard side at ninety miles per hour with a force of seventy pounds per square inch. During that chip

[2]Test Baker, vital statistics: detonated July 25, 1946 at a depth of 90 feet, in 200 feet of water. Yield was 20.3 kilotons (approximately one Hiroshima). The blast displaced 2.2 million cubic yards of water and excavated a 25-foot-deep crater in coral silt, with a crater radius of 500 feet. This was near the island of Bikini, a Pacific atoll subsequently known as "Nothing-at-all atoll." Impressed by "the American fireworks displays," French fashion designers quickly named a new swimsuit they had in mind after the island.

of time, sheet metal and air and water behaved as if they all belonged to the same spasm of fluid motion. Portions of the island stack and flight deck bear scars hauntingly reminiscent of damage seen on the *Titanic*'s deck houses and hull plates. On the battleship *Arkansas*, which was even closer to the tidal wave (and the shockwave), steel deck plates were hammered down in the shapes of underlying bulkheads and engine heads, before the sheer mass of overlying water flipped the ship over and, popping out rivets along the entire length of the *Arkansas'* six-inch shell plating, drove her 180 feet to the bottom. Nine hundred feet from the epicenter of Test Baker, the *Arkansas* was stamped flat by a collapsing water column whose weight was measurable in the realm of megatons and yet, owing to a phenomenon no one quite understands, but which accompanies all explosive events—shock cocoons—the five-inch guns' range finders and spider-silk sights survived. Two rounds remained in the ready rack, and a light bulb sat unbroken on the inverted ceiling.[3]

The *Titanic*'s stern appears to have been disrupted by similar forces, the equivalent of a very tall wave jetting down upon it (and appearing also, in a manner reminiscent

---

[3]I once knew a priest who apparently found himself standing in the middle of an explosive "shock cocoon" around which the most destructive of the surrounding forces had miraculously diverged, leaving him perfectly unharmed . . . physically. One moment he had been standing in a hospital in Hiroshima, a moment later he seemed to have blacked out and the entire building in which he had been standing was simply gone. So was every building on the block. As far as his sight could penetrate, through the rising dust, the entire cityscape had become describable in one word: "flat." He realized that, as far as the eye could see, he was the sole survivor. Underfoot, he found a little tin carousel music box—which, when he wound it up, still played, "Let Me Call You Sweetheart." He held onto the music box and decided to seek a safer place, picking as his destination the city of Nagasaki. (This turned out to be a rather obscure definition of the word "safer." My friend became one of only eighteen people known to have survived the bombings of both Hiroshima and Nagasaki.)

of a cardboard box full of water dropped on a hardwood floor, to have exploded out of its lower decks) at somewhere in the realm of fifty miles per hour . . . or equivalent to being close—terrifyingly close—to an atomic bomb blast.

This impression—"like Hiroshima and Baker"—was there from the start, from the day Bob Ballard first surfaced with videotapes showing steel decks hammered down to reveal the outlines of underlying bulkheads[4] and the contours of a reciprocating engine's head beneath, as if the deck itself had, for an instant, behaved like a soft membrane stretched over the face of a dime. We knew then that the emerging jigsaw puzzle of *Titanic* debris—twisted and cracked and blasted about—would fuel a dozen careers' worth of research on that mammoth, half-frozen artifact from the Edwardian world.

In the center of *Titanic*'s broken-off stern section, the relatively thin walls of deckhouses were still standing straight up, with ladders and light-fixtures intact, while everything standing off to the sides, even a few feet to the sides of the walls, was bulldozed out from the stern's center and either flattened or uprooted—much as in the pictures I had seen of trees caught under the Tunguska blast in 1908 . . . or the still-standing walls of the science museum, directly under the Hiroshima blast in 1945 . . .

Oh, yes. The thousands of pictures Bob Ballard had snapped (puzzle pieces) would certainly keep scientists busy for a very long time—

(*Tunguska? Hiroshima? Baker? Titanic?*)

—and I wondered if Ballard and I would ever find answers to any of the mysteries crowding around the *Titanic*'s

---

[4]Just forward of the poop deck, which is peeled up and over itself on the aftermost part of the stern, the floor plates of the third-class general room are pressed down in such a manner as to reveal, somewhat like a map of city streets, the vertical bulkheads of the third-class cabins on the deck below.

last three minutes. In 1986, the field of deep-ocean archaeology was so new that we were its sole practitioners (meaning that the field did not even exist yet). The aftermost part of the stern had been peeled up and raked back as if sheet metal and water had joined to form a uniform wave front. I remember looking at the pictures, shrugging, and asking, "What the hell happened down there?"

FULGURITES. IN 1995, when I discovered a twisted chandelier and a rippled serving platter in the French LP3 laboratory (where objects recovered from the *Titanic*'s debris field were being curated), I could not understand why, out of nearly two thousand artifacts filling drawers, shelves, and water tubs, only two pieces of metal showed signs of having been reshaped by water jets.

Found near the stern, the chandelier and the platter had preserved what were, to me, beautiful ripple patterns—but to museum curators those same patterns were regarded as "ugly" (read this to mean "it's broken") and it turned out that the serving tray had been collected merely as "scrap" from which rectangular slivers could be (and had already been) cut for "sacrifice" in metallurgical tests.

I showed the tray to Matt Tulloch, one of the curators on the French-American expedition team, and I said, "The bottom of the sea, near the stern crash site, ought to be littered with objects like this. Why are there not more of these?" And he mentioned that during one of his flybys of the stern's starboard side, he had looked down from the submersible *Nautile* and seen more than half a dozen rippled platters, and although it occurred to him that the ripples might be the result of a fascinating and apparently violent process, he was under instructions not to gather any more objects than the conservators could afford to preserve and repair. It was a fact of life that the conservators preferred objects that were unbroken and could be made to look new in a museum display.

The chandelier—water-jetted until its arms resembled leaf-stripped saplings twisting in a storm—turned out to have been recovered only because it was sheathed in brilliant gold leaf. There were two of them, originally. The conservators had already restored one to its original shape, so that it looked like it was ready to sail aboard the *Titanic* brand new, only a few steps away from stateroom A-36 in the stern, where shipbuilder Thomas Andrews still dreamed of building the world brand new.

No one had ever seen before what happened to large objects when they fell through two and one-half miles of water, apparently accelerating, during the first half mile or so, to spectacular terminal velocities. No one had dreamed it would be like this: the starboard side of the stern ruptured wide open, and the hull plating, though once an inch thick, peeled back like the skin of an orange, exposing the rooms within. Down there, near the starboard peel, is where Matt Tulloch discovered the rippled, seemingly out-jetted serving platters. When he and Captain Paul Henry Narnageolet sent the robot *Robin* into the bakery and pantry compartments, they found the rooms squashed and entirely empty. Even the bakery door was missing, torn from its iron frame and squirted out through the rupture in the stern's side.

Charles Joughin, the ship's chief baker, happened to be standing on the 330-foot-long stern section after it broke away from the bow. He remembered feeling, through the deck plates, the steady roar of uncountable loose objects thudding and tumbling underfoot. During the first seconds after the break, until the stern settled gently toward the propellers and appeared, from Joughin's point of view, to be leveling out and trying to float again, hundreds of plates, platters, and teacups gushed from the rend (many of them miraculously unbroken) and, along with the entire contents of the kitchen's coal bunkers, began falling toward the bottom in a spreading shower formation, globular and huge.

According to Joughin, the *Titanic*'s stern took fully three minutes to sink, rolling onto her port side, then pointing her propellers straight up at the sky again, and her kitchen and dining areas straight at the sea floor again, before she finally gulped under. Undoubtedly, the down-pointing break in her stern spilled one last cloud of debris—like a slit throat spilling blood—before she died.

Some of that near-surface "gush debris," which includes undamaged saucers, platters, teacups, and a cabinet full of buttercups, can be seen lying on top of the stern, suggesting that the stern, despite the fact that at least one of its debris clouds had been given at least a three-minute head start, arrived on the bottom ahead of its own clouds. The picture we begin to receive, as videotapes and snapshots merge into panoramic scans, and as panoramic scans become the jigsaw pieces of an archaeological map, is one in which objects lying on and around the stern were subjected to vastly different physical forces: simple spillage near the surface, and (if they remained inside the ship) complex jetting on the sea floor. And thus is it possible to recover mud samples studded with steel and glass shrapnel, including part of the bakery door, and a chip out of a child's marble.[5]

Standing on top of the shrapnel-laced mud, a ceramic Dutch boy holds a shoe. Neither the boy nor the shoe exhibits any sign of chipping or cracking. Amid a mountain of steel piping lying in twisted agony on the seabed and mighty steam engines cracked in half, a jar of olives stands unbroken, with the olives inside still plump and apparently edible. A miniature blue pitcher, whose glass is every bit as fine and delicate as a paper nautilus' shell, settled to the

---

[5]Explorer Arnie Geller was a rather stocky man who did not cry easily, but when he discovered a broken marble in a handful of mud, he wept as if he were a child again. This is a common sight at the *Titanic:* machos bursting suddenly into tears. If a man travels there and he tells you that he did not weep, he is either dead inside, or he is a liar.

bottom perfectly intact, apparently as gently as a leaf, just a stone's throw from the heavy keys to Charles Joughin's pantry.

Major Peuchen's wallet was found lying in the debris field, with his paper money still spendable, his business cards and his Toronto streetcar tickets still readable. In hindsight, his words to Richard Norris William II—"I might as well preserve at least this"—have turned out to be hauntingly prophetic. His act of preserving also provides a useful probe into the timing of events that night. The major's wallet went overboard somewhere between the first of his two or three deckside chats, commencing about 12:30 A.M., and his boarding of boat number six at 12:50 A.M. Eyewitnesses aboard both the *Titanic* and the steamship *Californian* (which were, with very little doubt, within sight of one another) watched each ship showing, alternately, its starboard and port-side running lights, suggesting that both vessels were twisting in the Labrador Current. Yet the major's wallet tells us that the current was not strong enough that night to push the *Titanic* (and presumably the *Californian*, and the icebergs) more than a half mile in an hour. An hour and one-half (at most, two hours) passed between the wallet's arrival on the bottom and the creation of the *Titanic*'s debris field. The field is roughly one mile in diameter. And Major Peuchen's wallet fell within it.

A minor archaeological puzzle piece, perhaps, but I wonder if it will fit into two other mysteries that have been haunting maritime historians ever since Bob Ballard planted the debris field's coordinates in a global positioning satellite: Was that *really* the *Californian* within sight of the *Titanic*, within actual rescue distance, and if so, *what went wrong?*

And another mystery unfurls, another contradiction of preservation, another trick of nature: A hook and pulley are

Symphonic destruction... yet a jar of olives lies perfectly intact in the Titanic's debris field.

lying on the bottom with their line of hemp intact. The iron hook is still shiny white, but it rests on a pile of splintered hull plating that has melted into rivers of molasses-like, bacterial sludge.

And I have seen a derby hat raised. It had, like much of the ship's hull, fallen prey to a bacterial assault, yet still visible on one side was a large dent. I could not bring myself to touch the hat. Two neatly folded pairs of pants, found in a suitcase along with a tie and a pair of shoes, had the same effect on me. Being luggage, the clothes could not possibly have marked places where bodies had fallen and decayed, but I confessed to curator Rhonda Wozmiak, with slight embarrassment, that I could not put my hands upon them, for no reason that could be consciously articulated. Something deep inside, strong and

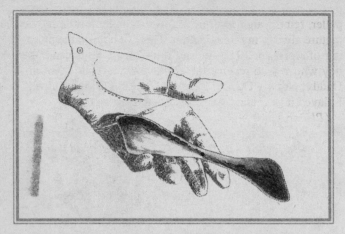

A wooden propeller from a toy airplane, along with rubber bands,
wing paper, and the cardboard box that contained them were preserved in a suitcase.

instinctive, recoiled and forced me to maintain at least a
one-foot distance. Rhonda nodded and confessed to me
that she was often halted by the same instinct. She, too,
found it difficult to come within touching distance of the
clothes, especially the shoes.

What I will always remember, when I think back upon
my first encounters with the *Titanic*'s many hundreds of
raised artifacts, is the toy airplane. That's the one that got
to me, like a punch in the stomach: a Harriet Quimby–era
airplane. During a visit to Paris, I once bought two rubber
band–powered replicas of a da Vinci ornithopter for my
niece and nephew, and it was easy for me to imagine the
owner of the suitcase in which the Quimby plane had survived carrying a toy flying machine across the Atlantic to a
child waiting at home. At such moments a toy plane—its
metal wires missing, but its rubber bands and doped paper
amazingly intact—ceases to be part of an archaeological

puzzle waiting to be solved. The miniature wooden propeller, felt through a surgical glove, brought a little movie picture alive in my imagination. There, a boy, on the morning of April 16, 1912—in my mind's eye, he became the boy who was to receive the airplane—cried out, "Not my Daddy! Not my Daddy! Please, God. Let Daddy be alive!" I played it over and over in my head, over and over—

(*Please, God*)

—and I kept coming back to a single line, dredged from the bottom of my subconscious and tossed up as if to answer the boy's pleas—

(*Please, God. Let Daddy be alive!*)

—"But the sea would not listen to the prayers of a child."

I MET "THE *Titanic* Waif," Michel Navatril, in 1996, when he joined a French-American expedition, having decided that it was finally time for him "to complete the circle" and return to the tiny patch of ocean where he had last seen his father alive. In 1912 he was traveling as Michel Hoffman, but his family name was not really Hoffman.

Michel's father, also named Michel, was a tall man who, while sailing aboard the *Titanic*, seemed to prefer wearing the sort of inconspicuous brown suits no one remembered five seconds after seeing him. He had been seen, but barely noticed, by Richard Williams II, playing with his sons outside the broad, brass-framed windows of the ship's library, just before the last dinner on that first and last voyage. To all outward appearances the elder Michel was an ordinary father, taking a short break with his children before supper. His boys were three and four, and Mr. "Hoffman" appeared to be devoted to them, perhaps even a bit too devoted. If one looked just a little bit closer, he became, at second glance, a cruel, unsavory creature.

(*Not my Daddy! Not my Daddy!*)

The "Daddy" behind the Hoffman mask had left his wife in Nice, France, and was abducting their two children to America, where he was planning to raise them under his newly assumed name. At about 2:00 A.M., he found a group of sailors locking arms in a semicircle around a small boat on the port side—the last sixty seats remaining for 1,500 people still aboard.

He recognized Second Officer Lightoller, walked up to him directly with Louis and Michel Jr. in his arms, and said, "I've done all that I could."

He kissed his sons, whispered something in little Michel's ear, and then, without any warning or fuss, without asking anything for himself, he turned and darted into the night.

Michel remembered crying for Daddy after the *Titanic* "went away."

(*But the sea would not listen to the prayers of a child.*)

He remembered crying for Daddy long after the sunrise. But most of all, whenever he relived that night, he remembered Daddy whispering a message to him: "When you see your mother, you must tell her exactly what I am about to tell you . . ."

And in 1992, when a historian asked him what that message had been, he replied that he was only four years old in 1912, and eighty years had passed, but he still remembered every word of it. "Every word," he emphasized. And every word, he vowed, would go to the grave with him.

At first glance, a lifetime ago outside the ship's library, Mr. Navatril had been a doting father. At second glance, it was easy to see that he was not what he appeared to be at first glance. His body was found on the afternoon of April 15, floating amid deck chairs and deck boards, and providing us with a third glance. In his jacket pocket, he was carrying a loaded revolver.

Michel Navatril, Jr. told me that he had indeed delivered

his father's message, and all I knew beyond that point was that some years later his mother died in a mental institution. Relying on archaeological thinking alone, letting a handful of facts and artifacts dictate the reconstruction of events, the elder Navatril became, at second and third glance, a creature unfit for human company, slithering away under a false name, abducting his two little boys from their mother, and, perhaps, with one of his dying breaths, weaving a last sentence designed to drive his wife mad.

The second and third glances, like the first glance, scarcely provided a clue to what was happening, and why.

When Michel joined our 1996 expedition team, he had only recently learned that his father's body was recovered in 1912, and buried in Halifax. Before the expedition set sail, historian Charles Haas drove him to the cemetery, and as Michel stood over his father's grave, he suddenly recalled a song that Michel Sr. used to sing to him every night at bed time. He said, "I can feel my father standing beside me, right now; and he is singing that song to me, right now."

Complete the circle, Michel had said. And he told us that Daddy would see him again, and sing him to sleep again, soon; one last time. But first, he needed to break his silence about Daddy.

Michel Navatril, Sr. had been a tailor in Nice. He was very good at his craft, very successful; he believed that he would have had a happy life with Marcelle if only (as his son later learned from relatives) his wife had possessed a will of her own. Marcelle was, by all accounts, a very kind woman, dominated by a cruel, pitiless mother who never tired of reminding her that she had married below her station. Her efforts to drive a wedge into the marriage did not cease even after Michel, in an attempt to hold out the olive branch, took up the slack on his mother-in-law's debts. He noticed that Marcelle was drifting away from him, becoming more aloof, until at last the rift seemed irreparable.

Finally, he decided to take drastic action. He secretly altered his identity papers, and the identities of his two boys. No one would ever find them until and unless he decided otherwise. But the central fact of the matter was simply this: He did want Marcelle to find them. He had planned to send for her at the proper time, having already made arrangements for delivery of a one-way ticket; he had depleted the bank accounts in such a manner as to leave enough money for Marcelle to follow in reasonable comfort—alone.

Mr. Navatril's abduction of his sons had turned out to be, in all of its essentials, a last ditch effort to keep his family together. He seemed to have planned for every contingency, except the iceberg.

When you see your mother . . .

One could look at the loaded revolver he was carrying and try to guess from appearances alone the measure of the man—

You must tell her exactly what I am about to tell you . . .

—and one would surely fail to guess the true nature of the message passed from fleeing father, to abducted child, to estranged wife:

Tell your mother that I loved her dearly and still do.

Shattering.

I had measured the man with an archaeological yardstick, with purely archaeological thinking, and decided that Michel Navatril's father must have been lower than the animals. Archaeological thinking, in the absence of oral history, turned out not to be the proper measure of Mr. Navatril. It becomes a lesson I shall carry with me for the rest of my life, a lesson no archaeologist should ever forget.

Hard lesson.

Deep-ocean robotics, 400,000 ASA cameras, atomic absorption spectrometry—these tools of what passes today for superscience give us only glimpses, permit us only to make guesses about private life. People who love and perhaps even worship technology often forget humanity. The *Titanic* never lets you forget.

3

•

Travelers' Tales

•

The Worldly Hope men set their Hearts upon
Turns ashes—or it prospers; and anon,
Like Snow upon the Desert's dusty Face
Lighting a little hour or two—is gone.
> —THE RUBA'IYAT OF OMAR KHAYYAM, QUATRAIN 14
> (Lost aboard the RMS *Titanic*)

I am proposing that any future revisits to the *Titanic* which
would involve deep-diving submersibles dedicate a portion
of their diving time to carefully recording and recovering
those delicate items lying outside the hull of the ship itself.
The artifacts recovered should be used to create a museum.
> —ROBERT BALLARD TO CONGRESS, OCTOBER 1985

They should leave her down there, undisturbed on the
bottom—not just as my father's grave site, but as a monument to all the strangeness and arrogance of the human
animal.

> —EVA HART, *TITANIC* SURVIVOR,
> TO C.R. PELLEGRINO, APRIL 1986

And those who husbanded the Golden Grain,
And those who flung it to the Winds like Rain,
Alike to no such aureate Earth are turn'd
As, buried once, Men want dug up again.
> —THE RUBA'IYAT OF OMAR KHAYYAM, QUATRAIN 15

GHOSTS. I KNOW all about ghosts.

I first came to know Archie Frost through the papers of shipbuilder Thomas Andrews' family. During the *Titanic*'s construction, Andrews had saved the engineer from what promised to be a fatal accident, then accepted the danger himself, on a failing section of scaffolding during a gale, eighty feet above the ground. As Archie told it, ever thereafter he strove to equal Mr. Andrews' standard of duty and courage, hoping to one day repay him, to one day make him proud of the life he had saved.

Two years later, on the night the *Titanic* went down, Archie stayed below at his post, just aft of the four-story-tall steam engines, in the bottom of the stern. When Andrews had confided to Engineers Frost and Bell, to Electrician Parr, and to Greaser White that the ship did not have a chance of seeing sunrise, the men replied, "We'll stay as long as we can."

Till the very end, the lights glowed stubbornly, and there was power to keep the telegraph spark burning just as stubbornly, and despite an escalating chain reaction of miscalculation, miscommunication, and misadventure, the electric pumps kept the liner afloat an hour past Thomas Andrews' original estimate of when the end would come.

Beyond preventing a deadly panic, the persistence of the lights told Andrews that his engineers, electricians, and maintenance workers had indeed resolved to remain in a part of the ship that offered only the slimmest hope of escape. Once he realized this, he was dead already, although to everyone he encountered, alive-seeming still. It was impossible for him to leave and to live while Archie and the others drowned, and he must have decided, before he climbed out of the turbine room, that he would not behave with an ounce less courage than his men, and that he would never see his wife Helen or his little girl Elizabeth again. Thus did the *Titanic* kill Andrews with his own good nature, with Archie's achievement of his own high standards, with his loyalty to his friends, with his humanity.

When he reached the upper decks, he simply went about his task of trying to give the *Titanic* every last possible second of life. But chaos held sway over the night, and over Mr. Andrews. When a passenger mentioned that she had opened her porthole in time to see the iceberg receding aft, a shiver ran through him. A dozen other portholes—two dozen or more—as they slid underwater, would act as new wounds in the hull. Andrews gave an order that every stateroom be searched to make certain that every porthole was buttoned tight, but the order was relayed through only a handful of stewards, and never relayed at all by the captain. The one or two bedroom stewards who volunteered to assist found many of the stateroom doors locked, and no one seemed to know who had taken possession of the master keys. In desperation, the shipbuilder began kicking doors off hinges, racing the sea to the portholes. He passed at least two broken doors over to the crew, with instructions to throw them overboard, as potential rafts. He was seen dragging one door onto the deck and throwing it over the side himself, after he paused to help Crewman Samuel Hemming feed out the line and lower boat number six away. Stewardess Mary Sloan noticed that Andrews' clothes were soaked with sweat in spite of the freezing temperatures, in spite of the fact that he had not, by all appearances, taken a moment even to throw a warm coat over his back. Along the 882.5-foot length of the *Titanic*, he had no way of knowing that he toiled in virtual solitude, trying to plug leaks, while Second Officer Lightoller ordered his work crew to open a gangway door in the port bow (of a ship that was sinking by the bow), and forgot to tell either the captain or the ship's designer.[1]

---

[1]Officer Lightoller never did consider the danger of opening the gangway door because even as he lowered women and children away in lifeboats, even after learning that the water was flooding rooms on F deck, only one

On the lowermost decks aft, whatever time the engineers bought with their efforts to keep the turbine and the electric pumps alive was being at least partly devoured by the incessant opening of new holes in the *Titanic*'s sides. None of them—Frost, Parr, Bell, or their compatriots in the generator room—ever returned to Belfast. None of them . . . or so went accepted historical reasoning until, quite by surprise some years ago, filmmaker Bill MacQuitty (who as a child watched the *Titanic* being built and launched, and who as a man sank her a second time when he produced *A Night to Remember*), received a letter from a survivor's nephew, and made an acquaintance with him.

Along with the family history of Alfred White came a letter dated June 21, 1912, from Mr. White to the brother-in-law of Mr. Parr, the assistant manager of the *Titanic*'s electrical team. Though a decades-long tradition held that the entire team had gone down with the ship, Alfred White left the generator room about five or six minutes before the stern broke away, and lived to tell a fantastic tale—thanks to a combination of quick reflexes, quick thinking, and unimaginable good luck.

At 10:00 P.M. on the Sunday of April 14, 1912, he had come on duty as a greaser—as the man assigned to keep the generator and every other electrical apparatus well-oiled. Because he was listed on the crew manifest as "Greaser Al-

deck below the door, he did not believe that the ship could possibly be foundering—for he was, as far as he knew, standing on the unsinkable *Titanic*. During the British inquiry, the solicitor general pointed out to him, "If the boat was down by the head, the opening of those doors on E deck in the forward part of the ship would open her very close to the water . . . of course you know now the water was rising up to E deck. It appears to me that you would be very unlikely to order the forward gangway door to be opened. You might get the head so deep in the water that she might ship water through that gangway door?" Lightoller replied, "Of course, my Lord, I did not take [it] into consideration at that time; there was not time to take all these particulars into mind. In the first place, at that time, I did not think the ship was going down."

fred White," and because his retelling of a story he had heard
aboard the rescue ship *Carpathia* about Captain Smith's last
words ("Every man for himself!") was mistakenly reported
as his own eyewitness account of events on the boat deck at
2:10 A.M., history removed him from Frost and Parr, and
from the generator room, and then commenced to overlook
him.

His letter, written only two months after the disaster,
was not penned as a sensationalist tale for the press, but as
words of comfort to the grieving relatives of a friend who
had died trying to save others. And it was written while
events were still sharp in his mind, before decades of memory replays allowed imagination, forgetfulness, and muta-
tion to take over.[2]

At 1:00 A.M., three hours after he came on duty, an hour
and twenty minutes after the starboard bow made its acquaintance with the iceberg, Mr. White was instructed to
start one more generator in the main light room, so as to
guarantee enough power to lower all of the ship's lifeboats
on the electric winches. While Alfred White and Archie
Frost tended the generators, and while Mr. Parr worked the
main switchboard, the slant of the deck increased to
slightly more than ten degrees, then stayed at that angle for
a very long time.

So slight was the tilt that their minds and bodies quickly
adapted, allowing them to proceed as if nothing out of the
ordinary were occurring. Indeed, it seemed as if Thomas

---

[2]In 1986, though most of the first-hand survivor accounts I received corre-
sponded with what I was then reading in 1912 court transcripts, I was occasionally jolted by "memories" of the impossible . . . Eva Hart's recollection
that her father had sighted the ice field two days before the accident . . . another woman who saw a gaping hole swallowing lifeboats (there were no
missing lifeboats) . . . and another who vividly recalled a nine-hole golf
course on the boat deck (no ship ever saw the like until the launch of the
Grand Princess in 1998, the largest passenger vessel ever built, 52.5 feet
longer than the *Titanic*, and "virtually unsinkable").

Andrews might have been mistaken in his prophecy of doom. It was possible to believe so, until about 2:10 A.M. That was when the bulkhead at the front of boiler room four ruptured, costing the bow the last of its buoyancy and prompting Marconi Operator Jack Phillips to tap out two "V's" in Morse code—

DIT-DIT-DIT DA
DIT-DIT-DIT DA

—the fateful opening of Beethoven's Fifth Symphony; Death knocking at the door, heard faintly by the *Virginian*; the last signal Phillips would ever send. At that very same moment, nearly five hundred feet aft of the Marconi shack, and ten decks below, Alfred White felt the floor tilt down two or three degrees and lurch forward, as if the three giant propellers had come suddenly to life again—but that was impossible, by everything Alfred knew. The boiler feeds to the reciprocating steam engines had been dead for more than an hour, and the three propeller shafts nearby were silent, and yet the *Titanic* made a forward acceleration of such magnitude that inertia flung Alfred, Archie, and Mr. Parr off their feet.

"What the hell was that?" Alfred hollered. A surge forward? Without engines? . . . *Forward* and *down*, he reminded himself . . . and the ship is damaged in the bows. Then Alfred understood. "Oh."

Archie grinned at him nervously and said, "It looks like we'll be putting in a little overtime on this one."

Gallows humor, Alfred guessed, and from this he knew that Archie, too, understood.

Mr. Parr was probably sure, by then, that his equipment would function for the rest of its life without the skills of an oiler, so he told Alfred, "Go up and see how things are going on—if there are any lifeboats left. Then come back and tell us."

As he ascended the turbine room ladder, the tilt of the

room was growing worse with each passing second, making a difficult job of his climb. By the time he reached the hospital deck, he became conscious of a distant rumble—partly groaning and snapping metal, partly falling glassware, and partly hundreds of stampeding feet—and the stampede too was growing worse as the seconds ran out, and this compelled him to climb faster.

There was no way out to the boat deck. A gate had been drawn shut and locked and on the other side Alfred saw a group of men huddled below in a corner, praying. They took no notice of his calls for help, and as the slant of the deck accelerated toward 23 degrees—which felt suddenly like 90 degrees—he discovered that he was unable to stand without the aid of rungs or rails. Alfred had no choice but to remain in the passageway until it became a trap, or to continue following the engine room ladder up to the fourth smokestack (which was known to the crew as the "dummy" smokestack because, save for a few vents meant to draw coal fumes from the kitchens, the stack's only purpose was to give the ship's profile a more raked-back, streamlined appearance).

Somewhere between 2:15 and 2:17 A.M., Alfred White emerged through a doorway, halfway up the fourth stack, and at first he found it impossible to comprehend—much less to believe—what his eyes revealed. The second smokestack and everything aft of it up to the third stack, including the compass platform amidships, had vanished into the sea. He watched the water take the tail end of the raised roof over the first-class lounge and lap a deckhouse at the base of the third smokestack. The lights still burned, though with only a fraction of their former glory, and from the stack Alfred had a grandstand view, starboard and port, of empty lifeboat davits awash. He saw a man in a white life-jacket clinging to a davit head, clinging to it apparently even after the sea crept over his shoulders and removed his hat. Directly below, a hundred shadowy figures had ascended a deckhouse ladder, seeking higher ground on a glass skylight atop the aft rendition of the Grand Stairway. They fell in a heap against the rear wall of an airshaft disguised to resemble a deckhouse with doors and windows. Gravity pinned them there, against false windows, for the *Titanic* was pivoting around a center of mass located just forward of them, beneath the third smokestack.

As his perch angled down 40 degrees, and continued angling, Alfred's initial feeling of startled surprise was replaced by an overwhelming sense of unreality—which squashed all thought of panic and lulled him into a false notion that whatever happened next really did not matter and really should not frighten him, because it was happening to someone else. He felt as if he were standing somehow outside of the event, watching it on a screen in a nickelodeon movie house—augmented with a wide view, perhaps, and rendered in full color, with surround sound, but a movie picture nonetheless. And thus did he realize matter-of-factly that it was now impossible for him to climb down to his friends in the generator room. There was nothing left for him to do except tighten his grip on the handholds, watch the rest of the film, and see how it ended.

The skylight over the aft stairway yawned open and began to disintegrate. And before he could see what happened to the hundred flailing shapes heaped near "the yawn," the ship's lights winked out. In the darkness, during an interval that must have lasted a second, perhaps less, Alfred heard metal cracking explosively, accompanied by the hollow thud of water gushing in. Then the lights snapped on again, for perhaps a second, and in that second he saw the ship cut in half, as though a mighty cleaver had come down upon it.

In later years it would occur to him that the lights should never have come on again, once some vital connection had snapped, more than 120 feet below his perch, in the very bottom of the ship. The lights should simply have gone out forever. That they did not, told Alfred that Archie Frost and Mr. Parr and the others, during those final two or three seconds before the water reached them, had found the right switches and thrown them, giving the *Titanic* everything they had, with what must have been their dying breaths.

When the lights snapped off for the last time, Alfred knew that his friends were, at that very moment, below the ocean surface and drowning in a ship cut open like a gutted fish. He did not have time to think of anything else. The fourth smokestack's forward stays were anchored alongside the disintegrated skylight. They no longer existed, so the stack stood for a second or two in a precarious balancing act: whatever backward pull the afterstays provided was being counter-balanced by the deck's forward tilt. With the stern set free, floating on its own terms, from the reciprocating engine room aft, the balance suddenly shifted. Alfred White never was able to remember what happened to him next, but others saw.

From boat number one, six hundred feet away, Lookout George Symons watched the stern settle back and "right itself without the bow." The deck leveled out so perfectly that he believed it might actually float and save everyone, but two or three minutes later the rudder and propellers went up "as straight as anything," and there was "a sound like thunder and soon she disappeared from view."

Two hundred feet nearer, Able Seaman F. O. Evans, in boat ten, vividly recalled the ship breaking between the third and fourth smokestacks. The stern section then fell back horizontally, then tipped, then plunged.

At a distance of only 180 to 200 feet, in boat two, Frank Osman, too, saw the after part of the ship settle on an even keel, but he was also close enough to actually see, during the moment in which Archie Frost's team managed to get the lights burning again, pieces of the skylight and stairway and other objects in the rooms beneath Alfred's perch sliding out of the stern and tumbling into the severed bow.

At this same moment, George Rheims and Richard Norris Williams II were swimming within a hundred feet of the wreck. They had stopped to watch, spellbound; and despite the horror of hundreds of people clinging to the railing like flies—and one man up there, impossibly, on the fourth smokestack—they could not help feeling that this was a majestic sight. Just before the lights went out, the *Titanic* reached an angle of 45 degrees, by Richard Williams' account. Then the stern broke free and leveled out, and the fourth smokestack canted up as if an unseen hand had yanked it back toward the well deck.

Within thirty seconds, the deck started slanting forward again, this time rolling to port. The smokestack rolled away with a loud rumble and disappeared, but Richard and George did not see this; their attention was riveted to the rudder and the brass propellers towering overhead, glistening. A man in white was ascending the six-story rudder— George supposed he had swum to it and grabbed on when the stern leveled out, and now it was hoisting him more than a hundred feet into the sky. *If I get out of this alive*, he thought, *there's one man I'll never see again*. And then the ship—what remained of it—seemed to twist in a semicircle, giving up the last signs of its list to port and pointing its keel skyward at a 90-degree angle. There it seemed to pause, hanging motionless for what felt like minutes but must actually have been seconds. Gradually, even a little gracefully, it slid straight down and was gone, "as if swallowed down a mysterious throat."

No one ever did see the man on the rudder again. Richard Williams was just as certain that no one would ever hear the tale of the man on the smokestack, but somehow Alfred White had rolled overboard with the stack without getting rolled upon and, though receiving a blow to the head sufficient to erase his memory of having done so, he managed either to be thrown away from the stack, or to swim away from it during the critical five or six seconds remaining before it could slip under, and form a slipstream, and drag him down.[3] Without remembering how, he reached the canvass-hulled, collapsible lifeboat called "A," half flooded, with its sides broken, and at least three dozen people, including Richard Williams and George Rheims, scrambling to get in.

From afar, Richard had written Alfred off as the last man he would ever see again, and yet the *Titanic's* only surviving electrician became one of the first people Richard met.

THE STERN, WHEN George Rheims observed the last of it, went down with such surprising grace that Chief Baker Charles Joughin was able to step off the *Titanic's* tail without getting his hair wet. The only sound George heard from the ship, in that final second, was a faint gulp. When it broke away from the bow, the stern must have bobbed

---

[3]It seems reasonable to suspect that Alfred White received his head injury upon reaching the half-flooded and dangerously overcrowded collapsible A—which was reached originally by "more than thirty people," only fourteen of whom paddled away. Another boat A survivor, Rosa Abbott, also received head injuries. Cold water is known to revive people knocked unconscious, meaning that it is possible that Alfred White and Rosa Abbott received their injuries during the actual sinking and were awakened by cold shock; however, head trauma alone was severe enough to keep both of them hospitalized for months (Alfred was unable even to write a one-page letter until late June, to the family of Mr. Parr, who had saved his life). Another phenomenon frequently associated with head injuries is the erasure of memories immediately prior to the injury. Alfred White had total recall right up to the moment the smokestack began to fall, but could not remember how he came to be in boat A. Rosa Abbott, too, failed to remember being pulled into A. Were the injuries sustained during the ship's breakup, one wonders if Rosa and Alfred would have had enough strength remaining to reach the lifeboat. It brings to mind George Rheims' remark, "I will spare you the details [of boat A], which were horrible," and James Cameron's response, "Which means they had to kill people . . . with their oars."

up and down—repeatedly; and as the last of its buoyancy escaped, the hull was probably reaching the amplitude (or upswing phase) of its final bob, so that it was, relative to the ocean surface, virtually motionless when the Atlantic closed over the baker's shoes. For the first fifty feet of its descent, the stern (seemingly by miracle) produced no suction at all. If it had, Charles Joughin could never have lived to tell the tale.

For the next two hundred feet, perhaps three hundred, the rudder and propellers continued to point straight up at 90 degrees, but as the 330-foot-long stern section gained momentum, accelerating past fifteen miles per hour by the time it reached a depth equal to twice its length, drag forces began to take command.

The power of water, like the power of ice, lies in its mass. A large bath full of water (say, seven feet long, two feet deep, and three feet wide) weighs three quarters of a ton. This means that a stream of water only two feet deep and seven feet wide can easily sweep a car away, even at the modest speed of fifteen miles per hour. For the ninety-foot-wide, ten-deck-high, open mouth of the stern's sever, the water was strong enough to begin peeling jagged hull plates out to port and starboard, as though the open mouth were trying to act like a parachute—which, in a sense, it was.

Further aft, at the very end of the stern, beneath the docking bridge, the roof of the third-class general room (where passengers Rosa Abbott and Gus Cohen had found nearly two hundred people in prayer) probably became unhinged at this time and began to peel back. Atop the forwardmost part of the roof stood two cargo cranes. These, too, probably began to unhinge. The starboard crane lies southwest of a boiler field (that is, in association with the contents of boiler room one), more than three hundred feet from the stern's point of impact on the bottom. From all appearances, as the bow and stern snapped apart, the boiler room (and coal bunkers) just forward of the reciprocating engines, and directly below the third smokestack, shattered into hundreds of pieces, like glass. The heavy boilers fell in a straight line to the bottom, whereas the stern, on account of its irregular shape, parachuted, fluttered, and spiraled down, somewhat like a giant leaf. Indeed, its mouth now points in a direction opposite the one in which it began; it points away from the severed bow, 180 degrees.

That the boilers (and the forward end of a reciprocating steam engine) are lying together indicates that they started their journey from roughly the same place, not very far from the surface, meaning that they came free before the stern had a chance to twist and spiral away from the *Titanic*'s breaking point. For the heavy starboard crane also to land hundreds of feet from the stern, it, too, must have separated early in the descent.

Boilers, engines, and cranes were not all that broke away. When the roof beneath the crane began to peel, the hundreds of people trapped in the general room, and the benches on which they had sat with their children and prayed, were swept through the opening. Probably, they became part of the ship's slipstream and continued to trail down behind it; but no one is sure. Almost certainly, none of them still stirred. They had by then reached a depth of 600 feet, just below the endurance limit of space-age saturation divers.

The peeling and ripping would have continued with increasing ferocity, had the stern continued down with its open wound facing forward. Given these conditions, the double-hulled keel on which the giant reciprocating engines stood was destined to be pulled out from under their feet and raked aft, breaking the engines free. Instead, the same forces that caused the stern's mouth to behave like a misplaced parachute, shot the "mouth" an upper-cut and swung the stern level again, probably within nine hundred feet of the surface. In essence, the wide, ragged, and blunt end of the hull offered more wind resistance and (in a manner of speaking) wanted to slow down, whereas the narrow end offered less resistance and wanted to fall faster. That the reciprocating engines and the floor beneath them remained in place means that the ship changed position quickly, before it had reached a velocity of even twenty miles per hour (with an attendant water jet effect equivalent to 21.43 pounds of water per square inch per second, or the weight of a small car pressing down on every square foot once every second—which is more than sufficient to flatten, and perhaps crack, the span of the Golden Gate Bridge).

Once the keel leveled out, the mouth ceased to behave like a parachute, and became more akin to the fins of a dart. The pointed end, with its rudder and propellers still attached, now became the leading end. The rudder twisted to one side, causing the stern to spiral, but a sort of truce had been reached with hydrodynamic forces, by which stability was achieved, and the ship could fall more freely now toward terminal velocity. No fewer than two and one-quarter miles remained in its fall.

The propellers were angled down 20 to 25 degrees, and the open wound was trailing, when the stern arrived on the bottom. The four decks directly above the blades were squashed until their total height was reduced to six feet. This occurred in less than a half second, an interval in which the propeller shafts were raised all the way to the first line of portholes, just below Middle Deck E. During the next second, the 20- to 25-degree angle of impact closed: the reciprocating engines and the keel beneath them came perfectly level with the sea floor. While this was happening, the *Titanic*'s frame—the equivalent of its spine—was bent, and then snapped, in no fewer than six places.

This was the source of the distant, cannonball-like detonations Assistant Purser Frank Prentice felt reverberating against his ribs. Richard Williams, as he swam toward boat A and Alfred White, felt the impact too, just barely. White's friends—Mr. Parr, Archie Frost, and Mr. Sloan—were still down there in the turbine room and the main light room. Of this the electrician had no doubt . . . and neither do I.

It appears doubtful, however, that they stayed there for very long. The stern struck the bottom with such force that a half dozen decks pancaked down, one upon another, and the hull was literally blown apart from the inside. The starboard shell plating was peeled away from the *Titanic*'s frame and bent into the shape of a wave cresting into the seabed. An evaporator from the turbine and generator room shot over the top of the crest, ejected on a hydraulic catapult. It came to rest almost a hundred feet away. More than two hundred feet of steel piping went with it, breaking as it went, and yet all the pieces landed within twenty feet of the evaporator.[4] A large condenser was also ejected from the

---

[4]With few exceptions, port-side hull sections (*those originating aft of the reciprocating steam engines*) and port-side contents are found lying near the port side; starboard near starboard. Exceptions include randomly scattered kitchen debris (typically released at the surface when the ship broke apart, exposing the kitchens, and thereby producing a cookware scatter field a half mile wide), and a pump from the starboard reciprocating engine, which lies 200 feet from the stern's port side, which suggests that it dropped free while the engine room dangled, wide open, at the surface. Some researchers have proposed that the *Titanic*'s stern remained connected to the bow section after the break, and was then pulled under so intact as to leave rooms and refrigerator compartments full of air—leading to a catastrophic implosion at a depth of approximately 800 feet. The distribution of stern debris (port-side debris on the port side; starboard debris on the starboard side) contradicts this. Implosion and scatter within 1,000 feet of the surface would have resulted in a far more random distribution (from the

generator room. It fell against the afterpart of the crest. Behind the crest, the room itself was left open to view. A sub's searchlamps revealed a turbine still rooted to the floor, but little else remained. Ladders, tool chests, wrenches—all appeared to have followed the condenser and the evaporator out the starboard side.

In 1986, the robot *Angus* photographed several pairs of leather shoes near the stern, on the starboard side. Bacteria and scavenging organisms can make bone disappear within a dozen years, cloth within two or three decades, but leather may sometimes require a century or two. The shoes, lying in pairs, are spaced eighteen inches apart, with the soles of each pair pointed in the same direction, as would be expected had they been attached to feet, as would be the case if they marked places where bodies had come to rest, then vanished, leaving behind only shoes.

One pair in particular captures my attention: They are a workman's leather boots, with one of the shoelaces still surviving and tied snug in a bow. Engine room debris and lumps of coal surround the pair.

Has *Angus* found and photographed one of Alfred White's fellow electricians?

We will never know. The shoes, and any identifying arti-

---

generator room aft, starboard hull fragments and contents would be strewn equally on the port and starboard sides, producing a pattern similar to the cookware scatter field). Instead, when Captain Paul Henry Narnageolet sent the robot *Robin* into the third-class quarters on the aftermost part of C, D, and E decks starboard, where an actual "skinning" of the ship—a peeling down of hull plating similar to that seen near the generator room—had opened entire staterooms to view, his cameras revealed the rooms to be absolutely empty, as if a tornado had reached inside the *Titanic*, stripping out its contents, leaving only bolts where the feet of bunk posts had once been anchored to the floor. On the starboard side, out to a distance of 100 feet, he discovered the contents of the rooms themselves, ripped and scattered and often blown apart into small artifacts—just as one would expect had the stern arrived reasonably intact on the bottom only to be rendered, two seconds later, unrecognizable.

facts that may lie near them, obscured by the upper inch or
two of sea floor "snow," should not and shall not be disturbed by the archaeologist's spade, or by its deep-ocean
equivalent. They remain one of the *Titanic*'s forbidden
zones.

There was a time, back in the days of the Cold War and
"Reaganomics," when I agreed with Bob Ballard's final
proclamation that *no* part of the *Titanic* should be probed
by anything more invasive than remotely operated cameras. The change began with submarine pilot Ralph Hollis'
suggestion that I approach the idea of raising and displaying the *Titanic* as strictly an engineering challenge.

I began to wonder, and with Brookhaven National Laboratory physicist Jim Powell, I soon discovered that even
raising the *Titanic*'s bow section intact would not be as expensive as most people had supposed, though I still had
very mixed feelings about it.[5]

The change was complete soon after I met Walter Lord,
in what became another of those odd, *Titanic* coincidences.

Late in the summer of 1986, about two weeks before I
bought a copy of Walter's sequel to *A Night to Remember*, I
mailed a sticker to his publisher for autographing and even-
tual pasting into my copy. On September 15, while in Man-

---

[5]A scaled-down variant of the Xerad Corp./Brookhaven design (unfortu-
nately, a bit too scaled down, with insufficient attention paid to distributing
the lifting force through a large number of anchor points) was applied by a
French-American team to the raising of a three-story-tall hull section that
once enclosed stateroom C-86. The resulting bending and fracture of the
metal overlaps and complicates, almost beyond recall, analysis of a system
of twists and fractures previously attributable exclusively to the original
breakup of C-86. By way of forgiveness, this was in fact a "flight test" of
new deep-ocean equipment. Like the first crashed Mars probes and the first
Apollo spacecraft, it was something that had never been tried before.
Though Powell and I had warned that there were not enough anchor points
and that objects rising through water could attain surprisingly high terminal
velocities, there were engineers whose views were opposed to ours 180 degrees, and the fact of the matter was, until it happened, no one truly knew
what would happen.

hattan, I purchased his book, stepped onto Lexington Avenue, and bumped head-on into none other than Walter Lord. One could easily have knocked me over with a feather when I realized that this was the man whose picture I had just seen on the inside flap of the dust jacket. It is a tribute to Walter's extraordinary graciousness that my awkward apology was followed by an immediate curbside conference about the *Titanic*. He was very curious about Bob Ballard, whom he had never met but with whom I had recently sailed. The conference lasted a half hour, despite the pain I had caused in Walter's left leg.

When he returned home, my letter of two weeks earlier was (by coincidence) waiting for him. "It is a pleasure to autograph and return the stickers for your copies of *A Night to Remember* and *The Night Lives On*," he replied. "This may be superfluous—can't remember whether I signed the books themselves when we met on Lexington Avenue."

It was the beginning of a long and special friendship. About three years later, we met *Titanic* explorer George Tulloch for the first time. He had found a curious object lying in the debris field, not very far from the stern: a leather satchel bearing the initials "R. L. B."—first-class passenger R. L. Beckwith, apparently. Richard Leonard Beckwith survived in boat number five. He had told his wife that he should return to his stateroom for the satchel, but in the end he decided to stay with the lifeboat.

Mr. Tulloch had brought the satchel to the surface, and he wanted to return it to members of the Beckwith family, but the Beckwiths had refused it, and returned to him a mystery.

Among the satchel's contents were a pocket watch, an initialed silver jewelry box, a gold-plated stick pin shaped into the Chinese symbol for good health, a pendant inscribed with, "May this be your lucky star," and a bracelet with the name "Amy" spelled out in diamond chips.

The Beckwiths protested that there had never been an "Amy" in their family, and added that all the other names and initials were equally wrong—belonging, by everything they knew, to non-Beckwiths. The misinitialed, misnamed assemblage "gave them the creeps."

"So," Walter said, "objects from the wreck site really can tell archaeological stories."

Indeed they could. When Walter and I first heard about the satchel, we had assumed immediately that it was ejected somehow from the Beckwith's stateroom (D-35, just forward and starboard of the Grand Stairway). Wrong assumption. Instead, the satchel's contents began to hint at widespread activity within the ship during its final hour— not all of it noble, and most of it unsuspected by people gathered in the open air of the boat deck, whence came most of our survivors' tales.

"Looting?" I wondered.

"Might be," said Walter. "Now, who do you suppose was carrying the master keys to first-class staterooms that night?"

"It could only have been crew," I supposed. "It begins to look like one of the crew was darting from room to room, filling Mr. Beckwith's satchel . . . until the water climbed up around his knees."[6]

"He and the satchel would have wound up on the top deck, then," Walter concluded. "Washed overboard, presumably."

That quickly, Walter and I were converts. The satchel seemed to fit like a matching puzzle piece into another mystery

---

[6] The Beckwiths occupied stateroom D-35, four decks below the first smokestack, very near the Grand Stairway on the starboard side. A silver box in the satchel bears the initials "D. G.," and with little doubt this belonged to the Duff Gordons, four decks higher, in staterooms A-16 and A-20, also located in the bow, just a few steps from the Grand Stairway. A sapphire and diamond ring, set in platinum and identical to a ring described in Mrs. Cardeza's insurance claim, was also found in the Beckwiths' satchel. Mrs. Cardeza's private promenade suite, B-53, was located just aft of the Grand Stairway. It seems likely that while Thomas Andrews and a small number of helpers were tearing doors off hinges—apparently trying to extend the ship's life by making sure all of the portholes were closed before any of the staterooms were submerged, and apparently unable to locate any of the master key sets—someone was quietly unlocking stateroom doors and loading the Beckwith satchel, following the Grand Stairway from D deck to A deck, his rate of ascent determined, most likely, by the dictates of rising water.

that had nagged my friend for many years: In 1912, the White Star Line notified the Blackwell family, of Trenton, New Jersey, that Stephen Blackwell's body had been found and the director of the Halifax morgue wanted someone to take him away. When his mother arrived, the deceased turned out not to resemble her son in height or hair color or style of clothing, and she could not understand how a man wearing a White Star Line crew jersey had been identified as a first-class passenger. "He wouldn't be seen dead in one of those!" she exclaimed.

"The jersey was wool," a White Star employee tried to explain, "and it would have provided much-needed warmth, and there were plenty of extras aboard. We thought one of the crew might have given it to him."

"Why did you think that?"

"Because of what he was carrying," came the reply. Inside the jersey's pockets were a silver shoe horn and a silver button hook, both engraved with her son's name.

"So, now," I said, "we have possibly *two* crew members pilfering staterooms."

Walter nodded. "And if we've found hints of two, you can be sure we haven't found them all." What continued to fuel the mystery, for Walter, was that he could not understand why a member of the crew rummaging through cabins would have chosen a shoe horn and a button hook. There were far greater valuables easily at hand. Edith Russell had left all of her jewelry in stateroom A-11, and anyone breaking into C-104 could have had Major Peuchen's $200,000 in easily exchangeable bonds (worth approximately $7,000,000 in 2001 dollars).[7]

_____
[7]As she left her stateroom for the last time, Edith Russell took a musical toy pig her father had given her as a "good luck mascot" after she emerged from a fatal car accident (one of the world's first) as a sole survivor. Major Peuchen brought with him, from C-104, two pairs of long underwear, a good luck pin, and three oranges. A partial census of what items passengers and crew thought most important to carry with them reveals a pattern, in descending order, of three categories: good luck charms, tobacco, and alcohol.

It seemed strange to Walter Lord that anyone in the crew would have engaged in such low-level pilferage. Even in the Beckwith satchel, there was nothing of particularly great value.

I was reminded of the 1977 blackout in Manhattan, which triggered the worst chain reaction of rioting and looting the city had ever seen. Robbers broke into the American Museum of Natural History and stole the brass railings near the dinosaur exhibit and the Hall of Gems and Minerals. Only a few dozen steps away from one of the stolen railings, the Star of India was on display with its alarm system dead, and the police busy elsewhere.

"Some curious things are done at a time like this," Charles Joughin had said. Walter and I really did begin to believe that our two apparent examples of looting were but a tiny indication of more widespread behavior, making it possible to suspect that the low-level pickings we saw in the satchel and the crew jersey were all that remained by the time the satchel-holder and the jersey-wearer arrived. The more valuable items, including Major Peuchen's bonds and Edith Russell's jewelry box, might already have been taken by others.

George Tulloch showed us a photograph of an aluminum megaphone found lying in the debris field, believed to be the funnel through which Captain Smith shouted his final orders. As legend had it, his last call had been, "Be British, boys! Be British!" In light of what the Beckwith satchel was beginning to teach us, the megaphone and the legend brought only an ironic smile.

As meteorites are a poor man's space program, archaeological artifacts are indeed a pauper's time machine; and while in the science fiction sense they may not be much of a time machine, they certainly get the job done. When you sift through objects that can reveal details about day-to-day life, or of their owner's final hours, you become part of the event, the first person to arrive on the scene after a struggle that ended long ago, in which each man had barely more than two hours to make a decision about how he was going to act.

Mr. Tulloch found a broken fuse panel lying near the evaporator and the out-jetted pipes from the turbine engine room. I noticed that one of its labels could still be read: WATERTIGHT DOOR BELLS. During the early morning hours of April 15, 1912, the panel had directed electricity from the generator to every part of the ship. Near the end, Archie Frost, Mr. Parr, and those who stayed with them had walked past this very same panel and even put their hands upon it. When I touched it myself, I did not merely touch it with my hands. I touched it with my heart. I reached out across time and touched the face of Archie Frost. And though he might only have been a boy that April night, barely into his twenties, I knew that the boy was ten of us.

A pauper's time machine . . .

I have seen a finger smudge of lamp-black left by the owner of a Theran bake shop thirty-six hundred years ago. I have held objects recovered from a Bronze Age ship lost during the time of King Minos and Eighteenth Dynasty Egypt. And what attracts me most to the field of archaeology, what addicts me to it, is the uncanny tendency for inanimate objects to pull you back through time and put you in touch with the people who used them.

I have grown accustomed to standing in the main square of Thera's buried city, holding an ancient oil lamp in my hand and, in my mind's eye, watching children come out to play. But not one of those Bronze Age children has a name, or a face: and though Plato called those children Atlanteans, and we call them Minoans, we do not know to this day what their civilization called itself. What makes the *Titanic* so different is that with each object I touch— Mr. Beckwith's satchel, Dr. Simpson's medicine bag, the

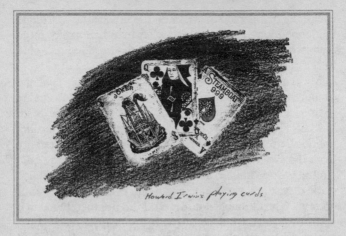

Howard Irwin's playing cards

davit from which my friend Eva Hart last saw her father waving good-bye—I know exactly who I am touching. And more haunting, still, are the pieces of crystal or china or brass that are perfectly recognizable; objects I remember seeing in my grandmother's house. The very familiarity of the material both chills and warms the bones.

Every shipwreck is a time *portal*, a seagoing town flash-frozen. As archaeologists, as we slowly conjure up lost worlds, and as gleanings from the debris field slowly bring us closer to those vanished people, our lives are intruded upon and occasionally deeply troubled by the past.

No, a Bronze Age city is nothing at all like the *Titanic*. At Thera and Knossos, though they grew with myth to become Atlantis, and at Mashkan-shapir, though it came down to us as biblical Sodom, I have never really felt as if I lived with . . . ghosts.

Oh, what I can tell you about ghosts.

HIS NAME WAS Howard Irwin, and in 1993 the leather and the wood trim on the lid of his steamer trunk were within five years, possibly within as few as five months, of final collapse, following a process of deep-ocean dissolution that had lasted eighty-one years. The bacteria inside the trunk were the sort that thrived in the absence of oxygen. They had already metabolized every scrap of iron, while at the same time preserving wood and cloth and wood pulp. Once open to the sea, and to oxygen and oxygen-loving bacteria, all the organic materials inside the trunk—which included reams of paper in pristine condition—would have vanished in the space of four or five weeks, as had happened to the contents of at least five other trunks on the abyssal plain, long before the first deep-diving robot flashed its strobes at the *Titanic*.

Had the bacterial environment inside Mr. Irwin's trunk changed before the crew of the *Nautile* found it and raised it, no one would ever have known how Mr. Irwin lived and died, or that he ever lived at all.

A preserved diary and a small, carefully wrapped bundle of love letters from his girlfriend tell the story of how, on New Year's Day, 1910, Howard Irwin and his friend Henry Sutehall began a round-the-world-trip from Buffalo, New York. They financed their adventure by taking up odd jobs and winning contests, moving from Buffalo westward through Cleveland, Chicago, St. Louis, and San Francisco.

Both men were musicians in their early twenties. Henry played the violin. Howard preferred the wind instruments—his clarinet and his sheet music survived intact inside the steamer trunk. In Buffalo, they had worked as trimmers for E. E. Dennistons, installing and repairing upholstery in horse-drawn carriages and early automobiles. They drilled holes for car parts in Chicago, picked peaches in California, won a racing sweepstakes in Australia. Early in 1912, they entered a talent contest in South Africa and were awarded a trip—which brought them to England in March, and to the *Titanic*.

Of himself, Howard was not particularly complimentary. He wished he could be more like his friend: popular, honest, an upright and quiet man who did not drink, swear, "or cast an evil eye upon the beautiful young ladies that crossed his path." By contrast, Howard viewed himself as an arrogant and aggressive man who would let conversations deteriorate into cursing, then deteriorate from that point into fist-fighting. It is apparent from his writings that he sought always to improve upon his character . . . and yet his deck of cards has survived, with one of the cards marked, and it appears that when he boarded the *Titanic*, he did so under an assumed name.[8]

Howard's love interest was a young vaudeville performer named Pearl. Like Howard, she traveled widely, and a letter from her mother, "Mrs. Ann Shuttle," reassured an apparently jealous Howard that Pearl was faithful and truly did love him.

During the Christmas of 1910, just prior to his voyage to Australia, Howard was briefly reunited with Pearl in Cali-

---

[8]On March 14, 1916, Henry Sutehall, Jr.'s father was awarded by the White Star Line the sum of $200 (approximately $7,000 in 2001 dollars) for the loss of his son's life. Howard Irwin's family received nothing, for it could not be proved until now that he had been anywhere near the *Titanic* at the time of his disappearance. In fact, his presence might have gone unconfirmed or unsuspected even by his family, for he does not appear on any known passenger manifest. The diary of his journey tells of a difference of opinion on the sights Henry and Howard wanted to see as they approached Egypt. On friendly terms, they parted on solo voyages, promising to meet in England in March 1912. Howard arrived about a week before Henry, and they spent time together before boarding their ship home. Henry had by now auditioned "impressively" for the London Symphony and was returning home with recommendations for what had all the appearance of a promising career as a concert violinist. Howard, for one reason or another, was apparently traveling under an alias. Many people were adopting assumed names as they boarded the ship—we are finding instances, more and more of them, spread throughout third, second, and first class. It seems to have been "the thing to do" in 1912, and because of this we may never really know who died on the *Titanic*.

fornia. In subsequent journal entries, he hoped that he would one day become the kind of man worthy of marriage to her. He had no way of imagining, of course, that his journal was fated to become the world's first example of readable paper recovered from a shipwreck, or that the wreck was to become a cultural icon, or that in writing of only one man's hope and love, he was actually writing history.

Crossing to Asia and then to Australia on tramp steamers, working their way "on God's good graces," from place to place, Howard and Henry circled the globe—apparently trying to live, a little slower but for real, Jules Verne's round-the-world adventure novel of only a few decades before. "With luck the trip will take us two years," Howard had written in his diary, as he plotted a course from Australia to Egypt, through the Suez Canal and the Mediterranean Sea to Southampton, England. "And with bad luck (WELL) we are going anyway."

With such hope and grace did Howard's words enter the vault of the ages, along with a calling card identifying him as a member of a men's club in Buffalo, New York.

The club still existed in 1993, still had records dating back as early as 1910. What chilled the club's secretary, when we mentioned the membership card, was that we were not the first to have recently inquired about Howard Irwin.

Some three years earlier, an elderly woman had called, asking questions about any letters that might be on file, from a man who had disappeared without trace in April 1912—a date that led her to believe, by 1990, that he had been an undocumented passenger aboard the *Titanic*. The secretary could not remember her name. He recalled only that she had asked him whether or not letters existed confirming that Howard Irwin had reached Southampton in time for the maiden voyage, or suggesting that, "for whatever reason," he had decided to complete his journey under an alias.

Before the document search was finished (no such confirmation was ever found; probably such letters still lie within the hold of the RMS—*Royal Mail Steamer—Titanic*), the woman had herself disappeared: "died of natural causes at advanced old age," the secretary believed.

The mystery must have troubled Pearl, or a sister of Howard's, or perhaps even a daughter, for most of her natural life. In the end, she had guessed the right answer, but now it is too late for the woman ever to know, and she has left us with the haunting and bittersweet distinction of having solved a mystery only a few short years after the last person to remember it had ceased to be.

Postscript: The similarities between Howard Irwin and James Cameron's fictional Jack Dawson are obvious, despite the fact that no one actually knew the story until after Dawson had become a cultural phenomenon. After this book's first edition went to press, the families of Howard and Pearl came forth with the poems and diaries of a man who seems to have Jack Londoned and Forrest Gumped his way through the first half of the twentieth century (see Dave and Barb Shuttle's article "Recovered Artifacts Recall a Story of Tragic Love," *Voyage,* Vol. 31, Winter 2000. The freeze-dried version of Howard's story, now authenticated beyond serious dispute, is as follows: Howard survived the *Titanic* on account of a last minute bar brawl that resulted in his being kidnapped to slave labor in the orient. He died in New Jersey in 1953, leaving behind, amongst his papers, a final poem to Pearl, whom he envisioned as married with grandchildren—"Step back . . . to recall the times of pure and innocent love . . . so many years earlier . . ." Howard passed without ever knowing that Pearl had died pining away for him, some forty years earlier.

4

•

Breaking Away

•

Do you remember that young man Emily [Badman] was flirting with on the *Titanic?* Well, you know he was lost, and his body was found, and Emily's eyeglasses were in his pocket, and his mother from England sent them all the way back here to Emily. Wasn't that nice of her?

—THIRD-CLASS PASSENGER S. ILES
TO MRS. FRANK GOLDSMITH

A horde of foreigners tried to break out from the bowels of the ship, all carrying their possessions on their heads. Horrible people. They must have been *fourth*-class passengers. Thanks to the vigilance of the crew and the officers with their revolvers, they were kept back behind the barriers and prevented from swamping the lifeboats.

—SECOND-CLASS PASSENGER EDWINA CORRIGAN

They could not have been more orderly if gathered in a church . . . There was not one woman who shed tears or gave any sign of fear or distress. There was not a man at this quarter of the ship who indicated a desire to get into the boats and escape with the women. The coolness, courage, and sense of duty that I here witnessed made me thankful to God and proud of my Anglo-Saxon race that

gave this perfect and superb exhibition of self-control at
this hour of severest trial.

—FIRST-CLASS PASSENGER
COLONEL ARCHIBALD GRACIE

Heroism and chivalry are the great myths about the
Titanic. This might have been true, somewhere on the
boat deck. But mostly, it was arrogance and madness that
night . . . madness . . .

—THIRD-CLASS PASSENGER MILLVINA DEAN,
YOUNGEST *TITANIC* SURVIVOR
(as told to her by her mother)

THE AMERICANS HAD come and gone. The Russians had
come and gone.

A French-American-Canadian team came and went.
And came again. And again.

Nineteen ninety-eight became the year of the ninth expedition, the year they raised a three-story-tall slab of steel
that had, until about 2:17 on the morning of April 15, 1912,
been the port-side hull of Mr. and Mrs. Walter Douglas'
stateroom. It broke away just aft of the third smokestack,
above the bulkhead separating the forwardmost reciprocating steam engines from the aftermost boiler room and coal
bunkers. Like other fragmentary sections from this region,
it appears (in a pre recovery, pre stress fracture survey) to
have bent ever so slightly, then shattered like glass. This is
consistent with how Frank Osman and Alfred White per-
ceived the separation of the stern: the result of a surprisingly clean cut, as if the ship—or at least that portion of it
left standing above water after all the popping and bursting
noises had died away—had been cleaved off by a butcher's
blade.

White had been looking down upon the sever from the fourth smokestack; Osman had watched from water level, close enough to see uprooted equipment and furnishings tumbling out of the French Cafe and the *à la carte* restaurant. Decades later, when an automatic dishwasher (one of the world's first) was recovered from the scatter field of *à la carte* debris, it still contained the glassware, silver forks, and dessert dishes from Sunday night. Half-penny coins (each worth about sixteen cents, when adjusted for inflation through the year 2001) were lying between the brass tubes at the bottom of the washer—"Tips left on plates for the waiters," George Tulloch realized. He supposed that the coins and the dishes had been left on a final wash cycle by staff who were in a hurry to "call it quits" and go to bed, expecting to find both the dishes and their buttercream-smeared tips clean the next morning. According to Helen Churchill Candee, the *à la carte* servers had put in an unusually long shift that night, continuing to provide dessert until at least 11:00 P.M., some forty minutes before the *Titanic* struck the iceberg.

Almost three hours later, Anna Sjoblom, an eighteen-year-old Finnish passenger from Third Class, was trying to lead a friend up an emergency ladder, meant for crew use, in a desperate run for the safety of the boat deck. The ladder brought them past the wide windows of the restaurant, and when Anna glanced inside, she drew her breath in astonishment. On every table, gilded lamps still burned. Their shades were rose-colored and fashioned from silk. The beautifully lighted tables were set with crystal and napkins and fine china for the following day's breakfast. Anna's friend had never seen the like, and she immediately forgot about, or went into denial about, what had brought her to be out there in the cold on a ladder in the first place. The room appeared to be completely deserted, and the girl suggested that she and Anna kick in a window and go inside "for a look around," but Anna convinced her that the room might not be so empty as it seemed, raising concerns that the White Star Line might fine them for any damage they did to the *Titanic*'s windows. Barely more than twenty minutes later, Walter Douglas' stateroom shattered and the windows of the *à la carte* restaurant broke of their own accord. Eighty-six years after that, the hull of stateroom C-86, following two days of drying on the deck of a recovery vessel, began to spill worms—hundreds of live worms.

They had infiltrated and colonized the mineral formations that Bob Ballard found hanging off the *Titanic*'s hull the way icicles hang from a house in winter. Ballard had named the formations *rusticles*. Then Roy Cullimore and I began dissecting them in 1996, proving that they were not mineral formations after all, but a complex consortium of various (mostly) bacterial species that were arranging themselves into actual tissue layers, complete with a functioning circulatory system. They were not quite animals, but they were certainly getting very close to becoming such, and they were built (impossibly) from bacterial cells.

We had never seen the like: a consortial lifeform. And if a three-billion-year-old living fossil nesting on (and devouring) the hull of the *Titanic* did not seem particularly strange or dramatic, then add to this picture the worms. Roy believed that they might have developed a symbiotic, mutually beneficial relationship with the rusticles, whereby the bacteria exuded a waste product edible to the worms and the worms, in their own turn, as they sought food, acted as miniature Roto-Rooter machines, "unclogging arteries," in a manner of speaking, and enlarging the rusticles' circulatory system.

"Our own white blood cells might have originated like this," Roy reminded me. "Instead of worms, imagine amoeba-like animals taking up residence in our remotest ancestors—creatures that were entirely 'non-self,' staying on until they became a vital part of 'self,' no longer recognizable as separate entities."

"The stranger within," I said, and let out a long, slow whistle. I had fully expected the *Titanic* to bring me back almost a century, but not millions of centuries. "Are you sure we can't make this story a little more strange and tangled?" I said, grinning. "You know, toss in another element?"

"Oh, the story is bound to get more strange," Roy assured. "It's already a very complex web down there."

ROBERT BALLARD WAS right about one thing: No one would ever leave the *Titanic* alone again—ever again, so long as humans and their machines continued to thrive on the continents above.

Almost every year since Ballard first saw her in 1985, lights have come out of the sky, like alien spacecraft, breaking the darkness and the silence. Even during the unusually historic summer of 1991, as the Soviet Union began to fragment, the Russian submersibles *Mir 1* and *Mir II* landed on the *Titanic*'s bridge, crewed by Americans, and soon-to-be-former-Soviets. The world's last empire was falling, and yet a surviving remnant of its navy was drawn, as if by some inner urgency, to a tragedy that should have been put to rest decades ago. One explorer described his attraction to the RMS *Titanic* as something inexplicable which he himself might never truly understand. Another attributed it to nothing more exotic than a uniquely human sense of mystery, and to him the *Titanic* was simply a ship full of secrets. One came because the hull plates appeared to have become the perfect culture medium for all manner of exotic organisms—which he was bringing back to the lab, hull plates and all, with the hope of discovering new medicines. Another came, years ago, mourning the loss of his wife and deciding, at the expedition's end, that he would give to the sea two wedding bands, and his wife's high school ring, and a golden necklace bearing two small diamonds: one as blue as Caribbean water, the other as red as blood.[1] And there was one who came because piloting a submersible was simply his job, and he liked being away from his wife.

There was a reason for each of them. They came to find something, or to escape something, or to learn something, or to forget something, or to take something away, or occasionally to leave something behind. Whatever their reasons, they came, drawn as if by a homing instinct, deep-rooted and impossible to ignore.

The majority of them could usually be found gathering an hour before dinner in the expedition ship's mess, retelling the story of the last night of the first voyage until at last one would have to believe that there was nothing new to be said. But the *Titanic* was indeed like a fractal equation, each of its details seeming to expand and pick up other details along the path, especially at those odd crossroads where archaeology met, and picked up, oral history. The *Titanic*, like the fractal universe, was a tale of expanding dimensions, a tale retold and revised and relived over and over . . . over and over . . .

With a gentle gulp. That is how it ended: with the rounded, aftermost part of the ship slipping under so quietly that nothing worse than a six-inch wave closed over Charles Joughin's shoes and there was not enough suction even to pull his head under and wet his hair, as he waded into the cold and the dark at 2:20 A.M. on Monday, the 15th of April, 1912.

Three minutes earlier, Charles Joughin and Alfred White had felt the stern break free beneath their feet. Seven min-

---

[1] The necklace was saved, at the last possible instant before being tossed overboard . . . though to this day it has not been worn, and to this day the mourner wonders, "How did James Cameron know?"

utes before that, at 2:10 A.M., the bulkhead between boiler rooms four and five (beneath the second smokestack) had failed with a loud thud, yanking the bow down hard. An hour and twenty-five minutes before that, directly below the first smokestack, the bulkhead between boiler rooms five and six buckled, cracked, then collapsed in a foaming white gush, driving out the firemen still toiling to draw coal from the boilers and shut them down. It was 12:45 A.M., an hour and five minutes after the impact. Lead Fireman Frederick Barrett knew that the last two feet of iceberg damage had come exactly two feet past the watertight bulkhead into boiler room five, producing a fire hose-like spray that the pumps could easily have handled, if only that last two feet of hammering from the berg had not crimped and so weakened the bulkhead that next door, in coal bunker ten, water was actually seeping up through the floor plates.

For decades, engineers and professional second-guessers would argue that the *Titanic* might have been saved, if only that last bulkhead had been built one deck higher, but there was no doubt in Mr. Barrett's mind that the vital, ship-dooming breach did not overspill the bulkhead but instead rendered the barrier's height utterly meaningless by shooting straight through it, "as if something that had been holding the water back gave way."

When the breach occurred, Assistant Engineer Herbert Harvey was helping John Shepherd, who had fallen and broken his leg shortly after the collision. He hollered for Fred Barrett and the others to "Get out of this!" and in a panic, Mr. Barrett raced up a service ladder, never stopping to look back, never seeing what happened next.

He did not have to see. What he would know, for the rest of his life, was that Mr. Harvey and Mr. Shepherd were still down there when he left, and that no one ever saw them again, and that they must therefore have been among the very first souls to be claimed by *Titanic*.

At that same moment, as Fred Barrett raced the tide to E deck and the first distress rocket went up, Mrs. Henry B. Harris noticed a group of armed officers stretching ropes across the aftermost part of the boat deck, to keep back the third-class passengers. This was being done, a crewman explained, because the ship was listing toward the bow and the weight of the steerage passengers in the stern could, in theory, be used to counterbalance some of the water entering the bow. A clever way to move water about, she supposed, for according to Darwin even the Archbishop of Canterbury was 95 percent water.

Theories about redistributing water weight aside, Mrs. Harris still believed the ship had not been badly damaged, and was anticipating nothing more dramatic than being towed to Nova Scotia for repairs. It couldn't be *that* bad, she told herself. Only two or three hours earlier she, Henry, and several close friends had been eating dessert in the *à la carte* restaurant. They had been surprised to find the banquet hall almost entirely empty, except for one table reserved for a large party that included the shipping line's managing director and Edward J. Smith.

"There is our captain," Helen Churchill Candee had said.

"That signifies his peace of mind," observed Colonel Archibald Gracie.

But Smith stood to leave after only ten minutes and when Mrs. Harris asked him to stay, he had replied, "I am going back to the bridge as we are among icebergs and that is where I belong."

No, the ship could not possibly have been hit very hard, she reassured herself, because the captain had known about the ice. Yet the door to her closet had been open at 11:40 P.M., and she remembered that her clothes were swaying on their hangers, swaying toward the starboard wall of stateroom C-83, to the accompaniment of a faraway rumble somewhere forward.

"We're going awfully fast to have my dresses sway like that," she had told Henry. "Much too fast among icebergs," and it was as she uttered these words that she noticed the engines shuddering into reverse and bringing the ship to a halt.

"This can't be all that bad," Hugh Woolner assured Helen Candee, as they peered over the rail at a glass-smooth sea that thwarted all sensation of motion and made the deck feel both rock-steady and rock-hard. This was an illusion, of course, but a stubborn and curiously dangerous one. At 12:50 A.M. the sea so resembled a slab of polished black granite that it reflected every star in the sky—"and made of the universe," Helen would recall later, "a complete unity without the break of a skyline. It was like the inside of an entire globe."

Richard Williams II's father spoke again about the *Arizona*, spoke with authority, spoke again and again of his faith in the unfailing bulkheads that divided the *Titanic* into watertight compartments and rendered her unsinkable, though he had no way of knowing, as he spoke, that one of those unfailing bulkheads had already drowned Mr. Harvey and Mr. Shepherd.

Nearby, Captain Smith was ordering lifeboats down to the A Deck promenade for the evacuation of passengers. Helen Candee had an impulse to remind him that there were several major differences between this ship and his previous command, the *Titanic*'s almost identical twin sister, *Olympic*. For a start, this ship's promenade deck was upgraded by weather-proofing: plate glass windows that enclosed, and sealed off from wind, the entire deck. They also sealed off egress to the lifeboats, Helen supposed; but he was the captain, she decided, so if this seemed like madness to her, there must surely have been method to it. A captain was to be obeyed, not informed.

Hugh Woolner did not stand so firmly on protocol. He walked up to Smith directly, saluted, and said, "I beg your pardon, Sir, but are you aware that the windows on the deck are unbreakable plate glass and that the boats cannot be reached?"

"My God, you are right!" said Smith, in anguished humility. "I'm not on the *Olympic* anymore!"

Richard Williams II shook his head. "I'm not much of a believer in symbols, Father, but when the letters spelling out the ship's name are sinking into the sea and the captain forgets which ship he is on, I don't think it bodes well for the future."

Driving the point home, the *Titanic*'s cellist passed by, dragging his precious instrument through the crowd, its metal spike banging on the deck planks. He had been off duty at the moment of impact, but was now dressed in full uniform, including a gold lapel insignia in the shape of a lyre. Within two hours he would be dead, and within two weeks his widow would be billed two crowns and six pence for the loss of the lapel pin. She would also receive a demand to "settle an account" for damage to his uniform.[2]

There was no doubt in young Richard Williams' mind that the musician did not care about tearing or damaging his instrument, or his uniform, or any other White Star

---

[2]Altogether, the "uniform account," which included White Star buttons (1 shilling), totaled 14s. 7d—or $3.50 in 1912 American dollars, or $122.50 when adjusted for inflation through 2001. Settling this account proved difficult for the band's widows, as corporate lawyers declared the bandsmen, "not crew, but officially passengers, therefore not covered under the Workmen's Compensation Act." They then heaped insult upon the widows' injuries by docking their husbands 75 percent of their agreed-upon salary for the maiden voyage, on the premise that they had been contracted for a two-way trip and had played only halfway through the outbound leg of the voyage.

Line property that night. He gave the sense of not caring about anything except joining the other members of his band, and Richard understood that he was watching a man who knew that he would soon be using his instrument for the very last time.

Richard decided that brandy might be "a sound precaution at this kind of time." He flagged down a steward and asked him to fill a flask for him, but the steward declined, saying, "I believe the *à la carte* restaurant has closed down for the night."

He was right, of course, but probably not for the reason he supposed. Another steward, by the name of Johnson, had seen the *à la carte* staff being shepherded into their quarters on the starboard side of E deck aft and locked in. Nineteen twelve was a time of British-American animosity and suspicion toward French and Italian nationals, and it was clear to Steward James Johnson that someone had made an evil but culturally consistent decision: These foreign kitchen workers should not be allowed an opportunity to "bring anarchy." Johnson knew that it would be difficult enough, under Lightoller's command, for men to find seating in the lifeboats—but to be locked below, without even a chance to swim away? It seemed grossly unfair to him; but orders were to be obeyed, not reasoned (and Mr. Johnson would live long enough to hear that thought—*orders were to be obeyed*—echoed over and over, from Nuremberg to Nanjing and My Lai).

Monsieur Gatti and his Assistant Chef Paul Maug'e managed to escape the *à la carte* death sentence by changing out of their uniforms, into top hats and evening jackets. Posing as first-class passengers, they had slipped easily through crew barriers and made it to the boat deck, shortly before Anna Sjoblom and another third-class passenger peered through a window and discovered that the restaurant was empty and apparently as silent as a tomb, save for the odd table lamp or tall water glass tilting forward and crashing. First one fell. Then another. Then another.

The people in Third Class had an easier race for the boat deck than members of the *à la carte* restaurant staff, but not by a very wide margin. As it turned out, first-class dogs were afforded a greater opportunity of reaching the lifeboats than third-class passenger Rosa Abbott's children. Just short of 1:00 A.M., someone freed all of the *Titanic*'s dogs from the kennel, whereupon J. J. Astor's airedale, Kitty, was seen making a mad dash aft along the boat deck. About this same time, the order was given to escort the first group of women and children from the aft steerage compartments (fifty-five were led to the boat deck, in only two groups, accounting for half the total number of women and children saved from Third Class). Another hour would pass before an officer opened the barrier between Second and Third Class and announced that "everybody" was at last free to go topside, giving third-class men, and more than fifty of their children, what amounted to an hour's handicap against the dogs.

This was shortly before 2:00 A.M., just as the last two boats to leave the ship upright and undamaged were being lowered from the forward port side, barely more than ten minutes before the bulkhead in boiler room four collapsed, nudging the bow into its final plunge. No one would ever ask Anna Sjoblom or any other third-class passenger to speak at the British inquiry, where it would be denied vehemently that gates had ever been locked, or that even a single "atom of evidence" existed to substantiate a charge of "any attempt [being] made to keep back third-class passengers."

Why not tell it thus? the officers and crew must have reasoned. *The boat is down there. The gates are down there. Who will ever know?*

What they did not know, could not have known, was that

historians of the future were launching robots deep into the *Titanic*'s bow and finding those murderous gates still locked—just as Anna Sjoblom and Emily Badman and Rosa Abbott said they had last seen them, on that cold, dark morning.

Three dogs, including publisher Henry Harper's Pekinese, Sun Yatsen, made it to the lifeboats. Rosa Abbott and her two sons did not, and Rosa's most lasting memory would be of poor Eugene, during the moments following an officer's declaration that the boys—"old enough to be men"—must stay, but that she, if she so wished, could go to the last boat on the port side. Nine-year-old Eugene, acting every bit the man, implored her to leave, but she refused, and the boy fell to his knees in prayer, not for his own survival, or for his brother Rossmore, but for his mother.

For every first-class dog that entered the lifeboats, twenty-nine steerage women and nineteen children died. Emily Badman and Kathy Gilnagh seemed destined to be counted among the lost, having found themselves penned in behind a drawn gate, deep within the stern. An armed, junior officer stood on the other side. "Following orders," he insisted. "It's not time for you to go up."

To Anna Sjoblom, such orders seemed neither out of place nor particularly sinful; she supposed those in charge were certain that the ship was indeed "unsinkable, as advertised," and did not think it wise to have more people on the upper decks than was absolutely necessary. Fellow countryman Olaus Abelseth was even more forgiving; to him, class distinction was merely a fact of life and visits to the boat deck were, "in the natural order of things," a privilege reserved for passengers in the first- and second-class cabins—even if the ship did happen to be sinking.

"To hell with your orders!" hollered a young Irish truck driver named Jim Farrell. "Great God, man! Open the gate and let the women through!" To everyone's surprise, the sailor turned suddenly meek, and lowered his gun, and unlocked the barrier—the sheer power of Mr. Farrell's baritone having been enough.

Kathy and Emily's troubles were not over, for there was no clearly marked path to the first-class deck, where the lifeboats were. They and a half dozen others from "Farrell's brigade" emerged, lost and frightened, onto the second-class deck, which was by now as deserted as the *à la carte* restaurant except for a man standing all alone near an open window. He offered himself as a human ladder to the A Deck, and that is how Kathy Gilnagh happened upon the first-class lounge, taking note of how deep and luxurious the carpet felt against her feet, as she dashed down the incline toward the last boats.

Below, in the turbine room, Alfred White and Archie Frost still toiled, giving almost no thought at all to reaching a lifeboat. Two chambers forward of the turbine room, beneath the third smokestack, other members of their team maintained the minimum amount of steam pressure necessary to keep the water pumps working, the lights burning, the telegraph transmitting. They had turned off all forty-five ventilating fans, transforming the climate below into a more humid version of Cairo, Egypt, on an August afternoon, but the electricity, they decided, was needed for more important concerns, and besides: their discomfort would not last very long.

Under these tropical conditions, Trimmer Thomas Patrick Dillon was dragging a new section of hose from the aft compartments (where the ship's generator and its most powerful pumps were located) to boiler room four, beneath the second smokestack, where the floodwaters were rising. To run the hoses where they were needed most, and to make it easier to move from compartment to compartment, Chief Engineer Bell had ordered all the watertight doors raised aft of boiler room four, reasoning that when the water began moving toward his generators, the doors could easily be lowered again. It was sensible reasoning, given what he and his team knew should happen next, but what should be and what would be were galaxies apart that morning, turning even the most well-reasoned and heroic plans into potent mistakes.

Above, in lifeboat number six, Helen Churchill Candee seemed the only passenger to have actually taken pause to wonder what was happening to the electrical engineers, as she watched two lines of portholes shining brightly under the water. The propellers were beginning to break the surface and the *Titanic* looked as if she were determined to raise her stern until it stood like a glowing skyscraper in the middle of the Atlantic. Like Richard Williams II and George Rheims, she could not help being astonished by the beauty of this city-ship that was no longer hers; and her astonishment brought with it an overwhelming sense of guilt, and her only comfort became the bright lights of another ship on the water, drifting only a few miles away, close enough for all to be saved. It had to be close enough—yes, Captain Smith had ordered one of the lifeboats to row toward it, so it had to be . . . should be . . . had to be . . .

First-class passenger Henry B. Harris, noticing that the crew were having a terrible time launching collapsibles C and A from the starboard side, escorted his wife to the opposite deck through the captain's bridge. Mrs. Harris, by now expecting something more than a detour to Nova Scotia, glanced at the clock behind the map room windows, and it became for her one of those curious, random moments when an image burns itself indelibly into one's memory, as if captured on a photographic negative: the hands had just passed 2:00 A.M.

"Why aren't you in a boat?" called an angry voice, and she turned to see that it was Smith himself.

"I don't want to leave him," Mrs. Harris meekly replied.

"How can your husband save his own life and yours too?" the captain cried, and motioned her toward collapsible D, on the port side. "You get into that boat—it's the last one, now. And lose no time. Give your husband a chance."

That seemed to be all she needed to hear, but as she and Henry exited the bridge, they met Mr. Straus, the owner of Macy's. His wife had also made a decision not to leave her husband, but Mr. Straus would not hear of Renee Harris repeating the act: "We've already *had* our lives," said sixty-seven-year-old Isidor. "You are young. You have your whole life ahead of you. You go and may God be with you."

Henry lifted Renee into his arms, kissed her gently and quickly, then shoved her into the arms of a sailor, throwing her the blanket he had been carrying for the past two hours.

When young Edward Lockyer escorted Emily Badman onto the scene, it was becoming difficult even for some children, especially steerage boys, to get away in the lifeboats. Only two of the Asplund children were allowed to depart with their mother: three-year-old Felix and five-year-old Lillian. Filip (age thirteen) and Clarence (age nine) were "old enough to be men," and remained on deck with their father. In those desperate last minutes, as Mrs. Asplund looked up from the lifeboat and begged someone to save her husband and the rest of her children, the distinction between boys and girls, men and women, filtered down to and divided even her five-year-old twins. Only the girl was fitted into a sling and passed down by the crew.

Nearby, Anna Sjoblom looked on as a Swedish couple—Alfrida and Anders Anderson—kissed each other and their five children good-bye. Then Alfrida clasped the youngest child, two-year-old Ellis, close to her breast. Anders held the next youngest, and all seven of them jumped overboard.

Emily Badman noticed a horde of mice emerging onto the boat deck and thought the scene "kind of cute," until Edward Lockyer pointed out, "They're not mice."

Years later, Emily would find it impossible to understand how the realization of rats being aboard the *Titanic* could have filled her with even a momentary horror, considering all else that was happening around her. She had thought of staying behind with Edward, but he told her that he could take care of himself and that she should climb down to the lifeboat, if for no other reason than to spare him any undue worry. He then pointed to the rats as proof that he would be safe: "You don't see *them* jumping into the lifeboat, do you? She's a strong ship. The rats don't want to leave."[3]

Calmed and convinced, Emily gave him the only item she had rescued from her cabin: her eyeglasses, for safekeeping until they met again.

Kathy Gilnagh almost missed the last boat. A crewman told her there was no more room in collapsible D. Remembering Jim Farrell's superb example of what initiative and voice-power alone could accomplish, she barged up to the officer and shouted, "But I want to go with my sister!" She

---

[3]Based upon average populations found in most newly constructed ships and buildings, there were, aboard the *Titanic*, approximately 6,000 rats, 200,000 to 350,000 cockroaches, and up to 2 billion dust mites (which means that the number of mites inhabiting a ship just under 900 feet long exceeded by about 500 million the number of people living on Earth in 1912). No rats or cockroaches are known to have survived. However, at least 50 million mites boarded lifeboats on the skin, and on the clothing, and in the blankets of survivors. Only one cat is known to have been aboard the *Titanic*, and she is said to have disembarked before the ship left Southampton (cat-lovers take note of further evidence that they *are* an intellectually superior species after all). A stoker named Jim Mulholland reported that he had cared for the ship's cat, and for its four kittens born enroute to Southampton. Mulholland signed off from the crew after "Mouser" carried her babies one by one off the ship. He explained to journalist Paddy Scott, "That cat knows something."

in fact did not have a sister, but one way or another she needed to move the man out of her way. It worked. He backed off an arm's length and submitted, and when she climbed down a rope, dropped into the boat, and stood up, she was surprised to see that she had not descended very far at all. Her head was almost level with the forward boat deck. The sea was about to reach the bridge.

"Look at her," a man said. "It's impossible, but I do believe she's sinking."

"Yes, she sure is," Kathy replied, and she would be amazed, in future years, at the matter-of-fact manner in which they discussed this appalling fact.

"I heard someone saying that the engines and boilers will break loose as the tilt increases," the man continued. "He said they'll crash down through the bulkheads and fall out through the bows; but if you ask me, they'll simply stay put, and their weight will crack the ship in half."

"Don't you just hate when that happens?" Kathy asked, and began searching for an oar.

Renee Harris, only two or three seats away, did not hear the discussion. Her only thought was that if she had struggled just a little harder against the sailors who pulled her into boat D, if she had waited just a minute longer on the starboard side, she would still be aboard with the man she loved. Mr. Straus' words came back to her: "God be with you."

"No!" she shouted, and Kathy returned her a puzzled expression. "God is not with me. God is going down with all those people who have no chance. God is going down with the *Titanic*."

On the opposite side of the bridge, Steward Ed Brown did not need to hear Miss Gilnagh's or Mrs. Harris' proclamations to know that he was in a very tight corner. The deck seemed to be settling beneath his feet like a very slow elevator and J. Bruce Ismay, the managing director of the

White Star Line, had just ducked away aboard collapsible C in an outburst of utter confusion underscored by the crackle of gunfire, or cracking wood, or both.

Presently, Ed Brown and a half dozen other men were struggling to push collapsible A to the edge of the starboard side, working against a list to port that had been developing ever since the sea reached E deck, and which had grown suddenly worse. The lifeboat felt to Ed like a truck that had lost its wheels, and he was trying to push it uphill.

One of the crew ordered the ropes that had just launched Ismay's boat slackened, so that they could be hooked to A and it could be *pulled* uphill, using the electric davits.

But the end seemed so near, now, "and tying our lifeboat to a sinking ship doesn't sound like a good idea," the steward protested.

"Compared to what?" someone snapped back.

Ed looked around . . . at the slanting decks . . . at the blocks of ice that had fallen near the forecastle, drifting free now that the forecastle was submerged . . . he then submitted and did as he was told. Before the lines could be secured, several passengers, including five women, added their weight to the lifeboat. It was almost to the edge and ready for push-off when Ed noticed Captain Smith standing behind him with a large aluminum megaphone at his side.

"Well, boys," the captain said, "do your best for the women and children, and look out for yourselves." He then turned away and walked onto the bridge. This was probably the last anyone ever saw of Smith. By Ed Brown's accounting, "a very few seconds after that," the bridge literally disappeared.

It was 2:10 A.M. Deep below the second smokestack, the bulkhead separating boiler rooms four and five had taken all the pressure it could hold. When finally it gave way, it burst like a child's rubber balloon, sending forth a thundering wall of water that could be felt through the deckwood under Ed's feet. In scarcely a second, the deep, interior tsunami shot sixty feet aft to the forward bulkhead of boiler room three, shredding pipes and uprooting boilers. Anyone caught in boiler room four did not survive long enough to believe, or even to register, what his eyes saw. Equipment lockers and coal bins and steel ladders blended undetectably with the hammerhead of water, as it mashed against, and cracked, the rear wall.

The sudden loss of buoyancy at this location caused the bow to plunge down, producing suction over the submerged forecastle and well deck, and yanking the entire hulk forward about six or seven feet. This was the surge of acceleration that, five hundred feet aft of the bridge and collapsible A, almost pitched Alfred White and Archie Frost to the floor of the turbine room.

At that same moment, the sea came rolling up in a shoulder-high wave over the boat deck. Collapsible A was still on the deck when the wave began to crest. Some fifty passengers standing nearby dove into the lifeboat. It was, to Ed, like riding a rowboat in the surf at Coney Island, with the added thrill of being dashed against the windows of the captain's stateroom.

This was the moment that made moot all the subsequent fury over too few lifeboats being put aboard the *Titanic*. Twenty boats or fifty boats—there was little difference, in the end. The crew had managed to launch only eighteen, with two (A and B) being floated in tatters off the decks as the bridge and the gymnasium went down, and one of these was still anchored to the ship.

Ed knew what was coming next. He did not have to see the davit slipping under; he did not have to feel the afterfall tightening in his hand.

"Cut that line loose!" he hollered to a crewman on the

forward end of the boat, and began slicing away at the afterfall. Then, just as the rope parted in his hands, just as he
began to breathe a sigh of relief, the forward fall straight-
ened and twanged like piano wire, pulling A's bow under
and washing everyone overboard—everyone except the
man on A's bow, who went down with the rope, still cutting
as he went.

Ed never did see him again. Collapsible A simply reappeared like a surfacing whale—empty, its forward fall cut
through.

The steward had never learned how to swim, but he
would tell a reporter later that as he held onto a lifejacket
he was momentarily fascinated by a row of rectangular
windows, toward which he was drifting, glowing bright
green under the water . . . momentarily fascinated—until
the windows burst inward and a hole seemed to open up in
the sea surface and someone ahead of him was snatched
down into the ship, snatched as if by a great undersea
predator. "No, I could not swim," he said, "but the snatching was a powerful motivation for quick learning . . . and
there were other people around me in the water. Yes, and
well I know it, because they tore my clothing away from
me with struggling in the water . . . I learned to swim like
an athlete, then."

He swam toward the large black object that had surfaced
near him: the battered remnant of collapsible A. No more
than sixty feet away, the already submerged bridge continued its descent, sucking and dragging through seawater. A
powerful riptide pulled Ed and A from the starboard side
over the place where Smith had made his last stand, bump-
ing A against the base of the first smokestack and spinning
it around to the port side. Collapsible B, also stripped clean
of passengers, approached from the opposite direction. The
two boats crisscrossed over the bridge, each headed
whence the other had come.

As Ed measured time, more than two hours would pass before he reached the safety of A, but in reality it was barely more than two minutes. The water was so cold that by the time he pulled Rosa Abbott and George Rheims into the boat and took hold of an oar, his feet would swell large enough to burst his shoes, and his hands would be just as badly damaged.

(—*And you volunteered to take an oar?* asked an incredulous Examiner Cotter at Lord Mersey's inquiry. *Yes*, came the reply. *And you took an oar?* Cotter pressed. *Yes . . .*)

And during those last six or seven minutes before the stern vanished, he saw the lights still burning. They burned even after the ship gave a loud report, like the report of a cannon. When he looked whence the sound had come, far away aft, he saw the stern give a tremble, and of this much he was certain: "There were lights burning then."

Between the 2:10 A.M. collapse of boiler room four's forward bulkhead and the 2:17 A.M. trembling motion—which Ed interpreted as a sign that "the bow had fallen off"—Chief Baker Charles Joughin found Dr. O'Loughlin near the starboard side of the *à la carte* restaurant, rummaging through the pantry and wine cellars on B deck, one deck directly above the ship's hospital. It was clear to Joughin that the ship's surgeon had stayed near his post most of the night, and that he knew this to be the hour of his death.

An hour or two earlier, the gentle old doctor had argued, in the curiously matter-of-fact manner of so many arguments overheard after the first lifeboat left, that when it came time to choose between freezing amidst panicked mobs in the ocean or dying inside the ship, he would meet his end indoors. By the time the ship reached a depth equal to its length, he reasoned, his lungs would be imploded and he would be dead. "Not necessarily painless," he had predicted, "but it has the advantage of being quick."

The baker was not so sure that this was the best way. A few minutes before the boiler room four deluge, he had thrown more than thirty wooden deck chairs overboard, as much for himself as for others. He stepped into the smoking room, then went again to the promenade deck, then ducked inside again, then made his choice.

As Ed Brown swam after collapsible A, and as Alfred White climbed toward the fourth smokestack, Joughin and O'Loughlin had but one thought in their minds: to find enough whiskey, and to drink it fast enough, to dull the pain that was certain to come during the next few minutes. The baker had no way of knowing this, but history was about to cast him as a man who survived the *Titanic* due to a remarkable convergence of alcohol, physics, and "fool's luck," and thus would he become the model for the adage that "God looks after drunks and fools," though he was in fact neither of those two things.

As soon as he saw covers being pulled off the lifeboats, Joughin reasoned that if boats were needed, provisions would also be needed. He then organized his staff of thirteen bakers to ransack the *Titanic*'s kitchens and make sure water and loaves of bread were delivered to as many lifeboats as possible. In those days the Marconi signaling device was very new, and though Joughin had been assured by an officer that rescue ships had been contacted and were on the way, he had his doubts about the so-called marvels of modern technology, and did not trust that the castaways would not be adrift for a very long time.

Like the old doctor, Charles Joughin was seen by many survivors that night, offering help wherever he could. He became one of the very few who had ventured down to Third Class. At 12:30 he came upon a group of immigrant women so distressed over the idea of leaving their husbands behind, should they reach the top decks, that they had resolved to take their entire families down with them, including the children. Joughin found the thought unspeakable, and on his own initiative he summoned a half dozen crewmen to help him snatch the children and haul them forcibly up to the boat deck. Their mothers naturally followed, and Joughin jumped into boat ten, helping to drag screaming mothers in after their screaming children.

"It's your lucky night," an officer called down. "You're assigned as skipper of that boat."

"Not on your life!" he called back, then jumped out of number ten and helped lower it instead. There was too much rescue work to be done aboard *Titanic* herself, and he did not want to set a bad example for the rest of the crew. Twice that night he had been ordered into lifeboats, and twice he had refused, while all around him many of those in charge—including the ship's owner—stood by wringing their hands or seeking the safety of the boats. When at last the baker saw empty falls dangling from the *Titanic*'s every davit head, and shrieks began going up into the night, he did what seemed most logical at a time like this: he sought out the nearest pantry, hoping against hope that he could drink himself into unconsciousness before the end came.

Minutes later, collapsible A was settling into position, within 200 feet of the port side, astride the fourth smokestack. Within the ship, floors slanted more than 20 degrees forward, but Charles Joughin would recall for Lord Mersey that he was more aware of the list to port. On the deck above, the sound of shuffling feet took on a more frantic, more sickening quality, and from not very far away, the baker thought he heard men scrambling atop the skylight of the after Grand Stairway, and a large glass pane breaking under the crush of people. Almost directly overhead, Alfred White was just reaching his perch on the fourth stack, and though the lights were dimming to a depressing red glow, they still provided enough illumination for Joughin to read the time on his watch. It was 2:15 A.M. The longest minutes of the night were about to begin.

On the deck outside, a gentleman in evening clothes threw his head back and let out a scream that a steward standing next to him found impossible to believe could be sustained by human lungs and vocal cords. The steward, a man of Charles Joughin's acquaintance (who happened to be named Brown, but was no relation to Steward Edward Brown of collapsible A), had, like Joughin, assisted with the lifeboats, calmly resigning himself to the fact of the ship's sinking. The slope of the decks, the burst of distress rockets, rumors of shootings—nothing he saw or heard had cost him his composure, until that inhuman scream.

Steward Brown bolted indoors and bounced over a table in the first-class smoking room. When he stood up again, he was surprised to find people still in the ship at this late stage. Publisher William T. Stead was going about the great business of sitting in a corner and reading as though perfectly oblivious to what was happening on the decks outside, and to the fact that his reading lamp was fading. Thomas Andrews was standing near the fireplace, staring aft at a large painting showing the approach to Plymouth. The designer of the *Titanic* had defied an order from Smith himself to enter one of the lifeboats, even when it was pointed out to him that there would be many questions no one else could answer.

"Mr. Andrews, aren't you going to have a try for it?" Brown asked. The sound of a steel bulkhead or a wooden wall cracking under the press of water came from somewhere disturbingly near. The steward felt the ship tilt forward and down another degree, and Andrews, in response, merely tilted his body another degree closer to the painting.

"Mr. Andrews?"

There was not a sign that he had heard. He just stood there with his arms crossed, his lifejacket threatening to

slide off a nearby card table, where he had apparently
tossed it. On his face was the expression of a man who has
just lost his child, whose energy and drive have drained
away utterly and without hope of recall.

Even as the sloshing and cracking noises came nearer,
Andrews did not move. After a moment of awed silence,
Brown decided to climb toward the aftermost part of the
stern, which was rising higher and higher and would
clearly be the last part going down. Time was racing. The
steward was not about to wait and see what happened to
Andrews. As he scrabbled away, water came crashing
through the aft wall of the first-class lounge, beneath the
third smokestack, punching through the bar on its way to
the smoking room and the A deck pantry. Mahogany panels and stained glass windows disintegrated. Parts of the
floor and all the furnishings of the lounge became a floating wood pile: pushed, lifted, rolled, and mauled.

Joughin was disoriented and alone on the starboard
side, somewhere near the *à la carte* restaurant, just aft of
the fourth smokestack, when the rooms tilted so irra-
tionally that the stairs became impossible to climb and he
no longer had a choice about whether or not he wanted to
die indoors. He grabbed himself another bottle of spirits
and leaned against a wall that seemed on the verge of becoming the floor. Seconds later, cups, saucers, and knives
broke loose from the cupboards aft and hailed down
around him. A monstrous fist of uprushing water was
aimed directly at his back, and in only two seconds more
it would have hammered through the wall against which
he reclined, if the hull beneath the third smokestack were
not undergoing such convulsions, such surges of twisting,
breaking iron, as to snap the ship in two.

One of the fractures went up through Charles Joughin's
quarters on the port side of E deck, immediately aft of the
third smokestack. It continued through a pantry on D deck,

through Mr. and Mrs. Walter Douglas' stateroom C-86, rose twenty feet aft of Benjamin Guggenheim's bedroom in B-96, and met the forward wall of the first-class smoking room on A deck.[4]

The last thing Thomas Andrews saw was his creation tearing itself apart where he stood. The card tables of the smoking room were bolted to the floor and should have been capable of supporting his weight against that impossible tilt, although if the fireplace were in use (and Steward Brown recalled this to be so), the backs of his legs would have been showered with hot coals. By the dimming but still burning electric lights, he would have witnessed the death of William Stead. Below and ahead of Andrews, walls and railings around the after stairway snapped in the middle and the designer stood in the grip of a surreal vision in which the eleven decks forward of the smoking room cast off and floated away, at first as gently as a ship casting off from a pier—and then the lights snapped off, and snapped

---

[4]This crack (or this branch of what might have been a network of cracks) probably began as a minor stress fracture more than a half hour before the actual break occurred. Between 1:30 and 1:45 A.M., Charles Joughin had returned briefly to his quarters, two decks directly below Walter Douglas' stateroom (apparently encompassed by the "Big Piece" raised in 1998). He was aware of a list to port that had started developing about the time E deck forward reached the sea, and water was lying ankle deep on the port side of his room, against the ship's hull. The *Titanic* was slanted down toward the bows, but when he stepped outside his "stateroom" and glanced down the long, port-side corridor known as "Scotland Road," he observed no water there; only in his room—which was, paradoxically, on higher ground than the corridor. He double-checked his porthole, making certain that it was locked, and that no water was creeping through it. Joughin did not stay long enough to solve the mystery of the leak, for there was still time for rescue work, but given that he happened to be standing where the bow eventually broke away, and that Joughin's port wall, then about six or eight feet under the sea, was actually the skin of the ship, it seems likely that what the baker saw was the formation of the first stress fracture beneath the *Titanic*'s aft expansion joint, the first drops of leakage (the first drops of rain, as it were) from an approaching storm, a terrible and hitherto unprecedented storm.

A grandstand view of the *Titanic*'s stern section suggests that it
bowed out like a water balloon dropped against concrete during its
first second of contact with the sea floor. In the foreground, two reciprocating engines mark the point where the stern broke away from
the bow.

on again—and the world tilted again with dizzying speed,
tilted like a dish, with Andrews standing on its edge.

A 450-foot length of ship was suddenly hurrying away
more than 1,000 feet below, picking up momentum as it fell.
Within the *Titanic*'s bow, the tires of William Carter's Renault Town Car had already caved in under the mounting
pressure. A cloud of debris trailed behind open dining sa-
loons, staterooms, and boiler room one—a cloud such as the
world had never seen before. It rained boilers . . . stoves . . .
tons of coal . . . cases of "dragon's blood," ostrich feathers,
rabbit hair, and opium . . . a grand piano and ivy pots from
the Cafe Parisien . . . the letters of George Rosenshine, an
American supplier of ostrich feathers (whom Mrs. Henry B.
Harris had identified as traveling with a young woman
named Maybelle, under the assumed names of "Mr. and

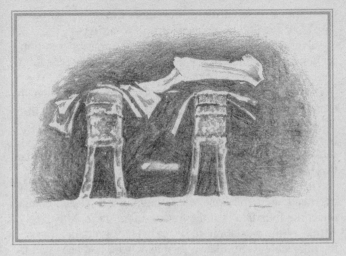

Four stories tall, the *Titanic*'s reciprocating steam engines are the largest ever built. They are seen from the forward part of the break in the stern; we are actually inside the engine room. Just beyond, on the other side of the bulkhead, is the turbine room, where Archie Frost and the rest of the engineering crew stayed behind until the very end.

Mrs. G. Thorne"—they were by all accounts happily married, but each to someone else) . . . three stained glass windows, two boxes of pencils, and a silver ashtray from the gentlemen's smoking room . . . three hundred cases of sardines . . . ninety-one pairs of gloves belonging to Mrs. Cardeza (a wealthy Philadelphian who normally sailed her own yacht back and forth across the Atlantic, but decided that the *Titanic*'s maiden voyage "might be more interesting") . . . Howard Irwin's clarinet . . . a cabinet full of buttercups . . . an aluminum megaphone . . . twenty-five cases of Bass Ale en route to America with the Molson Beer family . . . and thirty cases of golf balls for A. G. Spaulding.

One deck below Thomas Andrews, Charles Joughin did not see this, could not even hope to know of it until the day the realities of scientific achievement caught up with and surpassed the fiction of Jules Verne's *Nautilus*.

As quickly as they had started, all the roaring and popping sounds seemed to die away. The baker lay in sudden dark and a choking soot that was rising everywhere.

People in the lifeboats thought they saw the *Titanic* cutting short her plunge and settling back again toward her propellers, few of them guessing that what appeared to be a miracle—the great ship coming back up and righting itself—was only a moment's respite bought by a spectacular loss of weight.

The next sound Joughin heard was a great rumbling overhead, as if someone were dragging a thousand chains under the foundation of the fourth smokestack. Apparently, Alfred White was about to begin his unforgettable journey to collapsible A. Suddenly, the baker, who had been reclining against a wall-transformed-into-a-floor, chugging down whiskey as fast as he could, noticed that the floor was the floor again, and the wall was the wall again.

"I can't be *that* drunk," he said to the wall, then bolted out a door, mystified, and in only a second or two he arrived at the starboard rail. The lights came on again. He would recall later that they came on for a very long time— minutes, it seemed—but as he told it, they stayed on only long enough for him to glimpse his watch . . . and it was still 2:15 A.M., or very near to it. He thought that ten minutes, perhaps more, had passed since he last checked the time . . . but it was 2:15 . . . or 2:17—no later . . . and beneath his feet, the cruelest tragedy of all was unfolding.

The stern's break point damaged or reshaped the steel in two different ways, depending on whether it was shed near the surface or accelerated, still attached to the stern, into the downblast. The hull section that enclosed Charles Joughin's bunk and Walter Douglas' stateroom tended to buckle slightly, then crack like fire-hardened pottery, as

Double hulled bottom thrust out through side.

A ground-level view of the stern's port side (showing the same length of hull ballooned out to the right side of the grandstand view on page 94) illustrates the violence with which the stern arrived on the sea floor.

would be expected if a great force were applied from only two or three angles (primarily from the bow and the stern) against a single fulcrum (the ocean surface).[5] Slabs of hull crackage from both the starboard and port sides of the break ended up randomly strewn about the stern, as would be expected of plates breaking loose at the sea surface, then spiraling and fluttering like leaves and snowflakes, two and one half miles to the bottom.

By contrast, those hull sections still clinging to the stern when it reached the bottom were exposed to the jetting effects of downblast (forty-three pounds per square inch, or three atmospheres, if impact occurred at forty miles per hour; sixty-four pounds per square inch, or 4.4 atmospheres, if impact was at sixty miles per hour). Downblast, as distinguished from crackage effects, distributes its force

---

[5]By accident, this section was put to virtually the same test a second time. When raised in 1998, too few anchor points focused too much stress (or bending pressure) along the center of the slab. It began to buckle in the middle, and then to break like glass.

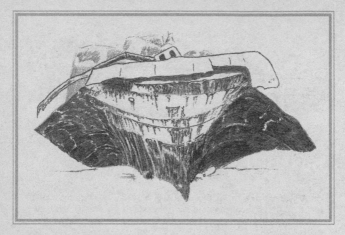

Viewed from the very end of the stern, the thrusting down and peeling outward of the port and starboard hulls becomes horribly apparent. Behind the aftermast, the entire contents of rooms exposed by the peel were ejected to port and starboard—where they sit today, indicating that the peel occurred at the moment of sea floor impact.

more evenly over the entire surface of a metal sheet, causing it to behave, for an instant, as if it were part of the water jet, more fluid than solid. During that instant, the steel would ripple and shift like tin foil or wax, forming new rivet-and-porthole-popping cracks only under the most extreme stresses (typically requiring a slab of steel to be bent back on itself, 40 degrees or more, or to be squashed, somewhat like the skin of an accordion). The explorers who came to this place at the end of the century would be pressed to explain, therefore, why long stretches of the stern's hull came to resemble slabs of warm taffy viewed in the aftermath of an explosion.

And this is where, today, tragedy and revelation unfold beneath the baker's feet, and mine: The hull sections splayed out nearest the mouth of the break, nearest the still-standing reciprocating engines, do not reveal a system

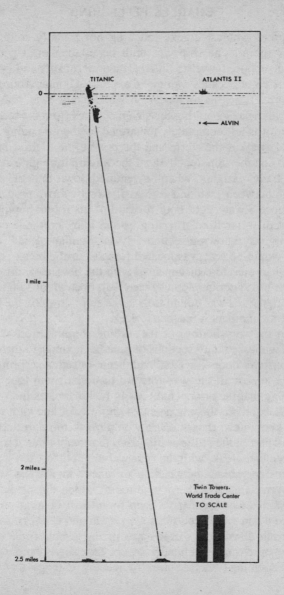

of pre-downblast cracks radiating horizontally from the break point. The ship was built better than most people have supposed—better, in fact, than oil tankers and ocean liners eight decades more evolved than Thomas Andrews' designs. It begins to appear possible, likely even, that the aft bulkhead separating the steam engines from the turbine room was left completely unharmed by the up-ending and breakaway of the stern; and these were the highest bulkheads on the ship, reaching all the way up through E deck.

Charles Joughin, when he ventured down to his E deck bunk between 1:30 and 1:45 A.M., saw two men preparing to close a watertight door forward of his room, hoping to prevent water from traveling up the long, port-side companionway known affectionately as "Scotland Road"; but the would-be seal was located forward of the break point, and had therefore disappeared with the bow, meaning that if the broad companionway were still open aft of Joughin's room, the sea was bound to drag the stern down by the port side the moment it reached E deck.

In the very bottom of the turbine room, Alfred White had witnessed long sections of pipe being dragged through watertight doors—which had been raised and propped open almost all the way forward to boiler room four. Believing that the doors could easily be lowered as the water progressed aft, the engineers had no way of knowing what we know now: that the ship would break through the forward part of the reciprocating engine room, or that it might be a clean break, with the next wall aft able to form a protective membrane between the turbine room and the sea.

Were it not for the door through which the pipes ran, 1,500 people might have been found still floating on the stern when the rescue ships *Carpathia* and *Californian* arrived at dawn. The surface area of the turbine room door was approximately eighteen square feet, slightly more than the combined surface area of iceberg damage that had

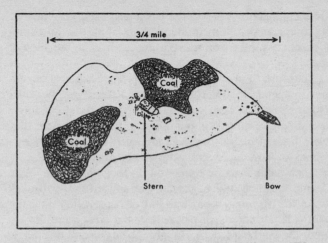

3/4 mile

Coal

Coal

Stern

Bow

drawn the bow under and snapped the *Titanic* in two. Water entering through the doorway would have begun to short out emergency batteries and other electrical equipment within three seconds of the bow's departure, and the subsequent filling of that room was bound, by mathematical certainty, to reach E deck and the port side opening aft of Charles Joughin's bunk within the next thirty seconds.

With no other sources of flooding but the turbine room door, and the aftermost extension of Scotland Road, the stern would have rolled onto her port side and disappeared about three minutes after breaking away from the bow. Charles Joughin's next act, after reaching the starboard rail and checking the time, was to put his watch into his back pocket. Three minutes later, the hands stopped.

He found himself standing in a sudden swarm of jostling bodies, unable to understand how a ship that had been diving like a duck in one minute had managed to level her decks in the next. Perhaps she truly was unsinkable after all, Joughin guessed, but there had come to him an incredible sound—the same loud report Steward Ed Brown heard from collapsible A—and the baker had been very near to its source, and to him it sounded not at all like an explosion, but "as if the iron was parting . . . like the breaking of metal."

The crush of people swept him up. They began stampeding in the dark toward the aftermost part of the ship. Dozens of them were leaping down from the deck above and simply running without taking any heed of where they were headed, as if they had just seen something, somewhere forward, and were trying to get away.

Their panic became contagious to Joughin, and he fell in behind the mob and began moving toward the well deck when the *Titanic*—what was left of her—rolled onto her port side. Hundreds of passengers and crew were thrown from the starboard deck. Joughin, being drunk of course, managed to be the only man who kept his balance. Under the glow of a lone kerosene lantern on the flagstaff, he watched everyone else impact "like swarms of locusts" against the port bollards and rails. The baker hauled himself over the starboard rail and the stern continued heaving to port until at last he was standing on the actual side of the ship. He began clambering toward the flagstaff lantern, sometimes bending down on his right knee to grab a tilted rail-rung and steady himself, other times noticing that he was stepping over up-turned portholes. A disquieting number of them were open, threatening to snare a leg and snap a shin if he misstepped. They vented jets of air, increasingly powerful jets—which became gauges for the volume of water pouring in underfoot.

By the time he reached the white-painted steel plates of the rounded, aftermost part of the ship, the stern's nose had corkscrewed straight down, swinging Joughin and the ship's rudder more than 120 feet above the water.

The *Titanic* now stood perfectly perpendicular in the

night, silhouetted against the stars like a tall building.
Joughin casually tightened his lifejacket and faced the inevitable. Below him, nearly fifteen hundred screaming
people had already spilled into the ocean. At 28 degrees
Fahrenheit, the water stung each of them like a thousand
steel teeth biting at once.

The *Titanic*'s chief baker was a man of average build,
and he was not wearing exceptionally heavy clothing. His
ratio of skin surface area to body volume dictated that his
rate of heat loss, just like everyone else's (unless, of
course, one was exceptionally overweight and possessed
the advantage of a relatively smaller ratio of skin surface
to body volume), would probably kill him within a half
hour of reaching the water, yet he would be found paddling alone more than two hours after everyone else, including the heaviest of *Titanic*'s occupants, had died.
During the years that were to follow, experiments con-
ducted by the United States Navy would demonstrate that
men sitting in ice baths lose heat even faster if they drink
alcohol, which increases circulation and therefore brings
more blood to the skin surface, where body heat is radiated away. But the Navy volunteers would be calmly listening to music and reading magazines. They would not,
as were Joughin and the *Titanic*'s 1,500 swimmers, be par-
ticipating in a major shipwreck—which was bound to
make the heart beat far, far faster than alcohol. Anes-
thetized as he was, Joughin's level of panic and hence his
heart rate, and hence his rate of heat loss, must have been
considerably slower than for any sober person pitched into
the sea that night; but even so, the calming effect of
whiskey alone would probably never fully account for his
survival. Shortly before dawn he would make his way to a
half-sunken, overturned lifeboat on which there was no
room for him, and he would spend an hour more in the

water, with fist-sized chunks of ice bobbing around him, while in other boats men who had only gotten their clothes wet died, their last words being, "I'm going to die. I'm going to die."[6]

The baker must have been a man of extraordinary will, such will that throughout the night, when the unbreakable laws governing heat loss said that he should die, his mind was somehow able to keep him alive.

During his final minute aboard the liner, about two minutes after he jammed his watch into his back pocket, the stern—which seemed to have bobbed up slightly and held steady for a while, as if hesitating before making its final plunge—began slipping away beneath his feet, bringing him closer and closer to the most bone-chilling sound he had ever heard or dreamed of: the shouts and pleadings of hundreds upon hundreds of people scrambling atop floating debris and atop each other, of children being dunked under, having ribs broken and arms dislocated, of mothers crying out for their missing sons and daughters. All that combined agony reverberated up the *Titanic*'s sides, up her cliffs of inch-thick steel, to Joughin's ears, as a single unendurable moan. He blinked

---

[6]Perhaps the more important role of whiskey, in Charles Joughin's survival, was to dull the pain of freezing water until after the water itself had numbed him. Never quite feeling the pain, it did not occur to him that he was supposed to die, making it more possible for him to live. Rosa Abbott might have been similarly numbed to her own predicament by the loss of her two children. She never did think of the cold water, or the severe injuries suffered (apparently) from timbers and people falling down upon her as the stern's port side dunked under and took her with it. She thought only of her children. After she was pulled into collapsible A, men who were uninjured, who suffered from barely more than frozen, swollen feet, began complaining about the "unbearable" cold and insisting that one could not survive such conditions for very long. If ever there existed a situation in which a little knowledge and self-centeredness could be deadly, it existed on the North Atlantic that night. Two of the men in collapsible A began speaking as if in their mind's eye they actually did see themselves as dead, and then they died on cue.

wildly, as if blinking would somehow put this whole inhuman nightmare away; but it stayed. And stayed. And stayed.

Looking about him, he could just barely see, in the light of the flagstaff lantern, a man trying hurriedly to descend the six-story rudder. Far below on the starboard side, a dozen men struggled for footholds on the white-painted keel of an overturned boat—collapsible B. The *Titanic* was drifting away from the crowd and toward B, threatening to take the raft down with her if she made a whirlpool. The little island on which Joughin stood grew smaller with each passing second. The man on the rudder was still hanging on when it glided under and no one ever did see him again. As the sea rose to Joughin's ankles, he gave his lifejacket one last tightening and stepped calmly off the stern. Then the lantern hissed under, leaving him in darkness and with the eerie sense of loneliness that comes to everyone who has been left in mid-ocean without his ship.

He was puzzled and thankful that the stern had not created the anticipated whirlpool, and had allowed him to step off without even a scratch. His watch did not fare so well. As soon as the water reached it, the gears seized up, freezing the dials at 2:20 A.M., and marking forever the moment at which Charles Joughin, chief baker, became the last man to leave the *Titanic*.

THE NIGHT HAD been less dramatic, but not necessarily less interesting, on the nearby steamer *Californian*. In the future there would be much argument over exactly how nearby: Captain Stanley Lord (who was no relation to historian Walter Lord) would naturally try to place his ship as far as possible from the scene of the *Titanic*'s foundering—"forty miles or more"—yet Apprentice James Gibson could swear that he was close enough to see deck structures illuminated by rockets as they lifted off, close enough to discern individual white stars in the air bursts, close enough to see that the rockets (as attested to by *Titanic* survivors) climbed barely higher than the foremast and smokestacks.

As the *Californian* lay to because an ice field blocked its path, a strange ship—which Captain Lord would go to the grave swearing could not possibly have been the *Titanic*—had come up from the east. Third Officer Charles Victor Groves watched the forward mast light appear on the horizon at 11:10 P.M. Fifteen minutes later a second mast light, and rows of bright deck lights, and the green running light on the "mystery steamer's" starboard side had risen into view and the ship continued to steam closer, revealing more details of itself as the minutes passed. Groves estimated that the steamer—a large passenger liner, he was certain—had approached within five to seven miles when, at 11:40 P.M., it seemed to change orientation and come to a stop, leading the third officer to conclude that he had just witnessed an attempt "to escape some ice."

The visitor started up again, then stopped again, and then proceeded to mystify Second Officer Stone and Apprentice Gibson throughout the remainder of their shift. Between 12:10 and 12:20 A.M., she appeared to be trying to signal the *Californian* with a Morse lamp and Gibson, who would testify that he could distinguish individual portholes at that time, tried to Morse back but could not understand what the stranger was trying to say. Only Groves thought of trying the ship's Marconi apparatus, but after listening for about thirty seconds, he heard nothing ("nothing at all"), so he removed the earphones, shut down the receiver, and went to bed. He remembered that the time was 12:15 A.M.—which was also the time Captain Smith entered what had, up to that moment, been a Marconi shack continually on the air with "maiden voyage chatter." Smith told the *Titanic*'s two operators that there had been "a problem with icebergs," and for a minute or two, as the captain spoke, the Marconi apparatus transmitted "nothing at all." Charles Groves must have missed, by a margin of only ten or fifteen seconds, the moment Jack Phillips tapped out: THE TITANIC HAS STRUCK A BERG . . . COME AT ONCE . . .

At 12:45 A.M., the ship fired the first of eight rockets, and at 1:20 Stone handed Gibson the binoculars, saying, "Look at her now. She looks very queer out of the water. Her lights look . . . strange."

The mystery steamer's lights did not seem natural to Gibson. He had seen vessels rolling in storms at sea, and their lights did behave in like manner: some dipping very low on the horizon while others were being raised—but there was not the whisper of a breeze and the sea was as calm as a quarry pool.

"Do you think something is wrong?" Gibson had asked.

"A ship is not going to fire rockets at sea for nothing," said Stone, but Captain Lord, resting in the chart room, did not believe his officers had seen anything more alarming than the shifting perspective of a ship's lights as it steamed away, firing company signals as it went. Stone simply left Lord to judge, believing that authority was to be obeyed, not questioned.

By 2:05 A.M. the visitor's side light had disappeared near the bow. The stern's white lights continued to burn for a little while, but they, too, appeared to be fading.

"Have a look at her now," said Stone.

"Strange," said Gibson, as he examined her through binoculars.

"What do you see?"

"She looks rather to have a big side out of the water."

"That's what I thought," Stone said, then ordered Gibson to wake the captain and advise him that the ship they had seen firing rockets "is disappearing in the southwest."

As he headed for the chart room, the apprentice prayed that he was reading too much meaning into Stone's words: The ship "is disappearing."

Oh, it can't be that bad, he tried to convince himself. *A ship disappears when it steams out of sight. Everyone knows that.* But one thought gnawed at him: A ship also disappears when it goes down to the bottom.

A minute later, Captain Lord both assured and unsettled him by insisting that nothing out of the ordinary had occurred. Sitting up sleepily on his couch, he asked, "Were they all white rockets?" and when Gibson confirmed this the captain muttered, "Company signals, that's all," leaving Gibson embarrassed and worried as he walked back to the bridge, believing then that awakening the captain unnecessarily was the most dramatic thing that could happen to an apprentice this morning. He supposed that for breakfast there would be "a hardy helping of crow to eat," a day of reckoning for his overactive imagination.

And yet, when he arrived on the bridge, Stone was still studying the visitor through binoculars. "Deck lights all gone, now," he announced. "I can still see the stern light . . . no, wait a minute . . . It just disappeared."

"What time do you have?" Gibson asked, his imagination active again.

Stone told him it was 2:20, and as if materializing on cue, a silver meteor ran down the sky, breaking up into a swarm of fading red sparks over the southwest, where eight white rockets had gone up.

Stone shook his head and declared, "That other ship is definitely gone."

"Gone to the bottom, do you think?" the apprentice asked.

The second officer's silence, and a second flurry of falling stars, seemed answer enough.

5

•

Iron and Silk

•

That noise ... All those years, and I could never put that noise out of my head. Not even drink could put it out.

—CHIEF BAKER CHARLES JOUGHIN

The stern stuck up in the ocean for what seemed to me like a long time ... then keeled over and went down. You could hear the people ... thrashing about and screaming and drowning. I remember saying to my mother once, "How dreadful that noise was," and I'll always remember her reply: "Yes, but think about the silence that followed it ... because all of a sudden the ship wasn't there, the lights weren't there, and the cries weren't there ... Silence. The silence was worse."

—SECOND-CLASS PASSENGER EVA HART

How ineffective human innovation was—and is—against the powers of nature.

—FIRST-CLASS PASSENGER MARJORIE NEWELL ROBB

THE CAVITIES IN the iron were a puzzle.

George Tulloch had told me that the rate of the *Titanic*'s deterioration appeared to be accelerating, and when I examined iron bolts and boiler casings at the French LP3 laboratory in 1995, I began to see a pattern very similar to that seen in a tooth overcome by decay.[1]

If a man decides not to brush his teeth for about six months, he will notice that the resulting bacterial assault will destroy more enamel during the last month than during the previous five months combined, in spite of the fact that the microbial assailants' rates of growth and digestion will remain essentially unchanged throughout the decay process. The apparent acceleration rests upon a well-established mathematical principle. Its effects are universal (governing everything from rates of heat loss in Jupiter's moons to the conquest of the land by Coal Age insects), although the results are often surprising when one is confronted for the very first time by the nature and power of surface area/volume relationships. Their power—their simplicity and their beauty—lies in mathematical certainty: as objects of the same shape increase in size, volumes increase faster than surface areas.[2]

By this rule, a perfectly spherical colony of iron-seeking bacteria growing on or in the *Titanic*'s steel would eventually be halted by a relatively smaller surface area (for nutrient intake) through which to feed an increasingly larger (and malnourished) volume of bacteria. The obvious way

---

[1]A paleontologist by training, I was almost as a matter of definition, well acquainted with rotting teeth. Indeed, teeth—which decay so readily in a living, bacteria-laden mouth—generally outlast all other body parts after death, often becoming the only trace of a mammoth, a shark, or a dinosaur. And thus does it happen that some fossil species are known only from their teeth, and the parade of life that has marched across this planet sometimes becomes snapshots of ancestral teeth evolving into descendant teeth.

[2]Keep surface area/volume relationships in mind when buying anything that sells by the pound. Live lobsters provide a good example: tossing aside any urban mythology about lobsters becoming less flavorful as they grow, mathematics dictates that larger lobsters will always have a greater amount of meat (volume) relative to shell (surface area). Relatively speaking, small lobsters are mostly shell.

around this problem is to excavate pits or wells in the food source—which will, much in the manner of a weed's tap roots or a bacterial plaque's cavities in a molar, or a tumor's tendrils, keep the colony's ratio of surface area marching in step with its increasing volume.

Able to read only from the footprints of corrosion, without the living bacterial colonies themselves in hand, it seemed to me that the colonists had tended to flatten out, as they spread across the metal; and they dug pits. They also managed to infiltrate microscopic seams in the hull plates, finding layers akin to the lines of cleavage in a crystal. The seams were produced by the rolling, folding, and pressing of steel emerging white from a factory furnace. It should have been impossible to fit anything between those molecule-thin layers, but the bacteria did not know this, and they squeezed inside anyway. They were fruitful and multiplied, and they pushed the seams apart in a process Roy Cullimore and I would come to call "biological wedging."

Each wedge immediately doubled the surface area available for digestion. Through a process of cavity growth and bio-wedging, approximately 20 percent of the *Titanic*'s mass had disappeared by the time I arrived at the LP3 laboratory. The rusticles were consuming at least 200 pounds of iron per day, and the rate of iron consumption seemed bound to accelerate rapidly, even if the rate of bacterial growth remained the same. Sooner or later, and probably sooner rather than later, the ship's hull plates would come to resemble a house of cards waiting to collapse at the slightest touch of a submersible's landing skids. During the years since Bob Ballard first saw the *Titanic*, Lightoller's gangway door on the port side had fallen away, the gymnasium roof had caved in, a forty-foot length of the promenade deck had dissolved quietly out of existence, and a ledge of steel at the after-

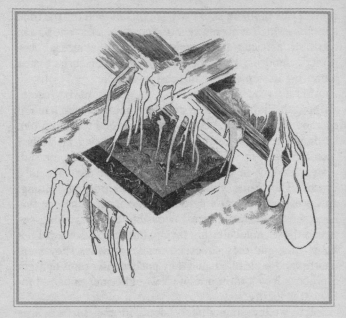

A house of mysteries: In the glare of a robot probe's searchlamps, a garden of rusticles streams down from the steel deck above. On their path to the sea floor, the rusticles pass wooden ceiling beams standing intact some forty feet from the (now missing) Grand Stairway.

most part of the stern, beneath which Ballard and Hollis had parked *Alvin* for a look at the rudder, was about to crash down upon "*Alvin* Base" and bury the giant brass propellers.

Surface area and volume: so went the *Titanic*—a victim of mathematics and biology.

On cast-iron bollards, pulleys, and a davit, I began to find evidence of colonization first by iron-oxidizing (or rusting) bacteria, which must have formed a deepening carpet of "slime" whose undersurface was inevitably cut off from oxygen. A second layer of reducing bacteria (thriving in the absence of oxygen) eventually took root at the bottom of the carpet, becoming the actual front line in the assault against the *Titanic*'s metal, and bleeding dissolved iron up to the surface, where it could be used by the outer layer of oxidizing bacteria. Thus through a symbiotic linkage (strange to relate), two normally opposing bacterial types were living and working together toward the final dissolution of *Titanic*. They thrived, one upon another, like the forerunners of tissue layers in multicellular plants and animals.

The "two-tissue layer" analogy seemed at first a bit crazy to me. Like most hot speculations it was probably wrong, and as it turned out, it really was wrong, apparently because it was not crazy enough to be right. George Tulloch suggested that I would need to see the *Titanic*'s dissolution in a rather larger dimension than the strict boundaries of a bacterial sandwich. He told me about two bacteriologists, at Saint Mary's University in Halifax, who had been examining rusticle scrapings collected from the hull of a Russian submersible after it collided with the *Titanic* in 1991. Henrietta Mann and William Wells had identified, not two, but *twenty* different bacterial species, and two fungal species, and a representative of the Archaea (bacteria-like organisms, often called thermophiles, that normally inhabit geysers, deepocean volcanic vents, and the plumbing systems of nuclear reactors).[3]

---

[3]In yet another odd coincidence, the consortial lifeform tentatively known as *Rusticalus titanicus* is almost exactly what I was looking for when I sailed with Robert Ballard and the robot *Argo* to the Galapagos Rift volcanic zone in the fall of 1985. Brookhaven National Laboratory physicist Jim Powell and I had hoped that our own robot submarine, then under design, would find similar lifeforms near volcanic vents under the ice of Jupiter's moon Europa. I never did find what I was searching for at the Galapagos Rift in 1985, and yet it was staring out at me from every picture Bob had taken of the *Titanic*, only two months before. Eleven years would pass before we knew.

The game I thought I had been playing was not the game at all. The real story went a bit deeper than two bacterial colonies, and was more complex than the one I had begun to tell; and it was a little sadder as well.

"The first thing we need to do is recover and dissect some intact rusticles," I told George Tulloch. "The second thing you'll need is a really good microbiologist who is not just a microbiologist. You want someone who is also an evolutionary biologist, an invertebrate zoologist, a botanist, and a paleontologist—in other words, a true polymath. They're not easy to find, George."

"But I think I've already found one," said Mr. Tulloch, as if he had known, a year before I knew, what the digested metal would reveal; as if he had been a step ahead of me all along, but had kept quiet about it.

Almost ten months later, I met Roy Cullimore for the first time as we stood together on the dock at St. Johns, Newfoundland, waiting to board the research vessel *Ocean Voyager*. The conversation started off with the weather . . . the weather on Mars . . . about 3 or 4 billion years ago.

The previous evening, a reporter had called my home asking about a (probable) Martian meteorite I had examined fourteen years earlier.[4]

"Sorry," I protested, "but I can't talk about Mars today. I have a plane to catch. I'm going back to the *Titanic*."

When I arrived at Kennedy Airport, I saw newspaper

---

[4]The volcanic rock I examined in 1982 had solidified between 1.1 and 1.3 billion years ago. Though I made a search specifically for blobs of carbonate (a sign of bacterial life, ubiquitous in the *Titanic*'s rusticles) and bacteria-like or "protocell" fossils (already discovered in icy, 4-billion-year-old carbonacious meteorites from the asteroid parent bodies), the search was doomed to failure because the life-producing phase of Mars' existence had ended at least 2 billion years earlier. This first Mars rock (which was brought to my attention by two aptly named Antarctic explorers: Drs. Andy Frost and Peter Snow), despite being more than a billion years old, was actually too young.

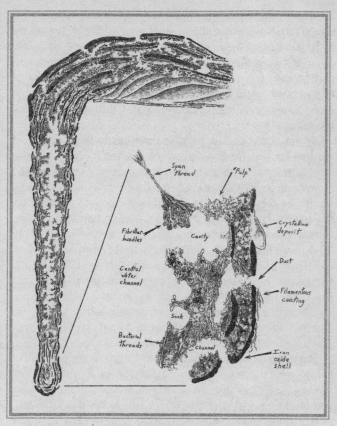

Cross-section of a typical rusticle, much like the ones hanging from the reception room ceiling on page 112. The rusticle interior gives us a glimpse of how multicellular consortia (things that became us) might have begun on this planet 3.5 billion years ago. Current research is focusing on potent new drugs produced by the rusticle's immune system. By acting as a culture medium for the "iron eaters," the *Titanic* might ultimately save more lives than it originally took. (Illustration by Cullimore and Pellegrino)

headlines announcing the discovery of ancient, bacteria-induced mineral formations in what seemed for all the world to be a piece of asteroid ejecta from the surface of Mars. *So, that's what the reporter wanted to talk about*, I thought, and on the way to the plane I bought the largest bag of Mars Bars I could find, for celebration with the crew of the *Ocean Voyager*. Independently, Roy Cullimore had done the same.

As we stood on the pier, sharing candy bars, Roy told me that he was discovering whole bacterial ecosystems—worlds no one had ever dreamed existed—thriving and competing in ordinary clouds directly overhead. The planet Venus, he theorized (if it still possessed some trace of atmospheric hydrogen), might support a habitable zone, somewhere in its cloudtops, where the temperature fell to 70 degrees Fahrenheit and bacteria could survive.

Places like Mars, and Jupiter's moons Europa and Ganymede, represented the opposite extreme to him: able to sustain life only beneath their icy surfaces.

"What makes our own planet unique," Roy stated, "is that it is able to sustain life from its cloudtops all the way down to the surface, and deep under it."

The conversation moved on to Saturn's moons Enceladus and Titan, to Neptune's Triton, to ice worlds circling the hundreds, perhaps thousands of cold, Jupiter-like stars that might be drifting between the sun and Alpha Centauri. A half hour and several light years later we finally came around to introducing ourselves. Four days after that, we had arrived on site. Three days later, we had dissected our first rusticle.

That my idea about two vastly different bacterial colonies living one atop the other was wrong should have been obvious from the start, as are most of nature's surprises, when viewed with twenty-twenty hindsight. The first rusticle (and the second, and the third)[5] turned out to be hollow, and hollow spaces were of course among the simplest means by which organisms (in a world on which every nation, every city, every individual cell, was attempting to live beyond its means) could expand the surface area through which nutrients were transported and absorbed.

It was Roy who discovered, and began to map, an animal-like organization in those hollow spaces, who charted the paths of reservoirs, ducts, structural threads, and— could that be? Precursors to, or analogues of . . . arteries?

"Look under the microscope and tell me what you see," Roy said.

The . . . *thing* under the scope was more complex than a sponge, and a sponge was sufficiently complex to be claimed by the field of invertebrate zoology. The difference between the two was that a sponge cell, torn loose from its brethren, would die much in the manner of an ant separated from its colony, whereas the rusticle's cells were individual bacteria, and each bacterium could presumably survive on its own. What I began to see was the probable ease with which independently living, bacteria-like species might weave themselves into multicellular arrangements.

Years earlier, when Jim Powell and I had made our first sketches of a Europa space probe, we would have been happy to one day find simple bacteria—even fossil bacteria—in an ocean hidden beneath the ice of a Jovian moon. I would still be surprised to discover crab-like and fish-like creatures living in alien seas, but their existence would no

---

[5]As it turned out, Roy and I were an annoyance to the *Ocean Voyager*'s metallurgists, and they were an annoyance to us; as is typical on most oceanographic expeditions, biologists are at the bottom of the pecking order. Our best specimens came from bilge pumps and garbage pails, having been hammered off raised hull pieces by the metallurgists.

longer jolt me like a shock from a live wire; no longer, now that I had seen the rusticles. I began to believe that the phenomenon we called multicellular life could happen almost anywhere—anywhere that remained warm enough and wet enough for long enough. This was day three at the *Titanic*; day one of school.

"This is amazing," I said at last, trying to suppress a laugh.

Roy laughed, put a hand on my shoulder, and said, "Welcome to Mars."

THE GRAND BANKS are a cold wilderness, covered by two and one-half miles of sunless water, pressing down with a force sufficient to crush a fully-charged scuba tank. Even deep-penetrating cosmic rays have tremendous difficulty reaching down through ten World Trade Center Twin Tower lengths of water. Save for the submersible's searchlamps and the occasional visit of a bioluminescent jellyfish, the bed of the Atlantic is blacker than any mine shaft. If photomultipliers could be draped over the *Titanic*'s decks and left there, the only light transmitted to us would be the faint flashes of carbon, potassium, and thorium atoms decaying in the ship's timbers and iron plates, trying to nudge their little corner of the universe back toward chaos.

Darkness, crushing pressures, and—we should add— life, are the dominant conditions of the abyssal plains. Even before the *Titanic* arrived on the bottom and formed a reef, uncounted species of ribbon worms, bristle worms, slugs, crabs, and eyeless shrimp had lived here, few of them any larger than an aspirin. As near as Roy Cullimore and I could tell, the mud-dwellers of the Grand Banks were unaltered in appearance from creatures we had known as fossils in rocks nearly a half billion years old. The mud-dwellers' ancestors must have dined on plesiosaur skeletons long before the last tyrannosaur drew its last breath, and it was a fair bet that this parade of unchanging life would still be here—uncaring, unaware of whatever happened to humanity—long after the West-Atlantic plate, moving at the rate human fingernails grew, carried the *Titanic* eight hundred miles to New York.

The most ancient, most unchanged, and most dominant of all deep-ocean lifeforms have turned out to be the "lowly" bacteria. A census of life in mud and water sampled from the Pacific and Atlantic reveals that the bacterial biomass of the oceans (just the oceans) outweighs all the fishes, the crabs, and all the other living creatures in the seas combined—plus the mass of all plants, animals, and humans dwelling on the continents.

"SOMETIMES IT TAKES a 'low-life' to put humanity in its place," said Roy, with more irony than most people were apt to recognize. Peeling apart "bacterial tissue layers" in one of the *Titanic*'s rusticles—looking at them and uttering the words "amazing" and "impossible" and finding myself on the verge of jumping up from my seat and cheering at one of nature's great "wows" (a cheer cut short, before it began, by the sudden realization of where we were)—I remembered that the mitochondria powering almost every cell in my body more closely resembled free-living, self-replicating bacteria than parts of my cells. Roy believed he saw, in certain human regulator genes and cell structures, evidence that 90 percent of the cells and cell organelles in our bodies were bacterial in origin; "and so it may be said that we are an indulgence for the ten percent of the cells which are comprised of the bits and pieces over which we claim 'true' sovereignty."

Low-lifes . . . putting us in our place . . . Perhaps the *sine qua non* for our existence was simply a series of ancient infections transformed from parasitism to symbiosis.

From independence to dependence to total assimilation. It seemed to be happening before our very eyes, inside a living fossil scraped from the *Titanic*'s hull. Somewhere very far back in our ancestry, a bacterial consortium might have filled the Holy Grail of our multicellular origins. The rusticles told us so.

The rusticle consortium could not possibly have appeared out of nowhere, evolving now for the very first time aboard the *Titanic*. The *Titanic* was merely a friendly shore upon which the consortium took root. Bacterial cysts, some of them capable of remaining dormant, if requisite, from the time of Columbus, must have drifted in from deep-ocean volcanic springs, known to exist hundreds of miles east of the wreck site, known to stretch across some forty thousand miles of sea floor, everywhere around the world. Every submersible or robot that ventured into the hot springs uncovered, on every dive, creatures no one had ever seen before. Neither Roy nor I (nor anyone else) had ever seen a rusticle at the springs, but the presence of at least one spring-dwelling "thermophile" in the consortium taught us that somewhere out there, more than 400 miles away in the cold and the dark, a "throw-back" to the origin of multicellular life was still thriving on the mineral-rich exhalations and regurgitations of the planet itself, thriving on volcanically heated water and the dust of the Earth.

The closer Roy and I looked at the rusticles, the more we began to see in them "things that became us." As a new century approached and the steam era neared its end, few people would have believed that butterflies and whales, and the blood that ran in their own veins, had risen, as if by miracle, from the dust of the Earth. Unless they happened to be deeply religious. Or unless they happened to be scientists.

"Hast thou entered into the springs of the sea?" I said to Roy.

"What?"

"It's in the Bible," I replied. "Probably just another strange coincidence, but it's hard to be floating in a laboratory above the *Titanic* and not wonder about the questions penned in the Book of Job some 2,700 years ago."

I explained that, as the biblical scribes told it, when God met Job in the desert, He defined the wonders of the Earth, and the stars, and the depths; and He demanded of humankind that we go into the wilderness and comprehend those wonders: "For I will demand of thee, and answer thou me . . . Hast thou entered into the springs of the sea? Or has thou walked in the recesses of the depth? Or hast thou seen the doors of deepest darkness? Hast thou comprehended the expanse of the Earth? Declare, if thou hast understanding."

Roy nodded, and prepared another rusticle sample for the microscope. "Within and outside of our bodies," he said, "there is a universe to explore, within which we singularly or collectively as a species are but minor spectators."

"It's a strange, haunting, and a stirring message," I replied, "never quite driven home."

"Until now," Roy said.

"Amen to that."

AS THE STORM in the desert taught Job, nature is full of surprises, not all of them pleasant.

During the early morning hours of April 15, 1912, the Royal Mail Steamer *Titanic*, after breaking apart and losing its grip on the ocean surface, burst down toward the sea floor as a mighty death cloud. Were the waters truly transparent and were it possible to step back ten miles and take a grandstand undersea view, the *Titanic*'s death cloud, in both its shape and its expanding dimensions, would have seemed to anticipate, by seven decades, the aerial debris field produced by the explosion of the space shuttle *Challenger*. Huge pieces fell out of the cloud, trailing long streamers of dust and dead machines and broken metal.

When the stern pounded down, an ejecta blanket of coal, kitchenwares, luggage, fittings, steel beams, and granulated windows were coughed out of their respective compartments. The smallest, most severely pulverized fragments were mixed impartially with spreading cauliflower billows of deep-sea "snow" and gravel. They fanned out and settled to the bottom as sheets of anoxic mud, generally no more than eight inches deep.

Crashing down separately, within a quarter mile radius of the stern, boilers, and a mountain of piping and deck plating more than forty feet across sent forth their own jets of deep-sea ooze, ancient rock-hard clays, and artifacts. Sheets and billows of crater ejecta radiated from multiple impact points. Artifacts from the stern were therefore interred in a system of ejecta blankets, the very same structures normally associated with the high-speed impacts of meteorites.

The first boiler to arrive on the scene truly did fall like a meteor, pounding out a crater and deep-hammering itself into the Earth. A teacup settled on top of it, about twenty minutes later; it landed as gently as a feather spiraling out of the sky. A chamber pot from the steerage quarters fell nearby . . . and a case of ale . . . a silver ash tray from the first-class smoking room . . . and Charles Joughin's pantry keys.

Even as the dust clouds settled, nature began its final reclamation of Helen Candee's symbol of humanity's dominance over nature. Within hours, the first wood-and-iron-eating microflora attached themselves to boilers and deck plates. They joined, and probably competed against, populations of microbes that had come down with the *Titanic* and were thus already aboard. The would-be squat-

ters from the surface arrived as residents of the ship's
sewage collection and holding tanks, as avian bacilli living
in crates of ostrich feathers being imported by George
Rosenshine, as streptococci lining the tissues of Chief Engineer Bell's throat.

Bacteria are far more resilient to pressure changes than
other organisms. They do not live by the rules of megacel-
lular creatures, and routinely survive the eight thousand
pounds per square inch pressure impulse generated during
the homogenization of milk. The shift from a sea-level
pressure of fifteen pounds per square inch to six thousand
pounds per square inch at a depth of two and one-half
miles was, from the peculiar perspective of the bacterial
world, without meaning.

The only things that did have meaning to them were the
native, deep-ocean microbes—which either became superior colonists on their own sea floor turf, or directly killed
the outsiders with defensive anti-bacterial toxins, or both.
Within a decade or two, the *Titanic*'s hull plates had begun
to drip rusticles up to thirty feet long, each with an internal
circulatory system rooted in the plates themselves and
branching outward, through a network of bio-wedges and
constantly expanding surface areas, into the roots of neigh-
boring rusticles. Along the 450-foot-long bow section, they
became an interconnected system, a system that would ultimately rank itself as the largest multicellular organism on
Earth, converting more and more of the *Titanic*'s iron and
sulfur, carbon and phosphorus into its own living tissues.

By the time Roy and I had cracked open our third rusticle, we could indeed begin to believe that something was
alive aboard the *Titanic*, and that it was the *Titanic* itself,
coming to life.[6]

---

[6]Never ceasing to fascinate, the rusticles have evolved a circulatory system
sufficiently complex to produce, in a single ton of them, an internal surface
area of 350 square miles.

We found rivulets, the color of drying blood, radiating away from the hull and sometimes forming great alluvial fans on the sea floor. Taking the iron and sulfur with them, seeping down into oxygen-starved sediments, the rusticle outflows created a kind of biological concrete. Thus did the same organisms that were destroying the *Titanic*—literally eating it—also act as its preservers.

On August 16, 1996, a desk-sized hull fragment, seen lying near the stern in the shape of a curled leaf, was raised by the submersible *Nautile*. Part of the sea floor came up with the hull plate. Bacterial outflows, radiating from a larger source of iron nearby, had partially coated (as a rock-hard "concretion") and entrapped the plate, along with the surrounding sediment, and any debris that lay within the sediment.

Roy and I began dissecting the concretion with whatever sectioning and grinding tools happened to be at hand, and we could see immediately that the entrapped materials, including the hull fragment itself, were part of an ejecta blanket. Descending through the concretion, sometimes with scalpel and toothbrush, was rather like turning the pages of a very old and brittle book. The "pages" contained fragments of coal, splinters of glass, and nuggets of clay— the fossilized, archaeological signatures of events that occurred before, during, and after the *Titanic*'s arrival on the plain. The events were stacked layer upon layer, each recording a different chapter in a sequence descending backward through time. The youngest, uppermost layer was sprinkled with pieces of quartz gravel (few of them more than a quarter inch in diameter), memorializing for us a slow but never-ending hailstorm arising from eighty-four years of icebergs drifting and melting overhead.[7]

---

[7] The *Titanic*'s boat deck has accumulated a light dusting of gravel, in addition to a Miller beer can, two Coca-Cola cans, and a box of soap from passing ship traffic.

Directly below the quartz layer we exposed a bed of rubble that appeared, by volume, to be comprised of approximately 60 percent sea floor clays. Viewed under a microscope, in cross-section, individual nuggets of clay rubble displayed distinct layers, or strata, indicating that they were once part of a local bedding plane deposited by the slow accumulation of organic matter known as "sea snow." The absence of glacially derived gravel in the nuggets themselves suggested to us that the clay formed before the Grand Banks became a major pathway for melting icebergs, meaning that the clay beds in our concretion sample were laid down before the end of the last Ice Age, more than 12,000 years ago. A new clue had emerged, resolving for us a clearer image of the violence with which the *Titanic* arrived on the bottom.

We already knew that the pre-Holocene clay layer (dating back at least to the time of Europe's giant shrews and cave-painting elephant hunters) rested several inches—and in many places more than two feet—below the present-day abyssal plain. This led us to a second fact we did not know before: the concretion-embedded clay nuggets had been displaced from a substantial depth, originating from a shattered sea floor, at or near the stern's point of impact. That the artifacts concreted alongside the clay nuggets included coal, glass, and the recovered hull plate itself meant that this particular concretion was composed primarily of impact-catapulted clays mingled with shrapnel from the object that had catapulted them.

A second concretion bed, clinging to a second plate from the hull, revealed two separate layers of clay and shrapnel, one plainly covering the other, as if the debris in the first layer had begun to settle out, before being overshot, after only a minute or two, by a second layer of darker, siltier material. No one in his right mind any longer wished he could have been witness to the *Titanic*'s arrival under the Grand Banks that morning. Looking straight up, one would have received a duck's-eye-view of a shotgun blast: metal streaking down with enough force to tear holes in the seabed and form a multiplicity of ejecta blankets.

Near the stern's starboard side, a sheet of black, silty ejecta gave all of its oxygen to the bacteria, and the bacteria eventually hardened the silt into a rock. As the microbes dined upon iron beams, nickel pots, and copper telegraph chains, they left a drumstick of quail meat essentially untouched, as if to freeze a remnant from the last snack served in the *à la carte* restaurant and pass it to us across time, like a bit of strange gossip passed over a backyard fence.

This example of miraculous preservation, this miraculous horror, came to the surface within a concretion fragment, no more than nine inches in thickness, clinging to the base of a silver soup tureen. Save for a dent on one side, the serving bowl was as shiny and new as the day it left the dock at Southampton. The ejecta blanket upon which the tureen had landed was an anoxic bed only a few inches deep but somewhere between 90 and 200 feet wide. The blanket had become a massive siltstone concretion, and when Captain Narnageolet lifted the silver bowl from the plain with *Nautile*'s robot arm, a sample came with it, entirely by accident. That was how I finally did come to touch an item of clothing from the *Titanic*: entirely by accident.

This was mine and Roy's third concretion. Initially, a conservator had chopped the "dirt" away from the tureen and tossed it in a garbage bin. One difference between conservators and archaeologists is that conservators tend to clean artifacts and prepare them for museum displays, whereas an archaeologist may express infinitely greater interest in the dirt that surrounds the artifacts (put another way: we archaeologists take curious delight in pawing through dirt and sticking our noses into other people's garbage).

Seen through a porthole in the submersible *Nautile*, a robot arm raises a silver soup tureen in 1996. Clinging to the bowl's base is an unexpected sample from an anoxic "fossil bed" containing screws, buttons, shreds of clothing, splinters of china, and remnants of what might have been the last meal served aboard the *Titanic*: lamb and quail bones with some of their meat still preserved. Given the possibility that human remains may also be interred, expedition leaders immediately call a moratorium on further exploration of the fossil zone.

The first thing I noticed about the tureen concretion was that it exuded the unmistakable "rotten egg" odor of hydrogen sulfide. The second thing I noticed was that it had formed a remarkably detailed fossil impression of the tureen's underside—right down to a mirror image of the manufacturer's serial number impressed above the words WHITE STAR LINE. When I started scraping a corner of the concretion with a scalpel, following the path of a fossilized worm trail, a third thing I did not notice before came to light: a bent screw, and immediately below the screw, a gold-plated cuff link.

I told Roy that the fossil appeared literally to be studded with artifacts: a blue-painted sliver of dining-saloon china, apparently from Third Class, and a second cuff link, with most of its gold electroplate removed and recrystallized by the same bacteria that had removed it. There was no doubt that we would have to complete the excavation, digging into the concretion and exposing its secrets by eighths of inches, until at last the concretion itself no longer existed.

Only nine inches across, and yet artifacts continued to emerge from the stone, more and more of them . . . an iron cylinder, about the size and shape of a biscuit, whose function in 1912 could scarcely be guessed at . . . an unidentifiable scrap of organic matter enclosed by copper oxides . . . strands of silk . . . a splinter of bone . . . buttons . . . shreds of fabric . . . more buttons . . . more chips of bone . . .

(God almighty . . .)
STOP

SOONER OR LATER it was bound to happen.

"Chicken bones," I told the news camera, not wanting to consciously admit even to myself that two of the fragments, still linked by cartilage, did not belong to the clavicle of a chicken.

"We've got to tell George," said Roy in a whisper. And so we explained to the expedition leader that it did not matter whether or not we had found animal bones from the *Titanic*'s kitchens this time, because in this concretion field the operative phrase was, "this time."

"No one really knows how many passengers and crew were trapped inside the ship," Roy said.

"If they were swept up in the stern's ejecta blanket," I added, "and if their remains were interred in anoxic beds, then the next concretion lifted from the area around the soup tureen may very well contain someone's father or mother."

"We should attempt no more exploration of that area," Roy said, and George agreed. There had been people, waiting ashore in 1912, who were siblings and children of the *Titanic*'s lost—dozens of them still alive, and a half dozen more who were actually aboard. Out of respect for them, out of concerns that we might raise, by mistake, fragments of a loved one's grave, the anoxic beds would remain off limits beyond 2012. The ship and its debris field were adrift in a gray area between oral history and archaeological time frames, like the battlefields of Gettysburg and the Little Big Horn during our fathers' time.

"So, when we come to the anoxic bed," George decided, "we leave nothing except the submersible's footprints, take nothing except pictures."[8]

Many months were to pass before I finally analyzed pictures and videotapes of the bones, a singular act of procrastination that I cannot consciously explain. Inwardly, I had insisted that I was looking at kitchen debris, but I was unsure until vertebrate zoologist Bill Schutt determined with reasonable certainty that the two largest, finger-sized bones, though clearly not from a "chicken," were not human, either. We were looking at the humerus of a lamb, which was consistent with what we knew of the last meal aboard the *Titanic*: the first- and second-class menus included an entrée of spring lamb with mint sauce.

I drew a long delayed sigh of relief, held it reflectively (*it's not human . . . this time*), then let my thoughts linger on four other remnants of bone I had seen in the tureen concretion. One of them belonged to a bird. Three of them were barely larger than grape seeds and (given only photographic evidence) might never be identified; and though it

---

[8]Save for a recommendation from Roy Cullimore that the objects from beneath the tureen be embedded in a tiny block of concrete and returned exactly whence they came, no further plans were made even to attempt landings on the anoxic bed.

was true that quail and lamb had been stirred together under the tureen, buttons also formed part of the mix, and a shred of clothing—"a shred that gave me the impression of an undershirt," I told Bill. "A very small undershirt."

Bill asked, "How many children were lost on the *Titanic*?"

"Over fifty," I said. "Almost all of them from the third-class cabins. In the end, the crew were declaring even very young boys old enough to be men. There's a story about a pair of twins, only five years old. An officer sent the girl to the lifeboat—" and I noticed that Bill's attention seemed focused on a single photograph from the tureen assemblage: the one showing a bit of undergarment that looked too disturbingly small.

"And they kept the boy behind," Bill finished for me.

"Yes. His name was Carl Asplund."

Bill handed me the photograph and said, "You might have found him."

Has thou walked in the recesses of the depth?
Yes, we've done that.
Or hast thou seen the doors of deepest darkness?
Curse, yes.

When my friend Don drove me home from the airport, at the end of the 1996 expedition, I mentioned nothing of the bones. On a conscious level, I had forgotten about them, forced them out of my mind altogether. As we sped east on Rockaway Boulevard, I spoke instead of how Roy had pierced a rusticle with *Nautile*'s robot arm, and how it had spilled red pulp in a watery gush, like a slashed vein spilling blood. I told him how it was impossible to watch that red gush without believing that the *Titanic* itself was bleeding.

"We haven't figured out how the circulatory system

works," I said. "But a pump exists—no doubt of it. Roy thinks dissolved carbon dioxide may be involved, but I think we've also got a gravity-fed system, in which water made heavy with dissolved iron drops through the rusticle, and after its iron is absorbed by the microbes, and incorporated into the rusticle itself, the lighter, iron-depleted water is either convected up again or ejected by the never-ending downflow of iron-heavy water. What I really need to know about this system is where physics ends and biology begins. I need—"

Don stopped me.

"How many pounds of these creatures did you happen to bring home with you?" he asked.

"Oh, about two or three," I said.

"Uh-huh. And when you filled out your customs declaration form, did anyone happen to ask you if you had visited a farm while you were away?"

"I *didn't* visit any farms."

Don nodded, and grinned. "And did they ask if you were importing any fruits, vegetables, or animal products from overseas?"

"I had none of those."

"Right. And, of course, no one bothered to ask about your new pet. Never mind that it's neither plant nor animal, or that it came from beneath the sea and it ate at the *Titanic*."

"Oops . . ."

"I thought so," Don said, and grimaced. "Now, let me tell you something: If I wake up tomorrow morning and find rusticles munching on my car, I'm gonna kill you—a lot!"

HUGE SECTIONS OF the promenade deck were being devoured. When Bob Ballard made his first reconnaissance of the bow in 1986, only the promenade windows were missing. When Roy Cullimore photographed the same section in 1996, rows of vertical supports had dissolved almost out of existence, and by 1998 a forty-foot length of the boat deck had collapsed into the promenade.

Stronger. The rusticles appeared to be getting stronger, and hungrier.

Paleontology teaches us that most of the earth's iron ores were precipitated out of sea water by bacteria, about 2 billion years ago. Bacteria living near volcanic springs, in the recesses of the deep, are still mining gold, iron sulfides ("fool's gold"), and silver from sea water; and in Western Africa, about 2 billion B.C., one bacterial reef managed to concentrate so much uranium-235 that it became, by accident, the world's first known atomic pile. The living reactor burned itself to death, then fossilized in a nuclear flame of its own creation.[9]

More than 90 percent of the world's deposits of iron were laid down between 2.5 and 1.8 billion B.C. Then the humans came along, took iron ore out of the Earth, fashioned it into hull plates and steel girders, and named them *Titanic*. Then the rusticles came along, took iron out of the *Titanic*'s steel, and were now returning hull plates to the Earth as iron ore.

"Substance is like a river in constant flow," Roy observed, recalling Marcus Aurelius of the A.D. second century. "The cycle is never complete. And there is hardly anything that stands still."

---

[9]At a depth of three miles lies a crashed Cold War–era Soviet submarine bearing the remnants of a melted nuclear reactor and 120 hydrogen bombs with plutonium triggers. A joint Russian-American expedition, using advanced miniature robot technology, is taking shape as this book goes to press. (Who, you might ask, would join such a mission? Count on it: They'll find a couple of damned fools somewhere.) Roy and I will be surprised, but we will not necessarily die from shock (fission, maybe, but not shock) if we discover that the rusticles now taking root on and in the submarine are able to metabolize plutonium—an element that did not even exist on this planet until humans created it.

It seemed as if Aurelius had anticipated our discoveries under the Grand Banks. It would have seemed perfectly natural to him that a consortial lifeform—shadowy, silent, and strange—should be festooning the *Titanic*'s decks, infiltrating every nook and cranny in the steel. But this was not to say that the process of dissolution was at last understood, and did not continue to bring surprises. A survey of the collapsing promenade deck, and the recovery of a concretion bearing only the hollow, fossil image of a three-quarter-inch slab of steel, led us to suspect that something in the deep-ocean environment—something in addition to mere surface area and volume relationships—might actually be speeding up rusticle growth.

Microbiologist Henrietta Mann had suggested that the rusticle was a very efficient, very opportunistic organism, with some of its parts able to metabolize, for the entire consortium, organic matter from decaying debris and other potential nutrients found in "sea snow."

And if the sea snow were suddenly to deepen, I reasoned, then the "snow eaters" would grow more thickly in the rusticle's tissues, and the rusticles might grow faster.

The snowfall from the surface was, in fact, intensifying. When Roy and I compared 1996 film footage with footage from earlier expeditions, we noticed, over a ten-year period, a fourfold increase in the amount of organic "snow" swirling in the submersible's floodlamps and covering the *Titanic*'s decks. Nineteen ninety-six brought a new element: the first time anyone had observed small, half-eaten and even wholly uneaten shrimp falling from miles above, as if it were possible for a major prey species to leave body parts behind, or even to die of old age, without being eaten by fish.

Looking to the terrain around the *Titanic*, a comparison with film from an expedition only two years earlier revealed an increase in numbers of large brittle stars in the sub's searchlights (which illuminated a radius of approximately forty feet) from two or three individuals in 1994, to more than thirty in 1996. Giant sea cucumbers were suddenly flourishing everywhere, and crab populations had doubled, then doubled again, between 1994 and 1996.[10]

Over the course of a decade, the snow flurries had literally become a blizzard, and a deep-ocean plain that (insofar as animals any larger than an aspirin were concerned) once gave the appearance of being a biological desert was in fact blossoming into a jungle.

The fault, I decided, was underfoot. At noon we could actually see the Deep Scattering Layer on the ship's sonar, about a quarter mile beneath the *Ocean Voyager*. It scattered and degraded our signals, and it was from this feature that the undersea meadow had earned its name. The Deep Scattering Layer was a vast, sunken cloud deck of tiny animals that covered two-thirds of the world. The cloud rose at sunset and fell at sunrise, inexplicably seeking the edge of darkness. Normally, it was the food source for almost all oceanic fishes, but to judge from the amount of "sea snow" falling out of the cloud and reaching the abyssal plain, Roy and I began to worry that the layer might now be thicker with copepods and other tiny animals (zooplankton) than ever before.

"The fault, Charles, is not underfoot, but in ourselves," Roy concluded.

"I know," I said. There was nothing else to say.

I remembered a fisherman from Halifax explaining that

---

[10]Two years later, the populations of starfish, sea cucumbers, and crabs had approximately doubled again. In 1998, up to sixty brittle stars could often be seen in the forty-foot range of the sub's floodlamps. At lease one crab and one sea cucumber were generally seen in this same range, whereas in 1994 they were seen, if at all, nearly 320 feet apart. The rusticle-induced degradation of the *Titanic*'s hull also appeared to be reaching a structural flashpoint, at which the entire aft end of the stern began to avalanche over the propellers between the 1996 and 1998 expeditions.

he was no longer landing adult cod. "We got them all," he said, with genuine sadness and realization. Almost daily, a Canadian Air Force plane overflew our ship, to make certain that we were not violating the fishing ban on what had once stood amongst the world's richest natural hatcheries.

Although the sighting of a small pod of pilot whales had given us hope that depleted fish stocks might already be recovering (as a food source for the whales), the deep-ocean blizzard told us otherwise. The blizzard existed because there weren't enough fish left in the top quarter mile of the North Atlantic to graze upon the animal plankton and thin the Deep Scattering Layer. Apparently, it was now expanding beyond all rational control.

We knew that the zooplankton surfaced every night, and upon what meat did this cloud feed, until driven below by the dawn? It grazed upon *phytoplankton*—single-celled plants living in the top few feet of the ocean—and herein the first portent of a biological chain reaction projected itself toward us, like a hideous, mocking grin.

"It looks like someone just pulled a major element out of the biological equation," said Roy.

"Yes. And when you pull out the pin, Mister Hand Grenade is no longer your friend."

And we knew that the Grand Banks could not be unique. As in the North Atlantic, so in the South Atlantic, so too in the Pacific, so in the Indian Ocean and the Mediterranean and South China Seas. Photosynthesis, the process that sustained life on this planet, did not depend upon the Amazon rain forest (or even upon all the forests of the world combined), but upon that planet-encircling membrane of greenery at the sea surface. It absorbed most of the carbon dioxide given off by us, and by our carbon fuels; it gave back most of the oxygen we breathed.

If overfishing, leading to a population explosion of uneaten zooplankton, was leading to overgrazing of phytoplankton, then the so-called "greenhouse effect" (assuming the atmospheric chemists were correct about an already alarming increase in levels of industrially produced carbon dioxide[11]) might be approaching faster than anyone had anticipated, and not necessarily for the reasons anyone had anticipated.

"Its earliest manifestations would be warming of the oceans," I said, "and shifting trade winds, with more powerful hurricanes than we've seen before."

Roy shook his head, very slowly. "I think we are, all of us, riding on the *Titanic* at the whim of human arrogance."

Eva Hart had expressed to me this very same thought, shortly before the expedition, shortly before her death. I had told her of the wonderful future I thought our civilization might build: of how the first interstellar spacecraft were already on the drawing boards, and that they could be flying by 2050; of how human beings might be perfectable, and that I did believe we were moving in that direction. What I said troubled her, for she thought I believed too much in the idea of "the Great Machine."

"There's too much of Thomas Andrews in you," she said. "So, pay attention to what I am telling you: Once upon a time there were men who believed they could sail a machine through the dark, at full speed, into an ice field they had been warned lay ahead. My life was changed forever that night, and I'm not sure we have learned very much since then.

"So move forward, yes . . . but if you scientists, engineers, and industrial geniuses do not finally learn how to

---

[11]In 1998, a team of atmospheric chemists working for the United Nations reported that the content of carbon dioxide in the atmosphere had increased by nearly 10 percent in less than a decade. Increased fuel usage by China and the United States could only account for a fraction of this rise, indicating that some process besides carbon-burning was layered on top of the usual suspects for atmospheric carbon dioxide increase.

temper arrogance with wisdom, and to pay very close attention, then I'm afraid there will be an even bigger *Titanic* in your future—for the whole world, maybe. And next time there may be no lifeboats—for anybody.''

And who would have believed, in the time of Eva's youth, that pulling too many fish out of the oceans might accelerate global warming, shift trade winds and agricultural belts, fracture Antarctic ice sheets, bring forth encroaching seas, warm the eyes of hurricanes?

I wondered.

The only good news in this picture was that we had received a warning—a deep-ocean blizzard—probably while there was still time to act.

(*This time . . .*)

I, for one, had firmed a resolve to eat more vegetables and beef when I returned to shore. If the ban on fishing off the Grand Banks continued to be enforced, and if people would voluntarily cut back by half on their fish intake, for about five or six years, then the fish stocks would recover quickly because, by everything Roy and I knew, there was plenty of food upon which they could grow. Recovered fish populations would, in their own turn, thin the exploded population of zooplankton—which, in turn, would halt overgrazing of the phytoplankton.

Roy supposed that we would be able to monitor the process by placing time-lapse cameras on the *Titanic*'s bow and charting rates of "snowfall" and rusticle growth. Presumably, a decrease in the nutrient-rich snowfall, resulting in a slight but measurable slowing of rusticle growth and a corresponding decrease in the *Titanic*'s rate of deterioration, would tell us that the Deep Scattering Layer was thinning, that the pressure on phytoplankton was abating.

That a warning had come from the decks of the *Titanic* prickled our sense of the mysterious, our love of irony. As during the night Eva Hart glimpsed the last of her, the *Ti-*

tanic continued to be of nature, not above it. Because the liner's rate of deterioration was being set, to one degree or another, by the health of the waters above, it was emerging as a useful and hitherto unanticipated tool for monitoring the pulse of the oceans.

"Hast thou comprehended the expanse of the Earth?" God demanded of Job.

Two and one-half miles above the *Titanic*, we had no choice. At dusk we could shine lights into the water and watch the living cloudbanks rising into the photic zone. When one floated in one spot on the ocean surface, instead of sailing through it, one witnessed changes not apparent to merchant seamen and *Queen Elizabeth II* passengers. Drifts of sargasso weed came and went. Bioluminescent jellyfish, whole swarms of them, rose to the surface after sunset, and went back down before sunrise. A reddish-brown lens of filth rose on the southern horizon and did not go away: the eastern U.S. smog layer—and we were eight hundred miles from shore.

On the evening of August 14 we discovered the tattered wreckage of a Japanese drift net floating among islands of boxes and sargasso weed. It was too large to haul aboard (nearly a quarter mile of netting still survived); all we could do was report its position. Probably years after being lost, it wandered the seas, continuing to trap (and kill) everything in its path. If it were anything like the typical drift net, then originally it was twenty miles long; and if we happened upon one only by chance, then it seemed statistically inevitable that there were others. Roy and I guessed conservatively at "only" five others, and realized that cumulatively (for several years until they decayed), the nets became a 120-mile-long "wall of death," or a "mouth" as wide as Long Island's length, going round and round the North Atlantic, strip-mining the water of whales and cod and tuna and anything else that got in its way. Was it any wonder that the slow, stately snowfall of the deep had become a storm?

EXCERPT FROM THE EXPEDITION LOG OF THE RESEARCH VESSEL *OCEAN VOYAGER*

Date: August 15, 1996
Location: Over the *Titanic*'s stern, with 2.5 miles of water below

We are living on a planet only 8,000 miles in diameter—that is, only 66.6 times as wide as "the wall of death." These, like all numbers, roll easily off the tongue, but people do not readily grasp how small our planet really is. No one and nothing can ever truly get lost on Earth.

Perhaps we can begin to answer, now, for Job; just a little bit. We have indeed come to comprehend the expanse of the Earth, to enter the springs of the sea and to walk in the recesses of the depth. And, yes, it can truly be said that we have seen the doors of deepest darkness—repeatedly.

And we know.

We who have gazed into the abyss.

6

•

The Dream at the
End of the World

•

My God . . . My God . . .
—THIRD-CLASS PASSENGER EUGENE DALY

Then said another—"Surely not in vain
My Substance from the common Earth was ta'en,
That He who subtly wrought me into Shape
Should stamp me back to common Earth again."
—THE RUBA'IYAT OF OMAR KHAYYAM, QUATRAIN 61

All philosophy ultimately dovetails with religion—which
is ultimately reducible to history. All history is ultimately
reducible to biology. Biology is ultimately reducible to
physics. Physics is ultimately reducible to mathematics.
And mathematics is ultimately reducible to philosophy.
—BISHOP AND PELLEGRINO'S FIRST LAW

JIM CAMERON'S EXPEDITION arrived a year ahead of me
and Roy Cullimore, with the Russian submersibles *Mir I*
and *Mir II*.

Officially, it was simply a filming expedition, and the
robots Jim brought with him were designed merely to be
photogenic; but the film-maker was—unbeknownst to almost everybody—a polymathic explorer and engineer (and
part-time rocket designer) who seemed to invent movie

140

projects intended to take him into the depths of the sea, onto Antarctic ice sheets, and eventually out into space. As a designer of deep-ocean robots, he could hold his own ground with the likes of Tom Dettweiler and Bob Ballard. As an archaeologist, he could hold his own with Nanno Marinatos and Trude Dothan. He resembled a latter-day da Vinci whose paintings moved and sang, so it came as no surprise when, with "a little tweaking," he turned a movie prop into a functional robot that penetrated deeper into the *Titanic* than anything hitherto invented by the French or American navies. Nor was it surprising that his results and conclusions turned out to be, archaeologically speaking, at least as important as those obtained from other expeditions sent to the *Titanic* specifically *for* archaeology.

Much of the evidence for cratering events and downblast effects resulting from high terminal velocities achieved by the *Titanic*'s remains came from the Cameron expedition. The first photographs of staterooms with their oak doors and wall panels standing erect were obtained by Jim Cameron's prop-turned-robot probe, in addition to clues that the Grand Stairway—which Ballard had concluded was missing and presumed eaten by wood-borers—had met a very different fate.

The expedition ended, for Jim, with an apparition the color of pearl. "A white rainbow," he called it, as ominous and peaceful as it was mournfully beautiful. He was acutely aware that it had materialized during the final moments leading up to his departure, over the very part of the sea on which fifteen hundred people died—materialized amid rising white mist and sudden dead calm, as if someone were trying to bid him adieu.

Jim Cameron was militantly agnostic on the subject of ghosts, but he had let something of the place—"the energy of this place"—touch him.

It did not happen without invitation, without his intention

of letting it happen. In the beginning there had been uncooperative weather, uncooperative deep-ocean currents, uncooperative submersibles, uncooperative robots. Each morning started with two and one half hours of free fall through the ocean just to arrive at the *Titanic*, and he was simply unable to obtain the film sequences he needed. None of the footage looked right when he reviewed it topside, on the support ship.

Jim began to wonder if he might have planned his shots too carefully, making them too vulnerable to shifting currents and shifting floodlamp angles, rather than letting the ship itself guide the shooting as exploration progressed and as opportunities presented themselves.

And so he began to let her in, began to let himself be touched by the *Titanic* until, in the manner of an archaeologist, he wandered the depths unstuck in time.

"Show me," he said, and as he sent a robot camera forward and aft of the Grand Stairway entrance, past once vertical steel columns kneed out by impact with the sea floor, it was easy to imagine those columns standing with their hand-carved oak claddings freshly waxed, and with people strolling beneath them. And in his mind's eye, the people really did seem still to be alive, as his robot entered stateroom B-51—which looked like a surreal grotto for all of its overhanging rusticle growth, until a chair, a fireplace, and other man-made objects emerged from the dark. Lady Cardeza had occupied the suite, had persuaded Officer William Murdoch to let her thirty-seven-year-old son and his valet enter boat three at 1:00 A.M., and she subsequently sued the White Star Line for the loss of a seven-carat pink diamond left behind.

A feather-shaped colony of hydrozoans grew on a wood-paneled wall, alongside a lamp whose bulb had imploded. An undersea breeze, blowing in through the empty Grand Stairway shaft and the broken promenade windows, made

B-51 a good nesting ground for filter feeders. There was enough oxygen in the water for white crabs to survive in Lady Cardeza's fireplace, and Jim imagined that the Turkish baths and swimming pool must also be inhabited by crabs.

Mrs. Ada Clark's stateroom was nothing except splinters. Jim could almost hear the young bride trying in vain to convince her husband that the ship was in trouble. Viewed through an archaeologist's eyes, there was no shortage of ghosts under the Grand Banks. Sometimes they moved Jim to tears and made him seek out a place on the support ship where he could be alone. But after a while, he became accustomed to them. After a while, he did not want to be away from them.

THE PEOPLE IN the smoking room just did not seem to understand. Mrs. Ada Clark of Los Angeles had been alone in her cabin when the crash came at 11:40 P.M. It came to her more as a shudder than a crash, as if the ship had just "rolled over a thousand marbles." When she stepped into the hallway, people were moving nervously about, and there was talk of a crewman having run past with his clothes wet. She decided to seek out her husband, whom she had left at the entrance to the smoking room, and find out what he knew about all the commotion. Nearly everyone in the smoking room had stood up from their seats when a thump and quiver carried up through the floor, shook their tables, and disturbed their drinks. A steward ran out through the aft exit just in time to see the iceberg scraping along the starboard side, quaking and sending chunks of ice tumbling into the water as it passed. Yet by the time Mrs. Clark arrived at the door, the usual card games and quiet discussions had resumed. Her husband was among the card players, who included Clarence Moore and the distinguished painter Frank Millet (two of the wealthiest people aboard), Archie Butt (President Taft's military aide and one of the big celebrities aboard), and twenty-year-old Alfred Nourney, who had booked passage as "Baron von Drachstedt" and snuck up from Second Class to mingle with the wealthy in First.

The room itself had all the cozy opulence of an exclusive men's club: A wide fireplace burned aft, and the wall paneling was rich mahogany in the Georgian style, inlaid with mother-of-pearl and enclosing sheets of stained glass depicting sailing ships and women in long, flowing dresses. The rules were against women entering the smoking room—even at a time like this, Mrs. Clark concluded. Rules were rules on British ships, and that was the be-all and end-all of the argument. So she pushed the door open and tried to attract her husband's attention, waving like some mean-spirited fan at a ball game who wants to irritate the pitcher or the batter. After responding with repeated angry stares, Mr. Clark put down his cards and walked to the entrance, where his wife stood waiting, not daring to step beyond the doorpost.

"What is this?" he demanded.

"We've struck something and there's talk of water in the mail room."

"We're on the *Titanic*, dear. Don't worry about it."

"But there's water!" said the young bride, in an abrasive, demanding tone that was entirely new to Mr. Clark, but which struck him without doubt as coming attractions for the next thirty years.

"I'm sure they've got it all under control," he said sternly. "But if it will put you more at ease, I'll check with the crew and see if everything is all right."

He then sent his wife away to bed, and never did check with the crew. Instead, he went back to his card game, at a table rimmed with raised edges to prevent drinks from sliding off in rough seas. It was just after 12:00 A.M., and the sea was as calm as a frozen pond. That there was not the slightest ripple in anyone's glass only added to the illusion of the *Titanic*'s solidity, but if one looked just a little bit closer at the drinks, it was easy to see that the ship was beginning to tilt down toward the bow. And in the center of the table stood a silver ashtray engraved with the White Star Line flag. A player's pipe and two cigars burned there. The first lifeboats would soon be lowering away, half empty on the starboard side, with Officer Will Murdoch calling for anyone, man or woman, to fill the vacant seats. Although there was room enough for each of the players, none but the impostor Baron stood to leave. The men he left behind would soon disappear into history. Only the pipe (found eighty-one years later with the tobacco still inside) and the ashtray would ever be seen again.

At 12:20 a steward knocked on Mrs. Clark's door and told her that all passengers were to put on lifejackets— "just as a precaution."

"Precaution!" She made no attempt to hide her alarm.

"Oh, there's no danger," the steward said. "It'll be a few hours and we'll be on our way again. An officer told me so!"

Grabbing an extra lifejacket for her husband, she pushed past the steward and headed for the smoking room, just as Charles Lightoller and the other officers began yanking canvas covers off the port-side lifeboats.

No danger, indeed! she thought. As before, she abided by the rule against entering the men's club. But she did not stop short of waving a lifejacket and shouting into the room.

"What is it this time?" her husband called out.

"Darling, they're putting people off in lifeboats."

That got his attention. He put his cards down and went outside to have a look.

In another part of the ship, Hugh Woolner tried to con-

vince Helen Candee that he and his friends would help her
aboard again when the *Titanic* "steadied herself." One of
those friends, a man named Kent, did not seem so sure of
the outcome. Another, whom Helen would simply remember as "Jolly Colley—the little Irishman who rarely spoke
but by some inner magic was able to spread warmth and
jollity, without chatter," simply gave a wan smile, then announced that he was returning to his cabin several decks
below and intended to stay there.

Kent (who had confided in Helen at "dressing time" that
no matter how well one disguised a ship as a first-class
hotel, he always took crossing the Atlantic as a possible
risk and therefore chose not to dress for dinner) urged her
to find a lifeboat at once, and scolded her for not tossing
her little leather "pocket book" to the deck.

"You can't take baggage with you!" Kent shouted, in a
voice of remonstrance that seemed to Helen very like horror.

"Baggage? This tiny case?" she said, and laughed. "We
women have no pockets, so please carry this for me." She
then pulled out the object of greatest value to her: a golden
locket with a miniature of her mother inside and, tossing
aside the "baggage," held the locket out to Kent, who stood
with his arms folded against his chest, his only reply a
frown.

Helen quickly tore out the ivory miniature of her mother
and, tossing away the gold casing, extended her hand.
Wordlessly, grudgingly, he took the miniature. It would
still be in his pocket when his body was found a week later.

To Hugh Woolner she gave a silver flask of brandy, explaining that it held a pint.

"Yes," said Hugh. "That might come in handy," and
then, after a pause, he said, "Take it, Kent." And Kent
obeyed.

At 12:30 it was difficult to know whether to snicker inwardly at a man who displayed grave concern, or to become gravely concerned oneself. From bow to stern, there were enough people aboard to range the entire spectrum of reactions.

On the starboard boat deck, George Rosenshine still fretted to his mistress about the unexpected changes they had witnessed in boa and hat styles at the spring fashion show in Paris. The unmailed letter he carried in his satchel would be found by archaeologists of the future, ending their own fretting about how several tons of ostrich feathers came to be lying on the sea floor. To his brothers in New York, Mr. Rosenshine had written about ostrich feathers going suddenly out of style, and about concerns that he might have squandered the family fortune by investing too heavily in them. To his mistress, he expressed grave concerns about life after bankruptcy, not yet suspecting how quickly a bad investment was degenerating into the least of his worries.

Colonel Archibald Gracie, as he paced the port-side boat deck, appeared to be distracted by his simultaneous efforts to find Helen Candee and to snatch up, and record in his memory, every detail of the night. A writer of history books, he had a strong sense that, this time, he would not merely be writing history, but literally wading through it. He had spent much of the voyage cornering anyone who would listen to him about his latest book, *The Truth about Chickamauga*. Helen Candee had tactfully referred to the copy foisted upon her as "remarkably detailed," and privately as "five hundred pages of labored minutae."

Gracie's tendency to publish such details as President Lincoln's year-by-year income and the types of window dressings preferred by Mrs. Lincoln would carry through to his next book, *The Truth about the Titanic*. Weighted down by such matters as departure times and listings of passengers in each lifeboat, the very feature of Gracie's writing that made him a favorite target of critics was about to produce the most valued of all firsthand accounts of what happened on the *Titanic*'s boat deck.

The Colonel never did find Helen Candee. Hugh Woolner saw her safely into boat six and said good-bye, minutes before the first rocket went up. With the ship's bow settling low against the horizon, Helen thought she could see dark, mountainous shapes eclipsing stars across the water. *No . . . Titanic was not the first to arrive here*, she told herself. *Down from the silent north that other sinister craft had slipped into her destined place. No wireless equipment, no port and starboard lights, no compass, no captain. But the power that is greater than man's has no need of man's methods.*

When O'Loughlin's assistant, Dr. Simpson, was found by Stewardess Mary Sloan, he was closing the ship's dispensary and setting out to help Second Officer Lightoller lower the boats. Dr. Simpson was best known for an uproarious sense of humor which had made him very popular aboard the *Titanic*, especially with the stewardesses.

Mary Sloan and her friend, another stewardess named Miss Marsden, seemed so nervous that he put off his mission for a moment, brought them into the dispensary, and gave them each a glass of whiskey in water. Mary laughed and asked the doctor if he thought this might be dangerous. "This alcohol, I mean," she said. "Will I need it? Is it necessary to have this?"

"Yes," said Simpson. "You might need it later on," whereupon Miss Marsden burst into tears.

"Are you scared?" the doctor asked.

Miss Marsden nodded and said, "I sure am!"

"I'm not scared," Mary insisted, and Dr. Simpson raised his flask in her direction, then toasted: "Spoken like a true Ulster woman!"

Some of the crew were not as chivalrous. At least two

men entered the lifeboats with "abandoned" babies in their arms, and would remain forever reluctant to explain exactly how they came to be in possession of the children. A Third Cabin Pantryman named Pearcey would claim three weeks later that he simply "saw" two babies abandoned on the boat deck, and when he brought them to First Officer Murdoch he was "ordered" to take charge of them in collapsible C, but no one could really believe in mothers simply leaving babies on the deck and running away to . . . to what? To something more important than their babies? The tale was bound to evoke images of crewmen recognizing infants as sure tickets onto lifeboats and offering to save the children if handed over, if they did not outright yank them from the arms of mothers locked below, before running up to Murdoch and declaring, "There is no one to watch after them except me."

At boat four, Assistant Purser Frank Prentice, who had helped Charles Joughin load cookie tins and drinking water into collapsible D and was about to do the same for number four, found the way blocked by men who were beginning to fight. The orderly evacuation "was a bit of a shambles then," so Frank left the tins strewn on the deck, as Second Officer Charles Lightoller (who would deny officially that he had ever used his pistol, while admitting privately to Colonel Gracie that in fact he had) fired into the air, then leveled his gun at a passenger's head, threatening to shoot the man "like a dog" if he made another step forward.

Nearby, a bundle dropped from a woman's arms and struck the deck with a sickening snap. To the relief of several onlookers, the bundle had contained only a toy pig, and not a baby. As a man picked the toy up and handed it to her with one of its little forelegs broken, Frank Prentice noticed that Ada Clark was having difficulty with her lifebelt. He helped her husband to tie it snug around her coat and, having heard from Thomas Andrews that the ship did not have a hope of staying afloat, said simply, "I think you'd better get into that lifeboat, now." He pointed to number four where Lightoller now stood virtually alone.

"No," said Ada. "I will not leave my husband."

"He—he'll be coming on afterwards, on a later boat," Frank lied. But she seemed to see through him, to the truth, and he doubted that Ada's husband would be able to convince her to enter boat four. Frank would spend much of the next hour wondering what eventually became of the newlyweds.[1]

At 12:45, as a wall collapsed and gushed on E deck forward and a wave of waist-high water sent Seaman John Poingdester and Fireman Fred Barrett scurrying for their lives . . . as Mr. Clark continued to urge his wife toward the edge of the boat deck and she scolded him with the words, "Now do you believe me?" . . . as Quartermaster George Rowe fired the first distress rocket and Chief Officer Wilde asked Lightoller to help him find more firearms, men could still be seen sitting around card tables in the smoking room.

Fifteen minutes later, as Lady Cardeza and her son departed in boat three, Colonel Gracie went on an impromptu "fact-gathering tour" of what he called "the whole length

---

[1]Years later, Ada Clark recalled that it was something in the force and urgency of Frank Prentice's voice that finally convinced her to listen to her husband and depart in boat four. Frank did not leave the ship; it left him. He stuffed an empty lifejacket and several pieces of floating wood under himself and realized, after a while, that all the moans and pleas had stopped and he was alone. Remembering that he had seen the lifeboats in the flashes of the rockets, Frank began paddling in the direction he thought they had gone, eventually coming within sight of boat four. "Some of the people on that boat were in a bad way," he recalled. "A fireman lay dead in the bottom. Another man was trying to get out and he was being restrained. And I sat in next to a woman and this was Mrs. Clark. She wrapped her coat around me and I think she saved my life. I'd probably saved hers and then she saved mine. But that was rather a coincidence, wasn't it?"

of the ship." It was in fact the whole length of First Class, for to him the *Titanic* ended at the gates to Second Class. In the gentlemen's lounge he found a steward still at his post, serving drinks that were now "on the house." William T. Stead was sitting in a leather armchair reading a copy of *The Virginian*. Major Archie Butt, Clarence Moore, Frank Millet, and a fourth man Gracie did not recognize were sitting around a card table, smoking and carrying on with a quiet discussion as if nothing in the world were going wrong. It occurred to Gracie that they could not help but know the facts, yet he was curiously certain that if he walked over to them and mentioned his own sense of alarm, they would rebuke him. He decided that the occupants of the smoking room really did feel among themselves that expressing alarm was not the way to behave on a foundering ship.

The colonel emerged onto the boat deck at 1:10 A.M., having finished his tour just as Mrs. Clark, standing finally, and hesitantly, in a lifeboat that was being delayed by a cascade of technical pratfalls, watched one of the boats just aft of her reach the water and cut loose from the falls. She heard a woman calling down to a friend, "When you get back, you'll need a pass. You can't get back on the ship tomorrow without a pass!" Only a few feet away, a woman in the next boat forward was not quite so optimistic. She begged her husband to join her in number two.

"No," the husband said. "The only honorable thing to do is to stay behind with the men."

The woman bowed her head in resignation, then looked up and gave a final, wifely order: "Then you must stay close to Colonel Gracie and Major Butt. They are big, strong fellows and will surely make it." Gracie bristled and, as quickly and quietly as possible, slipped away to the starboard side.

Mrs. Clark's own husband simply kissed her good-bye

and, without any further words, stepped back from the lifeboats and disappeared into a crowd of onlookers while, less than three hundred feet away, Steward Frederick Ray, who had ventured below to fetch his overcoat, made an unpleasant discovery. Striding down one of the long hallways of E deck, he found his way blocked by a lake that had no business being there. The whole corridor was slanting down toward the bow, and the lights appeared to be dimming, casting the water oily black as it lapped at the doors of washrooms and first-class staterooms. A passenger named Rothschild joined him.

"Where is your wife?" asked Ray.

"Gone off on one of the lifeboats. About fifteen minutes ago." She had in fact departed with Helen Candee on boat six, with a capacity for sixty-five people, carrying a total of only twenty-eight.

Lifeboats . . . "Gee, Mr. Rothschild. This seems rather serious. I don't know much about double-hulled bottoms and watertight bulkheads, but I'm beginning to get worried."

"I don't think there is any occasion for it," Rothschild said flatly.

And with those words, as the lake crept toward them, eating up twelve feet of carpet in only a few seconds, Ray's confidence in the *Titanic*'s unsinkable construction was buoyed upward by a man who had convinced himself that the ship would settle only so far and then stop sinking, in spite of everything his eyes were showing him.

Seaman McAuliffe did not seem to know any better than Rothschild when he sent number two away at 1:45. The ocean was only ten feet from the boat deck, and the members of the *Titanic*'s all-string band had just chimed in with a new Irving Berlin tune—*Alexander's Ragtime Band*—which was getting very close to being the last piece they would ever play. From the stern of boat two, Steward

James Johnson, unable to unlatch the falls, yelled up for a knife, and McAuliffe tossed down his own, calling, "Be sure to give it back to me when we get to Southampton!" Johnson shot back a puzzled look, shrugged at him, and began cutting. There were signs everywhere that the *Titanic* was never going to get anywhere near her home port. She was going down into the Atlantic with all the feel of a hydraulic ramp and a sound like windows imploding under the crush and swirl of water was trying very hard to overshadow Irving Berlin; and now in the midst of this oncoming horror that men did not want to bring themselves to believe, McAuliffe had demanded his knife back. Historians would later observe that McAuliffe must have been the last man aboard the *Titanic* so certain of returning to Southampton, but he was not the only optimist, and he was far from the last.

It was clear that Drs. O'Loughlin and Simpson knew the score, when Charles Lightoller found them "still assisting by showing a calm and cool exterior to the passengers." They came up to him and shook hands, exchanged the words, "Good-bye, old man," then headed aft. Frank Prentice also began walking aft, tightening his lifejacket as he went. In the glare of the rockets, he could see the lifeboats flashing out pallid white against black water. The flashes stood out in his memory like a series of snapshots in which he could detect motion, as if through time-lapse photography. Each successive snapshot showed the boats pulling further away, and Frank laughed quietly to himself, for it seemed to him that they were pulling their way full speed to New York.

When he reached the poop deck, the Assistant Purser found the place eerily quiet. At first there were only three other people up there, including his friend Ricks. Then, as he began to feel through the deck planks and the railings a powerful rumbling, hundreds of steerage passengers broke through from below: "The deck was *alive*. You could hardly move. And I couldn't do any more. I'd done all I could. They, like me, had nothing else to do, I suppose. There were no more boats. So they swarmed."

To judge from the very few third-class accounts to go on record, during the first ten or fifteen minutes after impact, the gates that separated the classes were apparently open and it was relatively easy for passengers to move out from the third-class cabins to other parts of the ship. Then, around midnight, orders were given for all steerage passengers to stay below and, for the most part, those orders were obeyed.

This was, after all, a time in which even first-class passenger Hugh Woolner was reluctant to question a command, much less to remind Captain Smith, without first saluting, that he had forgotten which ship he was on. The majority of the third-class passengers—employed as gardeners, chauffeurs, servants, and factory workers—were accustomed to receiving and obeying orders. Indeed, aboard the *Titanic*, for the first time in their lives, they had waitresses at dinner and many were astounded to be served by someone else—

(*If this is a taste of life in America*, Emily Badman had thought, *we'll be swank and spoiled in no time at all!*)

—and thus did a long habit of politely following instructions become as deadly as flood waters in Third Class, where a family lived or died that night based on choices made during the first fifteen minutes after impact, before the first gates were drawn shut. When Gus Cohen decided that death would be easier out in the open, and set out in search of an exit to the after poop deck, he passed through the third-class dining saloon, deep within the ship, just forward of the reciprocating engines, directly over boiler rooms one and two. What he saw shocked him. The portholes were under water—had been under water for a long time—and yet, "everyone was in this dining room, saying their prayers," many with strings of rosary beads in their hands.

Further aft, Eugene Daly, who had boarded the ship in charge of two young women from his hometown, had been held below by armed crewmen for what seemed to him an entire lifetime. Only when no one could deny that the water was advancing aft, and advancing fast, were some of the women let through the gate.

"But, as you know," he told Dr. Frank Blackmarr of the rescue ship *Carpathia*, "we had quite a number of hot-headed Italians and other peoples who got crazy and made for the stairs. These men tried to rush the stairway, pushing and crowding and pulling the women down—some of them with weapons in their hands. I saw two dagos shot and some that took punishment from the officers."

Within minutes of the shooting—probably within seconds, according to Daly, as recorded by Blackmarr—the crowd became a stampede. Avoiding the mass of people, Daly made his way to the starboard side and tossed a large wooden door through an opening near the *à la carte* restaurant—*something to raft away on later*, he thought. Then, noticing a set of empty lifeboat falls dangling from above, he climbed out and hauled himself up to the boat deck, knowing that the swarm at the stairs must be so thick that he would never get through. Reaching the top deck, just ahead of the crowds, Eugene Daly half ran, half slid and stumbled downhill to the bridge and collapsible A. He tried to assist Edward Brown in freeing A, but his world erupted into sudden gunfire, again—and nearby there was a sound like two or three trainloads of dishes crashing down from on high, superimposed over the suck and drag of water, and something like the crack of many bull whips . . . and the screams of women. Mr. Daly realized that he had just climbed from the frying pan into hell.

"My God . . . my God . . ." he said to Blackmarr, and the doctor noted in his journal that at this point in the tale, "the man fell back on his pillow crying and sobbing and moaning, saying, 'My God, if only I could forget! '"

"I THINK ISMAY, the managing director, wanted no one to remember what really happened near collapsibles C and A," observed Walter Lord, "even if this meant he would go down in history as a remarkable coward."

For years, the historian had owned a copy of a letter from a French passenger to his wife, written the day the rescue ship *Carpathia* landed. "So there wasn't really time to build up a lot of folklore," Walter explained. "One would ordinarily believe that what he described was pretty much the way it was, but what the letter described was hard to believe.

"He told his wife that as one of the last boats was being lowered on the starboard side, where First Officer Will Murdoch was in charge, a man tried to jump into it and the officer fired a shot at the jumper—not into the air—shot *him*, and then shot himself."

The witness' name was George Rheims, and his account of the shooting ended with the words, "As there was nothing left to be done, the officer said: 'Gentlemen, each man for himself. Good-bye!' He gave a military salute and shot himself in the head. That's what I call a man!!!"

"The story was so sensational that I didn't know whether to believe it or not," recalled Walter, "except for the fact that it did come from a man who was actually there, who had ended up swimming to collapsible A, and who was writing a letter to his wife. This was not some sensational, third-hand newspaper account."

And then, some time later, we came across Eugene Daly's accounts—which were dated, again, about the time the *Carpathia* landed—describing exactly this same incident. But this time the description came from a British third-class passenger who was not likely to have known a first-class passenger from France (especially as one of the first actions aboard the *Carpathia* was to once again separate the First, Second, and Third classes).

After escaping the shootings below deck, Daly told Dr. Blackmarr, "I reached a collapsible boat that was fastened to the deck by two rings [stays]. It could not be moved."

The guiding clue as to which collapsible was involved is the fidelity with which Eugene Daly's account matches Steward Edward Brown's recollection of A's launching. Amid pandemonium and loud cracking sounds, Daly worked frantically to cut the ropes. The boat was crowded with people—women mostly—clinging to its edges, when the bridge suddenly went under and the deck lurched forward and everyone was washed overboard: "I fell upon one of the oars and fell into a mass of people. Everything I touched seemed to be women's hair. Children crying, women screaming and their hair in their faces. My God, if only I could forget those hands and faces that I touched."

Edward Brown did not mention any shooting during the "great scramble" to cut A loose and get inside, but what was seen and unseen often depended upon which direction one happened to be glancing at a particular instant, and what was mentioned and not mentioned often depended upon one's loyalties to the White Star Line.

In a letter to his sister (which she sold to the *London Daily Telegraph* on May 4, 1912), Eugene Daly described what he saw in the moments before the *Titanic* lurched forward and A was pulled under:

"An officer pointed a revolver and said if any man tried to get in, he would shoot him on the spot. I saw the officer shoot two men dead because they tried to get in the boat. Afterwards there was another shot, and I saw the officer himself lying on the deck. They told me he shot himself, but I did not see him [do it]. I was up to my knees in the water at the time. Everyone was rushing around, and there were no more boats."

That both Eugene Daly and George Rheims were picked up later that morning from boat A places them in the immediate vicinity of a commotion that others described only from a distance:

"There was some disturbance in loading the last two forward starboard boats," wrote seventeen-year-old Jack Thayer. He saw a large crowd of men pressing to get into A and C. Thayer was standing near the starboard rail, almost abreast of the Grand Stairway, beneath the second smokestack, and from his vantage point, "It was really every man for himself." Then Ismay, who had been assisting with the loading of boat C, pushed his way into it.

"And I did not blame him," Jack Thayer told Walter Lord. "I would have jumped in myself, had I been nearer, and had there not been so many people blocking the way."

When two other men tried to jump into Ismay's boat, a man Thayer believed might have been Purser McElroy, standing up in C, fired twice into the air, then stepped out of the boat. "I do not believe they were hit," said Thayer, "but they were quickly thrown out." Oiler Walter Hurst identified the man who fired the warning shots from boat C as "the chief officer."[2] Hurst was in fact nearer to the "bit of trouble" than Thayer, near enough to have been assisting with the pushing of boat A from the roof of the officers

---

[2]It is difficult to discern (with no further identification given in his 1955 memoir) whether Walter Hurst was referring to Chief Officer Wilde, or to First Officer Murdoch, as the man who fired two revolver shots. Murdoch was the man Hurst had known as "chief officer" during the *Titanic*'s sea trials, and during the trip from Belfast to Southampton. For unknown reasons, Wilde, who was already chief officer on the *Olympic*, boarded the *Titanic* in Southampton, keeping his old rank for the Atlantic leg of the maiden voyage, during which Murdoch was temporarily bumped down a rank, to first officer.

quarters down to the boat deck, but not quite "near enough to see if anyone was shot."

Hugh Woolner was insistent that the warning shots at C (followed shortly, according to other witnesses, by actual shootings as A was being pushed off) came from First Officer Murdoch's pistol. In a letter written aboard the *Carpathia*, he described how he and a Swedish gentleman had just finished helping Lightoller load and launch collapsible D, opposite C's davits on the port side, when they stepped back and found three women huddled close together. Woolner and his friend rushed the women through the bridge to the starboard side, and "by sheer bluff," Woolner wrote, "we shouted our way through the press [of people], 'Make way for ladies!' and we hoisted them up, one of us on each side, and giving them a final heave in they had to go, head over heels. We then turned our attention to . . . where there was shouting going on. We saw the first officer twice fire a pistol in the air ordering a crowd of crew out of the boat."

With all the uproar at C's davit heads, one of the boats (number one) actually snagged a rope under its bow and seemed certain to tip over. Miss Francatelli, a passenger who happened to be sitting in the boat when "two American gentlemen and six stokers jumped in," believed it would have ended with her being spilled overboard, "had it not been for that brave officer still up on deck."

Lookout George Symons, who was ordered to row the nearly empty boat a short distance away—quickly, and then to come back for additional passengers when called to do so, had no doubt about the identity of the officer calling down commands from the deck, for his uniform was immediately recognizable. What distinguished William Murdoch from Henry Wilde and the other senior officers was what he shared in common with the *Titanic*'s skipper and designer: They neither carried nor wore lifejackets, so their clothing was fully exposed.

Miss Francatelli heard Murdoch holler for someone to cut the wayward rope with a knife, "but nobody had one and we were all in darkness, hanging in mid air; he shouted, 'mind your heads,' and threw a piece of heavy iron which shook our boat, and so set it free."

When the bridge glided down and the first smokestack threatened to topple, Miss Francatelli was within three hundred feet of the *Titanic*, watching from a vantage point outside the zone of confusion on the starboard boat deck, yet almost exactly level with it. Of Murdoch, she wrote in a letter dated April 28, 1912, "He . . . poor dear brave fellow, shot himself. We saw the whole thing."

"If you've ever tried to sort out eyewitness accounts at a car accident," Walter Lord pointed out, "you come to wonder if the two drivers and their passengers were at the same event. You learn very quickly that you cannot count on any single eyewitness account as truth. But if you've got the same incident described by a half dozen people, the chances are you've got a common consensus that is close to what really did happen. And so it really does appear that in the end, there was a shooting incident, in which warning shots escalated into serious business . . . killing business."

That the incident revolved around collapsible C was of particular interest, because this was Ismay's boat.

"As quiet as if gathered in a church," is how the managing director of the White Star Line described the people gathered around C. Only two other survivors from C were invited to testify at the British and American hearings—Quartermaster George Rowe and Pantryman Albert Pearcey—and they agreed emphatically with their employer: *there was no disorder at all.*[3]

---

[3]Indeed, Ismay and Rowe testified at the American inquiry that there did not even seem to be any people present. Rowe saw no passengers, not even men, gathered on the deck. Ismay claimed only to have seen no women, and both claimed never to have seen or heard Murdoch anywhere near C.

And yet Ismay claimed to have simply, on impulse, stepped quietly into collapsible C. The common consensus suggests that Mr. Ismay was near much more of an uproar than he has led historians to believe—which might explain the heightened state of panic that led him to jump into a lifeboat at that time.

During the days that followed, the rescue ship *Carpathia* went into a "news blackout," refusing even to answer a Marconigram from President Taft regarding the fate of his friend, Major Butt. Naval operators did, however, intercept three messages from the *Carpathia* to the vice president of the International Mercantile Marine, calling for delay of the steamship *Cedric*'s departure from New York, with the apparent intent of shipping all surviving crew members of the *Titanic* back to England without letting them set foot on American soil. All three messages were signed "Yamsi," a not very secret "secret code" used for Ismay's private messages.

Aboard the *Carpathia*, Carlos Hurd, a reporter for the *Post Dispatch*, found the news blackout both infuriating and challenging. Captain Rostron had ordered survivors not to speak with Hurd or his wife, but the pair managed to "sneak" several dozen interviews anyway. The captain imposed on Mr. Hurd periodic inspections of his cabin and his clothing for notes and other news-gathering materials (including pencils), but in accordance with formal Edwardian etiquette, the clothing searches ended where Mrs. Hurd began and, knowing this, Katherine Hurd hid, and wore, nearly five thousand words worth of notes in her underwear.

Captain Arthur Rostron was nobody's fool, and had assigned seamen specifically to watch after both Hurds when the *Carpathia* reached New York harbor, for he suspected that the *Post* would send a boat alongside, and that Carlos Hurd would toss his five thousand words down to its deck.

The skipper had guessed correctly, but Mr. Hurd was no fool either, and the two men became locked in a contest of wills and wits. Fearing that he might be interrupted at the critical last second, or that his story might miss the expected chase boat and be sunk, Hurd built a waterproof package wrapped in oilskin, fashioned a sling, and attached to one end a homemade buoy to guarantee its "unsinkability."

First-class passenger Spencer Silverthorne supplied a cigar box and gathered champagne corks from the *Carpathia*'s dining rooms, then helped Mr. Hurd build the buoy. Silverthorne was anxious to get out to the world his own version of how he had behaved aboard the *Titanic*, scurrying throughout the ship, dodging exploding boilers as he performed daring rescues, working "like a machine," loading women and children into the lifeboats: "Someone thought of the steerage folk and we helped save some of them . . . then it suddenly occurred to me that all the boats were filled and we had nothing to put the rest of the women and children in . . . I remember that as I stood on the deck the thought occurred to me that I might swim to an iceberg . . . I didn't have far to jump. I landed in the water. Somehow I got in a boat."

Silverthorne had in fact simply stepped off the boat deck and taken a seat in number five, the second boat down to the sea on the starboard side. At 12:55 A.M., boat five, with a seating capacity for sixty-five people, cast off with just forty-one aboard, only thirteen of them women and children.

One of the crewmen Captain Rostron had assigned to thwart Carlos Hurd got his chance when, just as Rostron had predicted, a boat came speeding down Ambrose Channel and joined the *Carpathia*'s side. A man Mr. Hurd recognized called for him to throw down whatever news he had been able to collect. Too fast for Rostron's henchman,

Hurd managed to sling the buoyed package at the chase boat, but its trailing line caught on a rope hanging from one of the *Carpathia*'s davits. The crewman climbed out on the davit, reaching for the line, while below him a hundred passengers shouted in protest. As his captain looked on, the sailor seemed deliberately to dislodge the package, dropping it straight to the deck of the chase boat, to cheers from the *Titanic*'s survivors.

In his dispatch, Hurd told of a first-class passenger who was "thoroughly dunked" before being picked up by collapsible A. After the ship's surgeon had examined him, the man "caused much amusement on the *Carpathia*, by demanding a bath."

The man's name was George Rheims, and from him, through Carlos Hurd, came the first word of "shots in the dark."

In the April 18 edition of the *New York Morning World*, Hurd wrote, "Revolver shots heard shortly before the *Titanic* went down caused many rumors, one that Captain Smith had shot himself, another that First Officer Murdoch had ended his life, but members of the crew discredit these rumors."

On April 19, the first rumors discrediting George Rheims as a coward who had survived by slithering into a lifeboat dressed in women's clothing were circulating in the morning papers, just as the U.S. Senate hearings on the loss of the *Titanic* were about to commence. Experts would be called in to speak about icebergs, coal, and radio waves, but no one would ever call Mr. Rheims to testify about what he had witnessed on the starboard boat deck, and no tabloid would ever publish a retraction clearing his name.

On that same April morning, ugly rumors were printed about how Miss Francatelli's group had behaved after the *Titanic* went down. Her employers, "Mr. and Mrs. Morgan"—who were really Sir Cosmo and Lady Duff Gordon—found themselves accused of bribing the crew of their boat, for fear of being swamped, to row away from the hundreds of people swimming towards them and crying for help.

Still recovering from his injuries, Eugene Daly awoke to read that he had snuck into a lifeboat, from which one of the *Titanic*'s officers had dragged him kicking and screaming and crying like a little girl.

Being pilloried by the tabloids was not the only thing Miss Francatelli (and the Duff Gordons), George Rheims, and Eugene Daly had in common. Bound for New York aboard the *Carpathia*, they had all spoken about what happened near boat C. Miss Francatelli and the Duff Gordons were in an especially good position to see, having departed on boat one, just ahead of C, rowing with their backs facing the sea and their eyes facing C's davits, Ismay, and Murdoch.

"We saw the whole thing," Miss Francatelli had said.

Four weeks later, at the British inquiry, the Gordons completely retracted their story of panic and gunfire on the decks of the *Titanic*. They, along with the crew of Ismay's boat, insisted on having no recollection of seeing William Murdoch near C, or anyone else, for that matter. Lady Gordon, who in an April 18 interview with a reporter from the *Sunday American* said she had been close enough to see the *Titanic* shiver, and break, and suddenly send forth a wave that forced her to clutch the side of the lifeboat, who said she had been close enough to see women and men clinging to bits of wreckage, who said she was close enough to distinguish a man's voice among the swimmers: " 'My God, my God' . . . he cried monotonously, in a dull, hopeless way," suddenly discredited the entire account as a fiction concocted by "a clever reporter." She told Lord Mersey's Commission that she, Sir Cosmo, and Miss Francatelli had in fact been too far

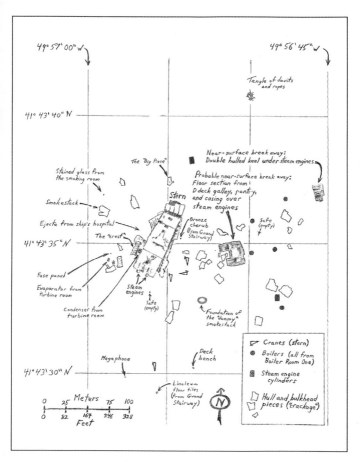

Archaeological map of stern debris field.

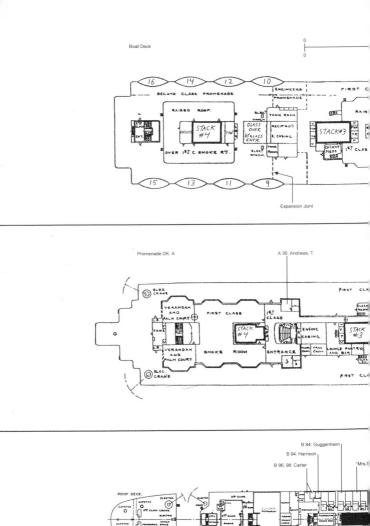

Boat Deck

0
0

16 14 12 10

SECOND CLASS PROMENADE

ENGINEERS
PROMENADE

FIRST C

RAISED ROOF.

STACK #4

FAN

TANK ROOM

GLASS OVER 1ST CLASS ENTR.

RECIPRO'S E. CASING

STACK #3

1ST CLASS

OFFICERS MESS

OVER 1ST C. SMOKE R'M.

ELECT. WINCH

TANK ROOM

15 13 11 9

Expansion Joint

Promenade DK. A

A 36: Andrews, T.

ELEC. CRANE

FIRST CLA

VERANDAH AND PALM COURT

FIRST CLASS

1ST CLASS

CLAS ROOM

FANS

STACK #4

ENGINE CASING

STACK #3

VERANDAH AND PALM COURT

SMOKE ROOM

ENTRANCE

TANK ROOM

LOUNGE PANTRY AND BAR

3

ELEC. CRANE

FIRST CLA

B 84: Guggenheim

B 94: Harrison

B 96, 98: Carter

"Mrs.

POOP DECK.

ELECTRIC

CAPSTAN

3RD CLASS CRANE

ELECTRIC

2ND CLASS

ELECTRIC

A LA CARTE RESTAURANT

RESTAURANT

CAPSTAN

PROMENADE SPACE

WINCH SPACE ELECTRO

2ND CLASS SMOKE ROOM

2ND CLASS

RECEPTION ROOM

CAPSTAN

ELECTRIC CRANE

CAFÉ PARISIAN

B 71, 73: Davidson and Hays

B 69: H

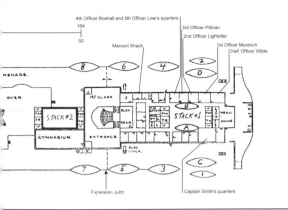

4th Officer Boxhall and 5th Officer Low's quarters
164
50
3rd Officer Pitman
2nd Officer Lightoller
1st Officer Murdoch
Chief Officer Wilde
Marconi Shack

MENADE.
OVER
STACK #2
GYMNASIUM
1ST CLASS
ENTRANCE
STACK #1
WHEEL HOUSE
ELEV
GEAR
ELEC. TOWER.
Expansion Joint
Captain Smith's quarters

8 6 4 2 D B A C I
7 5 3

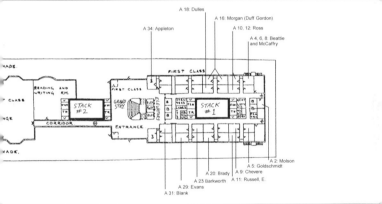

A 18: Dulles
A 16: Morgan (Duff Gordon)
A 34: Appleton
A 10, 12: Ross
A 4, 6, 8: Beattie and McCaffry

NADE.
READING AND WRITING RM.
CLASS
NGE
CORRIDOR
STACK #2
FIRST CLASS
GRAND STRY
FIRST CLASS
STACK #1
ENTRANCE
NADE.

A 2: Molson
A 5: Goldschmidt
A 9: Chevere
A 11: Russell, E.
A 20: Brady
A 23 Barkworth
A 29: Evans
A 31: Blank

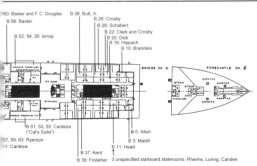

60: Baxter and F. C. Douglas
B 58: Baxter
B 38: Butt, A.
B 26: Crosby
B 28: Schabert
B 22: Clark and Crosby
B 52, 54, 56: Ismay
B 20: Dick
B 18: Hippach
B 10: Brandeis

BRIDGE DK B
FORECASTLE DK.
STEAM
CAPSTAN
WINDLASS
CAPSTAN
1ST CLASS
ENTRANCE

B 51, 53, 55: Cardeza ("Cal's Suite")
57, 59, 63: Ryerson
1: Cardeza
B 37: Kent
B 39: Frolieher
B 6: Allen
B 3: Madill
B 11: Head
3 unspecified starboard staterooms: Rheims, Loring, Candee

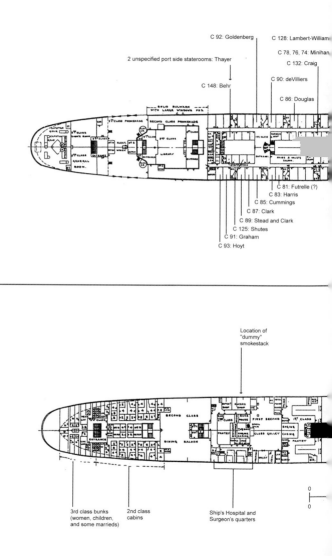

C 92: Goldenberg

C 128: Lambert-William

C 78, 76, 74: Minihan

2 unspecified port side staterooms: Thayer

C 132: Craig

C 90: deVilliers

C 148: Behr

C 86: Douglas

C 81: Futrelle (?)

C 83: Harris

C 85: Cummings

C 87: Clark

C 89: Stead and Clark

C 125: Shutes

C 91: Graham

C 93: Hoyt

Location of "dummy" smokestack

3rd class bunks (women, children, and some marrieds)

2nd class cabins

Ship's Hospital and Surgeon's quarters

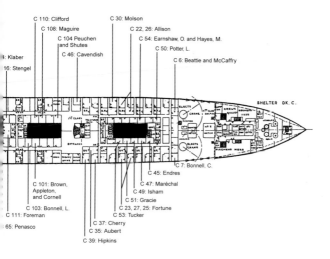

C 110: Clifford
C 108: Maguire
C 104 Peuchen and Shutes
C 46: Cavendish
C 30: Molson
C 22, 26: Allison
C 54: Earnshaw, O. and Hayes, M.
C 50: Potter, L.
C 6: Beattie and McCaffry
4: Klaber
16: Stengel

SHELTER DK. C.

C 7: Bonnell, C.
C 45: Endres
C 47: Maréchal
C 49: Isham
C 51: Gracie
C 53: Tucker
C 23, 27, 25: Fortune
C 101: Brown, Appleton, and Cornell
C 103: Bonnell, L.
C 111: Foreman
65: Penasco
C 37: Cherry
C 35: Aubert
C 39: Hipkins

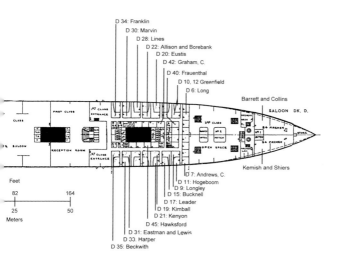

D 34: Franklin
D 30: Marvin
D 28: Lines
D 22: Allison and Borebank
D 20: Eustis
D 42: Graham, C.
D 40: Frauenthal
D 10, 12 Greenfield
D 6: Long
Barrett and Collins

SALOON DK. D.

Kemish and Shiers
D 7: Andrews, C.
D 11: Hogeboom
D 9: Longley
D 15: Bucknell
D 17: Leader
D 19: Kimball
D 21: Kenyon
D 45: Hawksford
D 31: Eastman and Lewis
D 33: Harper
D 35: Beckwith

Feet
82   164
25   50
Meters

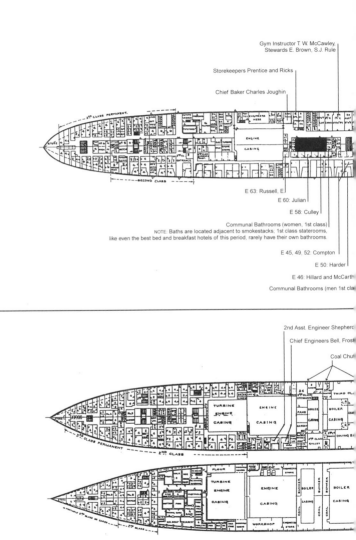

Gym Instructor T. W. McCawley,
Stewards E. Brown, S.J. Rule

Storekeepers Prentice and Ricks

Chief Baker Charles Joughin

E 63: Russell, E.

E 60: Julian

E 58: Culley

Communal Bathrooms (women, 1st class)
NOTE: Baths are located adjacent to smokestacks; 1st class staterooms,
like even the best bed and breakfast hotels of this period, rarely have their own bathrooms.

E 45, 49, 52: Compton

E 50: Harder

E 46: Hillard and McCarth

Communal Bathrooms (men 1st cla

2nd Asst. Engineer Shepherd

Chief Engineers Bell, Frost

Coal Chu

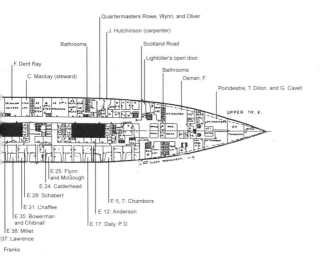

Quartermasters Rowe, Wynn, and Oliver

J. Hutchinson (carpenter)

Bathrooms

Scotland Road

Lightoller's open door

F. Dent Ray

Bathrooms

C. Mackay (steward)

Osman, F.

Poindestre, T. Dillon, and G. Cavell

UPPER DK. E.

E 25: Flynn and McGough

E 24: Calderhead

E 28: Schabert

E 5, 7: Chambers

E 31: Chaffee

E 12: Anderson

E 35: Bowerman and Chibnall

E 17: Daly, P. D.

E 38: Millet

37: Lawrence

Franks

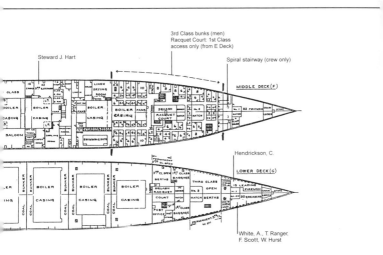

3rd Class bunks (men)
Racquet Court: 1st Class access only (from E Deck)

Steward J. Hart

Spiral stairway (crew only)

MIDDLE DECK (F)

Hendrickson, C.

LOWER DECK (G)

White, A., T. Ranger, F. Scott, W. Hurst

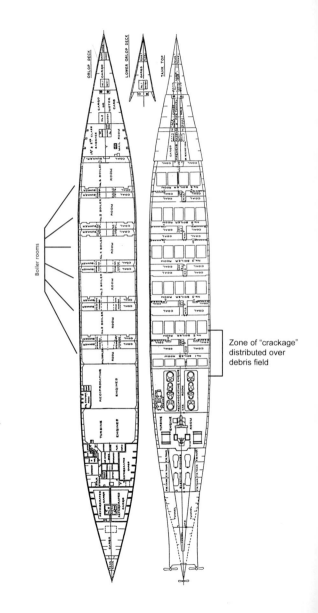

Boiler rooms

Zone of "crackage" distributed over debris field

away—two hundred yards or more—to hear any cries, or to see very much of what happened to the *Titanic* in the end.[4]

In his July 1912 summation, Lord Mersey exonerated the Gordons (from all rumors of cowardice), but George Rheims and Eugene Daly were destined to live in the shadow of the *Titanic* the rest of their days. Rheims stuck by his story, but scorn and ridicule destroyed his credibility beyond recall. Daly simply sought anonymity and obscurity.

Ismay also developed an affinity for the shadows. As one of the *Titanic*'s owners, he was ultimately responsible for the fact that even if the crew had been trained to launch all the boats quickly, there existed only enough space in the lifeboats for half the people aboard. The managing director would never live down his ultimate decision, given full knowledge of the mathematical discrepancy between passengers and seats in lifeboats, to seat himself in one of the last boats.

The uproar that others saw near boat C, if widely known, might have made his leap into C more understandable, might even have lifted some of the stigma that compelled the citizens of Ismay, Texas, to change the name of their

---

[4]The wave Lady Gordon described, apparently created by the stern when it broke free of the bow, was also described by Helen Candee in another boat close to the sinking (the wave washed over the sides of boat six and soaked Helen's shoes under a foot of water). Celiney Yasbeck, in a letter to Walter Lord dated June 15, 1955, described the view from Lady Gordon's boat thus: "When the ship sank it made a tremendous noise that I will never forget. The impact of the sinking was so great, it shook the waters and we thought our lifeboat would sink, too." Though officially denying before Lord Mersey's examiners that boat one had been near enough for her to feel the wave, or to hear and see the horrors, in her 1931 book, *Discretions and Indiscretions*, Lady Gordon wrote, "For a few seconds [the *Titanic*] stayed motionless while the agonized cries from her decks grew intensely and then, with one awful downward rush she plunged to her grave through fathoms of water, and the air was rent with those awful shrieks."

town. But apparently J. Bruce Ismay—"J. Brute Ismay" to the media—thought it better to be known as a coward than to admit that one of his hand-picked officers had killed a passenger or two, and then himself.

As he had, from the shadows, controlled the news black-out on the *Carpathia*, so too did Ismay control, through the press, the credibility of any aboard the rescue ship who had spoken of shootings. Rich, poor, or knighted, their reputations were doomed from the moment they set foot on shore. Given tabloids that were hungry for any facts whatsoever about the disaster (whether true or not), given all the power and cunning of the White Star Line, and given that even an amateur story teller like Spencer Silverthorne was able to recolor history in the *Post Dispatch* and *The Morning World*, it could not have been very difficult to keep Ismay and White Star's version of events—people who saw shootings have no credibility—in firm command.

"I suppose Ismay could be called many things," observed Walter Lord, "but 'natural born leader' was not one of them. There are natural leaders in the world, just as there are natural *non*-leaders. Bruce Ismay seems to be a good example of a non-leader who found himself in a leadership position."

Stanley Resor, secretary of the army during Nixon's presidency, happened to be visiting when Walter and I began to tackle "the leadership paradox." He picked up Walter's observation and ran with it. "We get inadequate leaders because the people *in* leadership are usually people who desperately want, and ruthlessly compete, for those positions. So the guys at the top are usually just good competitors."

"Which explains," Bill MacQuitty added, "why so many of the officers in charge of the *Titanic* that night proved to be of very little value. Just look at Captain Smith. For the first half hour he walked around in a state of shock. According to Marconi Operator Harold Bride, there was at least some steam left in the ship's boilers, keeping the turbines running almost to the very end. Once Smith saw, and pointed out to his second officer, the lights of another ship—"

("The passengers began asking why we were swinging the lifeboats out and lowering them level with the boat deck," Second Officer Lightoller explained to Walter Lord in 1946. "I told them it was merely a precaution and that very likely they'd all be . . . taken on board the ship everyone could clearly see only a few miles away—we could all see her lights quite clearly.")

"—That ship was the *Californian*. No doubt of it; she was only about ten miles away. Smith could have steamed toward it, rather than just tell his lifeboat crews to 'row toward those lights.' I've always thought it very odd that he didn't try. He only had ten miles to go."

"And this was not a unique situation," Walter said.

As apparently it was not. In Crete, I had visited the Greek cruise ship *Oceanos*, notable for its life-size, museum-quality reproductions of 1628 B.C. frescoes from the Isle of Thera. Some months later, the liner struck a rock off the coast of South Africa and began sinking by the bow. After two watertight bulkheads failed, the captain, in a state of shock, climbed into a lifeboat with his senior officers and left all of his passengers behind. The task of sending out the distress call and organizing the rescue was taken up by the ship's musicians and kitchen staff.

"I think you'll find this leadership paradox at work in every crisis," said Walter. "Be it a shipwreck, or an earthquake, or a war . . . Yes, maybe it takes a true crisis to bring an otherwise obscure man out of the woodwork and turn him into an Abraham Lincoln."

"Or a Charles Joughin," I said. "On the *Titanic*, it was the baker, the assistant purser, the electricians—people

who had never been groomed for positions of command—
who came forward and took up the task of rescue, asking
nothing for themselves, and even refusing seats in the
lifeboats. And there were the engineers, the stewards, two
or three housewives, Drs. O'Loughlin and Simpson, and
the ship's architect . . ."

"There have always been natural leaders who never,
under normal circumstances, get a chance to lead," said
Walter. "They are all around us. Under normal conditions, you may never notice them. They probably don't
even know themselves how they will behave until the day
they are needed."

"And when havoc strikes, it is the ones who are officially
in charge who often freeze or come unhinged," said Resor.
"That's when the true leaders, who might not be near the
top simply because they have the good sense to avoid com-
petitive, back-stabbing people, rise to the occasion and as-
sume the role of hard, risky leadership that no one else, in
time of crisis, really wants."

Stanley Resor knew, on a level deeper than words alone
could explain, what he was talking about. During the
Nixon administration, he had so admired his commander
in chief that he became a framer of the infamous White
House "enemy list," and put his own son (an anti-war
protester) on the list. Then the Watergate crisis struck, and
the President, between bouts of talking to paintings of Lincoln and Eisenhower, said, "Do they not realize that I
could get on that phone and in an hour and a half 700 million people could be dead?"

Resor did realize something, then. He really did. It astonished him that this "man" could even be harboring such
thoughts over what was, at bottom, nothing more substantial than a bad career decision. During the height of the crisis, the secretary of the army joined General Alexander
Haig in a plan to make doubly and triply certain that no

branch of the American military would obey a presidential order to launch missiles "without prior visual confirmation of mushroom clouds over American soil." And thus did Stanley Resor become a participant in what was, technically, one of the biggest antiwar protests of all time. Technically, it was also treason; but Nixon left the White House and died two decades later without ever learning the truth.

The human tendency to follow a J. Bruce Ismay, a Captain Stanley Lord, or the men in command of "the cowardly boat six" is not uniquely a failing of the Edwardian era. Perhaps the most important question facing our civilization over the next forty years is not how inadequate leaders become inadequate leaders, but what characteristics of human nature cause us to so consistently choose the most inadequate among us and elevate them to positions where they can inflict the greatest harm.

SECOND OFFICER CHARLES Lightoller had explained to Walter Lord that he lowered his first three or four boats half empty because (A) he did not believe the ship would sink and (B) he believed filling them to their full capacity once they were safely on the water would have been "a far easier job than lowering them with their full compliment from the tremendous height of the boat deck."

Too late, he realized that (A) perhaps the *Titanic* could sink and (B) the boats were not, as ordered, remaining near the gangway doors to take on more passengers. Fourth Officer Boxhall said he had rowed away from a gangway door because "there were so many people at the door that they would have jumped down and swamped us—and besides, we had only room for about two more." (His boat, number two, was in fact only 60 percent full and could easily have taken twenty more.) In number six, Helen Candee heard Lightoller calling her boat back to the *Titanic* with a whistle. There was additional room for thirty-seven, but

Quartermaster Hitchens said, "No, we are not going back. It is our lives now, not theirs."

"Hitchens was cowardly and almost crazed with fear all the time," recalled Helen Candee. "He made himself warm with a steamer blanket which he took from one of the women. Then, after the sinking of the *Titanic*, Hitchens reminded us forcibly that we were hundreds of miles from land, without water, without food. He said we did not even know the direction in which we were rowing.

"'We are going straight north,' I called to him with anger.

"'How do you know?' he taunted.

"'There is the North Star directly above our bow.' This answer silenced him. Strange that a sailor should be so ignorant."

Any peace Helen might have drawn from the stars and the still air was lost in the intense cold. One of the men snatched up almost every blanket in the lifeboat, leaving women and children without, until one of the women put a gun against his ear and explained in a quiet, almost kindly tone that she intended to puree his brains into fish food if he did not give up the blankets.

"One of the things that has intrigued me about that night," said Jim Cameron, "as more and more of these stories come forth [mostly through letters and old diaries held in survivors' families], is that so many people were packing guns aboard the *Titanic*."

"It seems to have been—at least among the passengers—an American custom," I said.

"I guess some things never really change. But if you look at survivors' accounts—Eugene Daly's aside—all of the gun incidents happened in the lifeboats and on the boat deck. But that's where all the survivors came from. Only one-third of the *Titanic*'s people lived to tell what they saw; so as a rough estimate we must be missing two-thirds of the shooting incidents that actually occurred, and those would have taken place below deck. I'll bet you that somewhere inside the ship, there was an incident somewhat like the one Daly described, in which the crew fired through the gate at the men in Third Class, and one of those men had a gun of his own. Given what we know of human nature, there might actually have occurred one or two gunfights below deck, but we'll never know of it unless one of our robots starts uncovering bullet holes in the walls and ceiling."

Finding those little holes, if they exist, would require the scouring away of rusticle encrustations from the walls, and the sifting of debris on the floors for spent lead. I realized that we could go on forever discovering new artifacts and new people and new stories simply by moving forward in any direction and looking at the *Titanic* on smaller and smaller scales—much as Roy Cullimore and I had moved forward, however accidentally, into the microscopic world of a rusticle's interior, or into the private world of Howard Irwin: two random snapshots of a ghost house filled with unanswered questions, leading to more unanswered questions, leading to yet more unanswered questions. To move forward in the *Titanic* was, as we had gone to sea suspecting and had now come to know for a fact, to be drawn into the archaeological equivalent of the fractal universe—which, insofar as our own human lifetimes were concerned, was indistinguishable from mathematical infinity. Archaeology's black hole. We were being sucked into it.

On the video monitor, Jim Cameron pointed to a panel of white-painted oak. "As our robot penetrated rooms and corridors forward of the great shaft, where the Grand Stairway used to be," he explained, "we found a surprising number of wood panels, and doorways, and sticks of furniture."

"It seems likely," I said, "that wood throughout the ship

is simply better preserved than we originally believed, based upon Bob Ballard's discovery that the Grand Stairway was gone." Missing and presumed eaten—we had all accepted Ballard's conclusion about the Grand Stairway's fate, and it followed, from this conclusion, that the rest of the *Titanic*'s wood had met the same fate.

But Ballard's robot, *Jason Junior*, had entered the shaft and descended no deeper than B deck, and had advanced no more than fifteen feet into the reception area on the port side of the stairwell. The decks were lettered A, B, C, D, E, F, G, from the boat deck down. The Grand Stairway had reached the base of E deck, meaning that *Jason Junior* had barely scratched the surface of the *Titanic*'s interior.

The Cameron robot, affectionately known as *Snoop Dog* ("he snooped around and he was on a leash"), moved aft of the stairwell, along the starboard side, into Mrs. Cardeza's suite, then forward of the well, along the corridor leading past B-37, the room occupied by Helen Candee's friend, Kent.

Once Jim strayed more than forty feet from the stairwell, wood began to appear, more and more of it the further he strayed. The camera did reveal trails left by wood-boring mollusks, many more of them had been bored through varnished boards than through those covered in toxic white, lead-based paint; but the general pattern Jim began to see was that all of the wood near the stairwell appeared to have been stripped away and blasted outward toward the hull and staterooms, as if by an explosion emanating from the center of the ship, from the stairwell itself.

Curiouser and curioser . . . Alice's plunge down the rabbit hole seemed barely to furnish criteria for the realities of a robotic descent to E deck. Areas sheltered from the blast—the walls and doors along the corridor leading to Frank Millet's stateroom E-38 (about thirty feet aft of the

stairway, against the casing for the second smokestack)—
stood so intact that the room itself could not be entered
without breaking down panels. The filmmaker had no
stomach for vandalism, so he moved on. The forward corridor, leading toward Norman Chambers' stateroom, was
in similar condition. At first, Jim thought weaker currents
in this part of the ship, and correspondingly lower oxygen
levels, might have made the wood-paneled corridors un-
healthy for scavenging organisms, but the deep-ocean
snow was blowing through the halls and silting a heap of
unrecognizable debris; and there was a rat-tailed fish hov-
ering near the ceiling; and fern-shaped hydrozoans growing on a wall-mounted lamp. Even six decks down and
forty feet forward of the well, it was a good place to be a
gilled, oxygen-breather or filter-feeder.

There was not much to be seen on C deck. A massive
structural shock, upon impact with the ocean floor, had
pressed B deck down upon C, bowing out, like rows of
bent knees, all of C's vertical steel columns and blowing
their oak cladding away.

"Downblast," Jim concluded: an inertial fist that came
down the shaft unimpeded . . . *Unimpeded*, Jim began to
see, by the stairway itself. A thin strip of bulkhead from the
boat deck had been swept back like a flag and raked down
the stairwell, fully two decks down. This could not have
occurred, Jim knew, if the stairway, or at least its upper two
decks, had been standing in the bulkhead's way.

If Bob Ballard's wood-boring mollusks were responsible for the stairway's disappearance, then one was hard
pressed to explain how they had managed to remove it
even before the *Titanic* arrived on the bottom. Not even pi-
ranha worked that fast.

A robot's-eye-view of girders and steel plates at the base
of the E deck landing revealed no traces of brass ornamen-

tation or linoleum flooring.[5] Had the stairway been eaten by wood-borers, the indigestible brass and linoleum should have been lying in piles at the E deck landing. The pattern Jim saw suggested to him that the stairway—a multistory, oak-framed tower built on a steel footing at the base of E deck—had become buoyant as the sea climbed toward A deck. The absence of brass trim and linoleum at the bottom of the shaft (and more, the absence of broken glass or even a single piece of iron frame from the crystal dome) led me to become a believer in Jim's emerging theory that the Grand Stairway had broken free of its mountings and floated up through the dome, carrying out everything on, and above, and around it as the boat deck and the main reception area glided down.

Through the eyes of Jim Cameron's electronic fish, through its hours of recorded images, the TV screens became, for us, a gallery of windows on sunken rooms. We moved under the arched entryway, into the corridor on the starboard side of the stairway's forward bulkhead on E deck. The bulkhead had formed the back wall or "spine" of the stairway. To our left were the elevators, and ahead, the very hallway in which Mr. Rothschild had explained to Steward Frederick Ray that the water would advance only so far and then stop advancing. Multiple generations of rusticles had formed on the ceiling and fallen to the floor, their features now softened by a dusting of deep-ocean snow.

Some of the oak paneling was in near-pristine condition, but here and there doors and walls and metal frames had been mauled by a great force. A solid wooden beam, fully eighteen inches across, had apparently come pounding like a battering ram into one of the rooms.

---

[5]Linoleum was a new invention in 1912, and had become "all the rage." In expensive hotels and on first-class ships, wood and stone flooring was being stripped off and replaced by linoleum.

"God knows where it came from," said Jim. "But the interesting thing to think about is, if it came from a catastrophic destruction—a column of water pounding down through the shaft on impact with the bottom—and then this beam came with it, sailing in from the stairwell—"

"Yes," I said. "A lingering fragment from the stairway—that's what I was thinking."

"Or it could have rotted loose and fallen from the ceiling years later, but—"

"But," I observed, there was a thick powdering of "snow," rusticle debris, and what appeared to be dissolved ceiling plaster lying on top of and around the beam, meaning that "the beam settled to the floor years before all this debris formed, meaning that it might very well have been hurled in here, that first night."

"Right."

"I'm thinking of a piece of the Grand Stairway that got lodged in the reception area as the ship went down, and was later blasted forward into this room, when the downblast effects kicked in." I pointed to a clean surface on one side of the beam. "And *this* piece of oak was not eaten by wood-boring mollusks, which means we have yet another clue that the stairway itself was lost top-side. Otherwise, a lot of uneaten wood (to say nothing of brass and linoleum trim) should be piled at least two decks deep at the bottom of the shaft."

Jim nodded. "If the stairway had a heavy steel frame, and if it went down with the ship, and was eaten by wood-borers, we would have found steel beams, too, on the E deck landing. To judge from every bit of information I've been able to get, the stairway was constructed almost entirely out of wood, so, once submerged, it acquired a tremendous positive buoyancy, many tons of lift—which leads to what I call 'my very radical theory about where the stairway went.'"

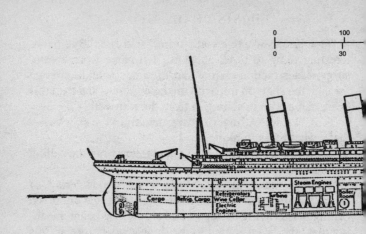

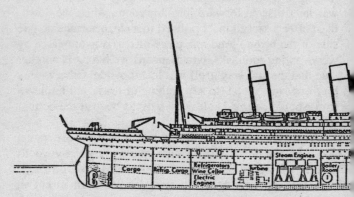

At 11:50 P.M., ten minutes after impact, 4,000 tons of water have entered the first five watertight compartments through twelve square feet of iceberg damage. Fireman Fred Barrett notes that water is entering the sixth compartment through a small hole behind the forward bulkhead of boiler room five. The water "enters five as if through a firehose," but the pumps are able to handle it.

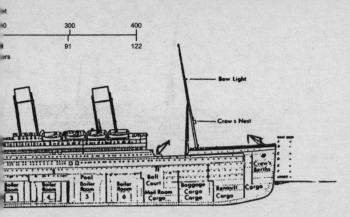

This cross-section of the 882.5-foot-long *Titanic* shows the liner in normal draft moments before the impact of 11:40 P.M. on April 14, 1912, opened up a series of leaks and punctures in the bow. Vertical partitions running from the keel to E deck divide the boiler rooms, mail rooms, and cargo holds into watertight compartments and render the ship "unsinkable." Advertised as the largest ship in the world, she is in fact only nine inches longer than her nearly identical sister ship, *Olympic*.

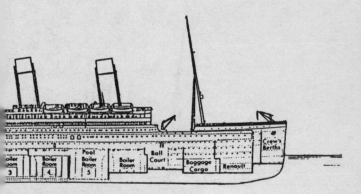

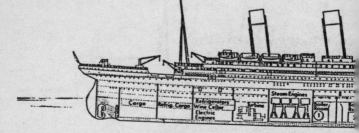

12:20 A.M. Forty minutes after impact: Two rows of portholes are now under the sea (and soon, Lightoller's gangway door). More than a half dozen of those portholes are open, increasing by at least 50 percent the original twelve square feet opened to the sea by ice. Even so, the ship is settling toward stability, at which point the sinking process slows to a near halt.

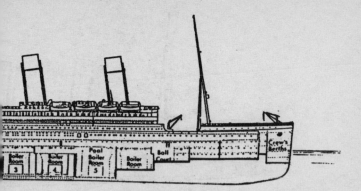

12:00 A.M. Twenty minutes after impact, 7,000 tons of water have entered the *Titanic*'s bow. The bulkhead between boiler rooms five and six, already embrittled and partly melted by a coal bunker fire, and warped by the lateral thrust of ice, is further weakened by increasing water pressure in boiler room six.

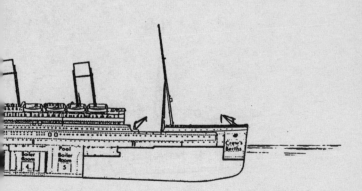

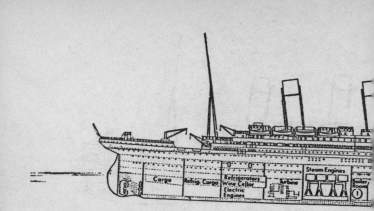

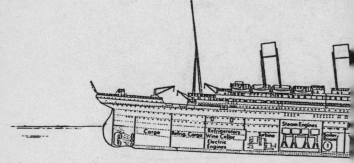

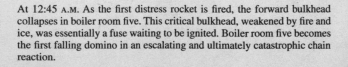

At 12:45 A.M. As the first distress rocket is fired, the forward bulkhead collapses in boiler room five. This critical bulkhead, weakened by fire and ice, was essentially a fuse waiting to be ignited. Boiler room five becomes the first falling domino in an escalating and ultimately catastrophic chain reaction.

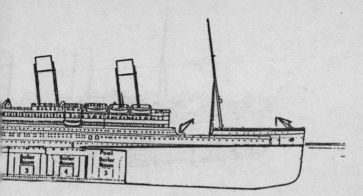

12:40 A.M. An hour after impact, water rises over the closed hatch at the top of boiler room five and creeps aft along the hallways. The first boat, number seven, is being lowered on the starboard side.

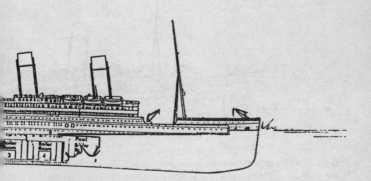

2:00 A.M. Two hours and twenty minutes after impact: Rowing along the starboard side, Mrs. Thayer notices a porthole open to the sea, and watches a cabin flood as the opening glides under. She realizes, with a start, that portholes left open by passengers who looked outside after the crash have increased the rate of hemorrhage. Third-class men are released from the stern at this time, an hour after first-class dogs were released from the ship's kennel.

1:20 A.M. On the port side, water is flowing in through Lightoller's open gangway door and running aft along Scotland Road. The ship is now listing to port. During the past thirty-five minutes, since the collapse of boiler room five, water has been spilling down stairwells on either side of Scotland Road. With the gangway door now providing a wider opening to the sea than the initial iceberg damage, nothing except the buoyancy of boiler room four keeps the *Titanic* stable.

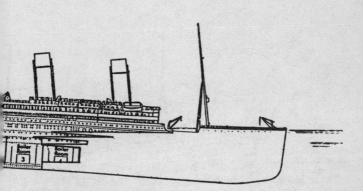

2:10 A.M. Building water pressure bursts boiler room four. The final plunge begins.

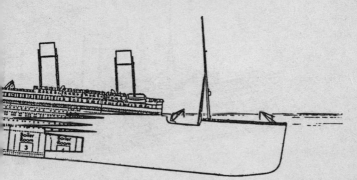

2:05 A.M. Hundreds of square feet are now opening to the sea along the upper decks. The hatch at the top of boiler room four has been closed for more than an hour, providing a brief respite to men working the pumps below—unaware, apparently, that they are working in a submarine.

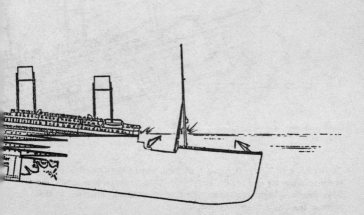

2:11–2:14 A.M. The entire five-story structure of the Grand Stairway becomes buoyant and breaks away from its mountings, presumably in large pieces. The afterstays for the first smokestack, attached to the spine of the stairway, are severed.

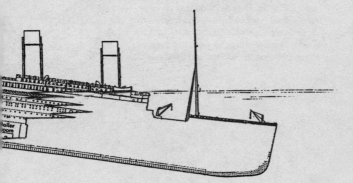

As the *Titanic*'s bow plunges under, Scotland Road and other avenues
of seepage stop transmitting water aft and send a storm surge forward.
Washington Dodge notes that water jets out through a window actually
located above sea level. Charles Lightoller notices that the roof of the
bridge, when it reaches the sea, is level with the crow's nest.

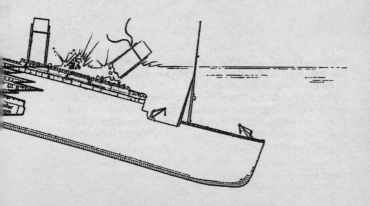

2:15–2:17 A.M. Boiler room three collapses. Eugene Daly sees dozens of swimmers about to be drawn down into the second smokestack. Below the surface, Colonel Gracie struggles near the compass tower, between the second and third stacks.

2:17 A.M. The sea surface becomes a fulcrum, snapping the *Titanic* just abaft of amidships. Between the reciprocating engine room and boiler room two, an eighty-foot length of hull and decking (including the kitchen floor on D deck and the double-hulled floor of the engine room and aft boiler rooms) cracks into hundreds of pieces, like glass. Drifting below the surface, just forward of the break beneath the toppling third smokestack, Colonel Gracie makes one of history's narrowest escapes.

2:17 A.M. Given what appears to have been a "clean" breakaway, the stern should have floated; but attempts to pump water out of the forward compartments through hoses attached to the aft engines have left the door at the bottom of the turbine room open, permitting water to gush in from the reciprocating steam engine room. The passengers might have fared better had the engineers done absolutely nothing to save the ship. . . . might have, if not for hot coals spilled from the smoking room fireplace during the forward plunge. The stern is now burning and sinking.

2:18 A.M. Thirty seconds after the break, the open doors of the engine rooms bring the forward section of the stern down to E deck.

2:18–2:19 A.M. As the E deck passage-way outside Joughin's stateroom floods the aft extension of Scotland Road, the stern rolls briefly onto its port side, then corkscrews "nose down." Furnishings, tools, fittings—even ashtrays from the first-class smoking room—begin raining from the nearly vertical opening. The last good news anyone will hear aboard the *Titanic*: The fire has been put out.

2:20 A.M. As water fills the stern, the last air pockets begin to compress. Refrigerator doors break. A few chambers, unable to fill quickly enough, undergo partial crushing, like beer cans, until the moment of breach. By the time the stern reaches a descent rate of fifteen miles per hour, drag forces are peeling back the fantail decking and trying to swing the keel level again.

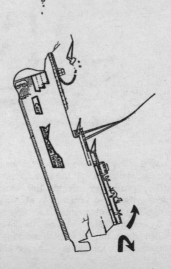

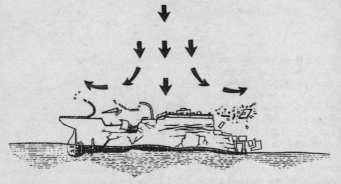

2:23–2:24 A.M. After falling two and one-half miles, the stern arrives on the bottom propeller end first, having reached a terminal velocity of at least thirty-two miles per hour, probably as high as forty miles per hour, and possibly as high as fifty or even sixty miles per hour.

2:24 A.M. As the propellers impact against hard sediment, the stern bends, compresses, and cracks all the way forward—all in the space of two seconds. The slipstream of water that follows the stern is still descending at the same terminal velocity achieved by the wreck before it stopped. The effect of the resulting downblast against the upper decks is like a tidal wave striking a skyscraper. Within the stern, inertia continues to push water toward the seabed where, finding its path suddenly blocked, it bursts out the sides and contributes the formation of an ejecta blanket.

2:22–2:24 A.M. Relative to the stern, the *Titanic*'s bow glides to the bottom. Nevertheless, it reaches a terminal velocity of at least twenty-five miles per hour, probably somewhere between twenty-five and thirty miles per hour, and possibly as high as thirty-five or even forty miles per hour. The nose plunges more than sixty feet into the sediment, crumpling as it descends.

2:22–2:24 A.M. Below the bridge, the hull bends like accordion skin and the double-hulled bottom is actually telescoped aft into boiler room six, rendering the archaeologist's separation of iceberg damage in this region from bottom impact damage an intractable problem. The only likely signs of iceberg damage are observed further aft: a): a twelve-foot-long horizontal scratch (apparently made by a small rock within the ice) drawn like a pencil point, during one third of a second, across the centers of three hull plates, and just ahead of the scratch b): a hole, the approximate size and shape of a plumb, near the bottom of boiler room five. A second after the bow levels out on the bottom, the downblast strikes, hammering down rooftops, pancaking decks, and (except on the narrowest deck profiles, near the point bow) blowing railings out to port and starboard.

"Not down a mollusk's throat," I said.

"No. Not at all," he emphasized, and he was able to prove it, more or less, in a manner that no archaeologist's budget would otherwise have allowed. "When we were filming *Titanic*, we built a full-size replica of the Grand Stairway, based upon the original Harland and Wolff plans. We then sank the entire set in thirty feet of water, at our best guess at what the angle of the ship was when the sea reached A deck—somewhere between ten and twelve degrees.

"We plunged the set as fast as we could, simulating the *Titanic*'s sudden dip and lurch at 2:10 A.M.; and as it plunged, we dumped fifty thousand gallons of water in through the crystal dome. The water plunged down less than ten feet, and hit the stairway—which was, at that point, submerged under eight feet of water—and the sudden additional down-force of water dislodged the stairway . . . and it floated up . . . Catastrophically, it floated up. It just came up through the middle of the set. Stunt men rode it right up out of the water. They were holding onto it, frightened. Nobody expected it to happen."

"At the library in Halifax, they have the letters of passengers on the *Carpathia*," I explained. "Amongst the floating steamer chairs, cushions, planks, and crates, they saw a large piece of what many believed was the after first-class stairway [the Grand's smaller, three-story replica, built into the after part of first class]. Because the after Grand Stairway was located between the third and fourth smokestacks, where the ship broke in two, I had always believed some portion of the after stairway to have been thrown free, which might still be true, but—"

"But if something like what happened to our set happened to the *Titanic*," Jim said, "if there was a sufficiently catastrophic inrush of water near the surface, then the real stairway, the Grand one, might have sailed up and shot out of the ship through the dome.

"And—oh, if you could have seen it happening on the

set. It was only a pale imitation of the forces actually working against the *Titanic* that night, and yet the noise was tremendous . . ."

JACK THAYER DID not know what to make of the noise. Occasionally there had been a muffled thud or the deadened "explosions" of walls giving way within the ship. At 2:10 A.M., without warning, the *Titanic* lurched forward at an angle of about twelve degrees. "This movement, with the water rushing up toward us was accompanied by a rumbling roar," Thayer recalled, "mixed with more muffled explosions. It was like standing under a steel railway bridge while an express train passes overhead, mingled with the noise of a pressed steel factory and wholesale breakage of china."

Thayer was standing by the starboard rail when this happened. He was abreast of the second smokestack, some twenty or thirty feet aft of the Grand Stairway entrance on the boat deck. A crowd of more than a hundred people had come spilling out of the entrance, startling Thayer, and his next startled thought, as something like a shoulder-high tsunami approached from the direction of the bridge, was to get away from the crowd and the wave. In what seemed to him a half minute, but could only have been three or four seconds, he leaped ahead of the wave and the people, into the sea.

Hugh Woolner also jumped overboard as the bridge went under, finding for himself a place in collapsible D. Elsewhere, oiler Walter Hurst saw a man next to him do a header over the starboard side and without a thought did the same. He was followed by Fireman George Kemish, who swam with such vigor after boat nine that he outpaced its oarsmen and managed to haul himself aboard. Trimmer Thomas Patrick Dillon had no choice about jumping. The stern's poop deck had already pivoted him far too high, but it would soon slip away beneath his feet, dragging him down with Rosa and Rossmore Abbott, then popping him to the surface alongside boat four.

During the minutes leading up to the final plunge, as Steward Edward Brown tried in vain to push collapsible A against a steepening list to port, uphill to the edge of the starboard boat deck, Richard Williams II and his father, seeking the warmth of the gymnasium, had found instructor T. W. McCawley idly practicing on the rowing machine. They followed his example by mounting two stationary bicycles and pedaling to throw off the chill in their bones, until the list to port made pedaling too difficult.

Just ahead of the 2:10 A.M. surge, Richard and his father wandered restlessly onto the starboard boat deck, within ten or twelve feet of Jack Thayer.

What happened next unfolded so quickly that, in later years, it would come to Richard mostly as compressed flashes of memory: *First there seemed to be not many people in sight, then I saw lots of them—passengers—and there's Captain Smith near the bridge with a seaman . . . sailor goes off on some errand—curious noise—I look up to see water sweeping onto the bridge—turn with father and start running aft—as we turn, I hear a shot from the direction of the bridge but I do not look back—and the water catches up with us and sweeps us up the deck toward the stern—the ship seems to be rushing forward and down, generating the wave that engulfs us and Father is swept aft and away—I'm carried over the side—hear a last shout from Father—strike out swimming . . . can't find Father—I think I swim a mile . . .*

Colonel Gracie was standing about twelve feet ahead of the starboard entrance to the Grand Stairway reception area, some forty feet forward of Richard Williams II and Jack Thayer, when the wave approached. Like Richard and his father, Gracie's first instinct was to turn and run toward the stern, but he found the way blocked by a mass of people, several lines deep, swarming out of the Grand Stairway entrance—women, men—mostly steerage passengers, as near as the colonel could tell.

Something—either water rising against the port-side windows and up the Grand Stairway, or the rise of the stairway itself (the source, perhaps, of the "wholesale breakage" that reached Jack Thayer's ears)—was stampeding them onto the boat deck. No one would ever learn who those men and women were or what they saw to make them stampede. Not one of them was to survive the next hour. Not one of them.

When the people saw the wave, they turned and ran, but they were not fast enough, the colonel realized. Fearing that he would be swept under them and drowned, the only way out seemed to be up—and in one small part of a second his attention turned to the roof of the officer's quarters, just forward of the angle made by the broad walls of the Grand Stairway Reception Room.

His effort to jump up and gain a hand-hold on the railing atop the officer's quarters was thwarted by the weight of two overcoats and a lifejacket. As he fell, the wave—almost as tall as the colonel—struck him on the right side. Instinctively, he moved with, rather than against, the water and, recalling a trick he had learned at Coney Island, managed to crest the wave, to body surf it until a whirlpool behind the Grand Stairway colonnade brought him within reach of the iron railing along the edge of the gymnasium roof.[6]

The surfer's instinct had served him well, uplifting him to the rail and allowing him to mount the roof. His next instinct did not serve him so well: a reluctance to ease his grip on the rail that had spared him from being dashed

---

[6]It seems possible that the colonel was disoriented by the wave, which should have been decreasing in height as it traveled uphill and aft. Archibald Gracie thought he had grabbed a railing atop the gymnasium roof (and for all anyone knows, he guessed correctly), but he might actually have been swept just a few feet further aft, to the railing *behind* the gymnasium and atop the first-class lounge, which was six feet lower than the gymnasium rail.

headfirst against fleeing people, jutting walls, and davits. Sprawled beneath the second smokestack, he went underwater still holding on to the ship.

The wave never reached the third smokestack. Everything aft of that point seemed to be swinging higher and higher, but Colonel Gracie and the gymnasium roof were pivoting in the opposite direction. As he plunged down twenty, nearly thirty feet, the pressure on Gracie's ears became very noticeable, then very painful. Bursts of warm air erupted through gratings at the base of the second stack. These, combined with the sound of water gushing down boiler shafts, raised in the colonel an irrational dread that he was about to be cooked alive by exploding boilers. He let go of the rail, and kicked away with all of his strength, but soon discovered that he was still being drawn in the direction the wave had gone—aft, and apparently down as well.

More than forty feet forward of Gracie's position, on the far side of the crystal dome, the two after-stays for the first smokestack had been anchored directly to the bulkhead at the top of the Grand Stairway. If the stairway did in fact break loose at this time, the anchor points, if not the bulkhead itself, could not have withstood the shock.

Paddling away from the starboard side, Jack Thayer looked back and saw that the sea had swallowed the base of the second smokestack. He also saw that the propellers—as wide as windmills—were actually clearing the surface. The rumble and roar continued, "with even louder distinct wrenchings and tearings," and suddenly the first smokestack—large enough for two automobiles to pass through abreast—seemed to be lifted off, emitting either a cloud of sparks from the furnaces, or static-charged soot.[7] In either case, the "sparks" seemed to

---

[7]From his point of view in boat thirteen, about nine hundred feet (or one *Titanic* length) away, passenger Lawrence Beesley became transfixed by the noise that immediately preceeded the collapse of the first smokestack: "It

Thayer like a cloud of fireflies . . . millions of fireflies . . . red fireflies . . . fireflies from hell . . .

At a time like this, the brain takes notice of the trivial. As the stack toppled forward and starboard, Thayer decided that the fireflies must actually be bits of red-hot coal, and he wondered how coals could still be burning underwater, even as the stack loomed toward him and splashed down, missing his head by only twenty feet.

The stack sank slowly, taking fully five seconds. It trailed a slipstream that pulled Jack Thayer down, thirty feet or more, and it would have dragged him all the way to the abyssal plain if not for the buoyancy of his lifejacket—which caused him to lag behind the stream, then to break away from it and float up. His head came up against something smooth and firm, the cork fender of the overturned collapsible B which had crossed over from the port side as the bridge went under. Firemen had climbed on top of the upturned keel. Oiler Walter Hurst was among them, half blinded by soot from the falling stack. It could have been a lot worse. The stack had missed Hurst and the boat by a margin of arm's lengths, producing a wave that washed B thirty yards clear of the *Titanic*, which, as she plunged and gurgled and dragged, seemed to be pulling everything floatable indoors.

---

was not a sudden roar as an explosion would be, as it came to us along the water. It went on successively for some seconds, possibly fifteen to twenty . . . but it was a noise no one had heard before, and no one wishes to hear again. It was as if all the heavy things one could think of had been thrown downstairs from the top of a house, smashing each other and the stairs and everything in the way." Jack Thayer, in the moments before the stack fell, thought he saw the whole superstructure of the ship buckle, "well forward, and blow or buckle upwards." He also believed he saw the point bow rising out of the sea almost as far aft as the place where the bridge had been (an impossibility), and from this he concluded that the *Titanic* had split near the Grand Stairway, pulling the prow backward and pointing it at the stars. With the bases of the first and second smokestacks submerged, what he might actually have seen was the Grand Stairway itself breaking the surface, followed almost immediately by the toppling of the first stack.

Eugene Daly realized with despair that for every ten feet forward he swam, for every ten feet nearer he came to the imagined safety of boat A, the *Titanic* appeared to be gaining on him by twenty feet. Finally, feeling exhausted, feeling as if he were being stalked by a particularly determined monster, he gave in to the inevitable and turned around to face his killer. What he saw stupefied him.

From the port side, above the place where boat two's davits and the first smokestack had been, he looked back and saw the top of the second smokestack being submerged, and those poor swimmers who were even nearer the monster than Daly—"those poor people who covered the water—were sucked down the stack, like flies."

From her vantage point aboard boat one, Lady Gordon was near enough to see Mr. Daly grab onto a piece of floating wreckage. He threw back his head and she heard him crying, "My God . . . my God!" in a hopeless, monotonous way.

Some forty or sixty feet below Daly, Colonel Gracie still hovered near the starboard boat deck, somewhere aft of the second stack. The suction had drawn him down from the back wall of the gymnasium and alongside the raised roof of the first-class lounge. Below him, the tall windows of the lounge were imploding—and because the ship was still listing to port, and because only the upper twelve inches of the lounge windows rose to the boat deck, the air pocket within the room below was aimed like a row of cannons in Gracie's general direction.

The colonel did not know whence the air bursts came, but he was quite aware of their presence, and their actions: "My being drawn down by suction to a greater depth was undoubtedly checked to some degree by the life preserver which I wore, but it is to the buoyancy of the water, caused by the volume of air rising from the sinking ship, that I attributed the assistance which enabled me to strike out and swim faster and further under water than I ever did before."

He was probably between twenty and thirty feet above the boat deck, about midway between the second and third smokestacks, when the *Titanic* snapped in two under the third stack. Gracie must have been located just outside the ship's boundary layer—a region in which even air bubbles could be overpowered by drag forces and brought down—when the 450-foot bow section broke free beneath him and rocketed toward the bottom. So many random processes now came into play—currents generated by cracking hull plates, by the upswing of the stern's sever nearby, and by the fall of the third stack—that it becomes possible to believe that had the colonel been located just two or three feet deeper, or two feet forward, or back, or right, or left, he would never have had a hope of living. As it was, after nearly three minutes underwater, he could not have known or cared that he, and he alone, had come within no more than thirty feet of the *Titanic*'s break point, and had been present when it broke, and was still alive to tell the tale.[8]

For lack of breath, he thought he would have to give in and die, and with that thought he seemed to have been provided with a second spurt of energy, but he could not be certain that he was kicking in the right direction toward the surface, and his next thought was that his last moment really was upon him. He kicked harder, praying inwardly and fast, wanting only to somehow convey the news of how he died to his wife and daughter, at home in New York. He prayed that his spirit could go to them and say "Good-bye,"

---

[8]As it turned out, the man who would pen *The Truth about the Titanic* was never to learn the truth about his survival. Indeed, Gracie went to the grave believing that the *Titanic* had gone to the bottom in one piece. No one could have told the colonel otherwise until his meticulous chronology of his movements on the starboard boat deck, combined with an archaeological reconstruction of how and when each major piece of wreckage broke, made it possible to take a closer look at the very strange escape of Colonel Archibald Gracie.

and he believed that if he prayed hard enough, his last wish would be granted.

At precisely that moment, Mrs. Gracie awoke from an uneasy dream, with a voice crying out in her brain: "On your knees and pray!"

She rolled out of bed and instantly obeyed, somehow knowing that Archie was calling out to her from the sea, praying for her. Eight hundred miles away, Colonel Archibald Gracie believed he could actually sense his wife's presence, and there came to him "a new lease on life and strength." Suddenly there seemed to be a light somewhere ahead, and as he drew near, a flurry of wooden planks ascended from below. He caught one and tucked it under his arm and the light increased in brightness and then it was gone—replaced by starlight. He bumped against another piece of wood and tucked this, too, under himself—the nucleus of a raft he contrived to construct from whatever flotsam and jetsam he might find.

When he looked around, he could detect no lights from the *Titanic*. The stern had by now upended and, silhouetted against the stars, was slipping under somewhere nearby. It went down with a gentle gulp, but Colonel Gracie did not hear this. The sea had done its work. One eardrum was hopelessly clogged. The other had imploded.

7

•

Fire and Ice

•

As man proceeds toward his imagined goal of the conquest of nature, he has written a depressing record of
destruction.

—RACHEL CARSON

Our deepest fear is not that we are inadequate. Our deepest fear is that we are powerful beyond measure.

—NELSON MANDELA

SCORES OF ARTICLES had been written about split seams and
popped rivets sinking the *Titanic*. Bob Ballard had pointed
out to me a crack in the starboard bow that ran for more than
a hundred feet, but the opening's combined surface area was
more than sixty square feet and, when added to at least two
similar rows of parted steel plates, should have flooded the
bow and snapped the *Titanic*'s spine in all of twenty minutes.
Follow-up expeditions by George Tulloch revealed that the
damage was bilateral, meaning that if one wanted to identify
ruptured seams with iceberg damage, one had to posit how
the port side—which, by all eyewitness accounts, never saw
ice—somehow suffered the same wounds as the starboard
side.

Impact with the sea floor seemed a more likely source of
bilateral ruptures. Pounding down at nearly thirty miles per

hour, the point bow was driven, within the space of a second, fifty feet deep into gravel and clay. The point bow entered at an angle of about 30 degrees, rebounding slightly upward but coming to a standstill within the next three tenths of a second. Everything aft, up to the superstructure at the base of the bridge, also ceased moving during that part of a second; but the rear end of the bow section, and all the water inside it, and the slipstream of water above it, was still plunging down and slightly forward at approximately thirty miles per hour. A tenth of a second later, directly below the *Titanic*'s bridge, the hull on both sides, from C deck down to the keel, began to bend grotesquely out of shape. Any splitting of riveted seams caused by the iceberg would likely have acted as zones of scoring, from which the original damage was magnified into spreading waves of deformity.

In 1986, Bob Ballard photographed a horizontal, starboard side crack running through almost the entire length of boiler room six, and continuing aft into the forward coal bunker of boiler room five, beneath the first smokestack. Thirty-five feet from the forwardmost extension of the crack, thirty-five feet nearer the point bow, he discovered the tail end of a similar hull breach located under the floor of the mail room. Ten years later, an attempt was made, using sonar, to peer beneath the thick layer of gravel and clay forward of the mail room. Six decks below the forecastle, several large cracks showed up on the sonoscan, but interpreting them was rendered all but impossible, because the keel, as it penetrated the earth, crumpled like the hood of a car driven into a brick wall at thirty miles per hour.

Alvin pilot Ralph Hollis, as he "flew" Bob Ballard along the lower starboard side aft of the bridge, below the *Titanic*'s water line, noticed that some of the steel plates seemed to be bent slightly inward. At the center of one bend, Hollis saw three little holes, the largest about the size and shape of a coffee mug's mouth. It looked to him as if someone had fired a bazooka shell through the inch-thick steel, into the side of the ship. Co-pilot Paul Tibbetts also noticed a hole where Ballard had said the "ice-gash" should have been. Tibbetts judged that it could not have been more than four inches in diameter—hardly large enough to sink an ocean liner. But more than a hundred feet of the forward bow—the part that took the brunt of the impact—had plowed under the sea floor and was hidden from Hollis' and Tibbetts' view. The iceberg need only have opened a dozen more as yet unseen holes, and sprung a dozen little leaks in the seams between plates, popping a rivet here and there, to have allowed 4,000 metric tons (roughly 4,000 cubic yards) of water into the ship during the first ten minutes.

According to naval architect Edward Wilding, who knew the *Titanic* almost as well as Thomas Andrews and who testified at the 1912 British inquiry, a series of punctures and leaks adding up to no more than twelve square feet (the approximate surface area of two sidewalk squares) could have accounted for all the phenomena seen that night.

The holes discovered by Hollis and Tibbetts in 1986 are the only punctures seen along the starboard bow that can be separated definitively from impact with the sea floor. Crashing into sediment may split steel plates or expand splits already made by an iceberg, but the sediment cannot possibly punch holes into the centers of dished-in plates.

After speaking with the *Alvin* pilots, I began to understand that far too much attention had been given to the *Titanic*'s side of the story, and not enough to the nature of the injuries inflicted upon the other participant in this drama: the iceberg.

That many tons of ice fell onto the forward well deck was evidence enough that the berg had been severely eroded by contact with the ship. As the berg passed Quartermaster George Rowe, on the afterbridge, its central peak looked to him exactly like a windjammer's sail and, indeed, at first sighting that was exactly what he thought the *Titanic* had struck. On April 15, the chief steward of the German freighter *Prinz Adelbert* photographed an iceberg whose central peak looked, in profile, like Rowe's "windjammer with its sails set." He did not photograph it because of the *Titanic* (he had not yet heard), but because of "the great scar of red paint" that ran along its base, about ten feet above the water line. He concluded that the berg had been struck, recently, by a passing ship.

The *Titanic* was painted red below the water line, and red paint *above* an iceberg's water line suggests that the berg had shed a significant amount of weight on its ship-facing side, causing it to recline slightly toward its far side.

If one spends a great deal of time around glaciers (as I have), one notices that huge slabs of ice are not particularly flexible and, when forced, tend to shatter into automobile-sized boulders. Those boulders of ice, if smashed between a rock (a rock-hard wall of ice will serve nicely) and a hard place (say, a wall of inch-thick steel reinforced with girders), will tend to shatter into football-sized boulders.

Irregular and huge, a block of ice shattering does not spread its force evenly, like the flat slap of a hand. Its effect is more akin to a highly magnified knuckle punch—generally lashing out in equal and opposite directions: at the ice boulder's parent body (the iceberg) and at the impactor (the *Titanic*'s hull). For a chunk of ice ten feet wide, the forces at the very center of converging shock fronts may rise to the threshold at which refined uranium undergoes fission and converts graphite into micro-diamonds. As a result of this, a ten-foot section of inch-thick steel plate may be dished in an inch or two by one face of the ice block (and this may, all by itself, cause a stretching and leaking of seams at the edges of the impact zone), while most of the boulder's punch will be focused on an area smaller than a man's fist. The effect is somewhat like the focus of an old-style phonograph needle, whose point exerts a force that is, square inch for square inch, comparable to the peak pressure of a fist against a skull during a karate strike (which explains why old phonograph records sound so scratchy). The point source impact of an ice block can be twice as powerful, which actually exceeds the penetrative power of bullets.[1]

Edward Wilding had calculated the total force exerted by the meeting of the *Titanic*'s hull with the iceberg as being equivalent to lifting the Washington Monument up and down thirteen times. Under such conditions, the iceberg would have begun granulating immediately into boulders of ice, and the largest of those ice boulders would have been smashed between the berg and the hull, instantly shedding most of their energy as dozens of point source impacts . . . and then the next smallest set of ice boulders would have behaved in the same manner. Once one began to see how the ice behaved, and to run this behavior like a movie picture inside one's head, the popular notion of an icy ledge slicing along the *Titanic*'s hull like a blade, producing a 300-foot "gash," or opening up huge horizontal splits between plates, simply fell away. So, too, did arguments about brittle steel, too rich in sulfur, having failed as if through the builder's negligence to stand up against the iceberg.

When I looked at the numbers and translated them into

---

[1]The peak pressure of a fist against a skull during a karate strike is 12,000 pounds per square inch (or 800 atmospheres, or twice the pressure exerted by the ocean on the *Nautile*'s hull at the depth of the *Titanic*). For comparison, the steam pressure in the *Titanic*'s boilers was 225 psi (15 atmospheres); the thrust of the space shuttle *Atlantis'* engines at liftoff is 6,000 psi (400 atmospheres); and the force of a bullet is only three times as strong at 18,000 psi (1,200 atmospheres, which is equivalent to standing sixty feet from the Hiroshima bomb).

pictures . . . enough energy to lift the Washington Monument up and down thirteen times . . . most of that energy translated into dozens, perhaps hundreds of point source impactors drumming against the *Titanic*'s hull . . . with 50, perhaps 60 percent of those point source impacts focused on a cumulative surface area smaller than two sidewalk squares, I could see immediately that the hull could never have stood up against such power, not even if it had been made of inch-thick titanium instead of steel, and sheathed in diamond. Here and there, at little focused points at the centers of dished-in plate fields, the ice punched through with the ease of hot steel through butter, making holes no wider than bazooka shells, sometimes no wider than dimes, through which witnesses indoors would have seen water spraying in as if through garden hoses and fire hoses. Here and there, within fields of dished-in plates, seams opened up, perhaps one eighth inch wide and three feet long, and gushed fan-shaped sprays into the ship.

The effect, as a half kiloton of granulating ice drummed across the wall of steel, was like a lethal symphony written by Isaac Newton and performed in Morse code:

DIT—DIT—DIT—DA—

DOT (a hole)—DOT (a hole)—DOT (another hole)—DASH (a split seam)—

What people on the other side of the wall saw, felt, and heard provided clues about how the granulation and Morse code effect worked. In the foremost part of the ship, just aft of the anchors, in the number one cargo hold, Crewman James Hyland thought the *Titanic* had struck the berg head-on. He saw steel and crushed ice kicked three feet indoors, knocking away the protective casing of the fireman's spiral stairs. About two seconds later, and nearly sixty feet behind Hyland, Walter Hurst was roused from his bunk by "a grinding crash along the starboard side." In a nearby bunk bed, Lookout George Symons was also awakened, but it seemed to him that the loud grinding sound had also come from beneath the floor plates, as if the ice were working its mischief along the keel as well as along the starboard hull. A hundred feet further aft on the starboard side, in a first-class stateroom below the first smokestack and above boiler room six, Mrs. "Ella" Stuart White was awakened about three seconds after Walter Hurst by "a slight shock . . . accompanied by a grinding noise as if the ship were running over a bed of pebbles." In the same row of staterooms, the initial shock, and the rumble that followed, almost knocked Helen Candee off her feet. Six stories beneath Helen and Ella, in boiler room six, Frederick Barrett saw a red "STOP" signal come down from the bridge and called out, "Shut all dampers!" But the crash came before anyone could stop the engines, and water began spraying into the room, sending Barrett and Engineer Hesketh scurrying aft, through a descending watertight door, into boiler room five. There, Barrett discovered a puncture two feet aft of the watertight bulkhead, inside coal bunker ten. It was a small breach, the furthest one aft on the starboard hull. Barrett had plenty of time to inspect the damage. He noticed that the water did not come through in a fan-shaped spray. It spouted in a stream through an opening as round (and as powerful) as a fire hose.

Eighty-five feet aft of Barrett, in boiler room four, Trimmer George Cavell felt a shock, and a second later he was buried in an avalanche of coal, from which he barely managed to extricate himself. He soon realized that his troubles were only beginning. For many minutes, the lights went out in Cavell's part of the ship, and as he searched for kerosene lanterns and tried to shut down boilers, water began rising through spaces in the stokehold plates, rising eventually to Cavell's knees, which meant that the *Titanic* must have rolled *over* as well as *against* ice, and that damage to the double-hulled bottom extended at least eighty feet aft of the last breach on the starboard side.

Two hundred and fifty feet past Cavell and boiler room four, the rumbling continued—all the way to upper deck staterooms clustered near the fourth stack, where Karl Behr felt the walls and floor "suddenly tremble all over." In the smoking room, above Behr, Hugh Woolner was talking with friends, "when there came a heavy grinding sort of shock beginning far ahead of us in the bows and rapidly passing along the ship."

The granulation and Morse effect could easily account for the rumbling and grinding sounds, for dished-in plates and split seams, for the occasional popped rivet, for the fire hose–like spray seen from Barrett's side of the hull, and for the fire hose–sized holes seen from Hollis' side. Instead of the traditional (and mythical) 300-foot-long "gash" or "split," the *Titanic* was felled by a series of punches, stabs, and bullet hole–like punctures adding up to only twelve square feet of openings, through which 24,000 metric tons of water entered the bow during the first hour.

Short of ramming a ship's starboard bow into an iceberg, actually producing (and testing) point source impacts against inch-thick hull plates can be difficult. Fortunately, in May, 1993, the captain of the *Regent Sea* was kind enough to conduct the experiment for me (albeit unintentionally) during our first night in the Alaskan fjords. This was the only sea voyage I had ever begun that was not part of a science project, and yet . . .

Shortly before midnight, the ship collided with a relatively small iceberg, standing about five or six feet above the water and extending some fifty feet down. Impact was along the starboard side at eighteen knots, about seventy feet forward of my stateroom. I did not hear this, or feel it, and I would not have noticed the collision at all had the iceberg not clipped off the *Regent Sea*'s stabilizer and were the engines not immediately thrown into reverse and shut down.

The next day, the cruise director allowed me to view the damage from a motorized rubber launch. The only leak (in the middle of a steel plate) was a hole of one-inch diameter, it was slit-shaped, like an eye half open, or like a laceration caused by a punch. Most importantly, it lay in the center of a zone of dished-in plates, about the diameter of a kitchen table, and no more than an inch or two deep. Compared with the *Titanic*, this was very low magnitude damage, but if one imagined the *Regent Sea* lengthened by a factor of three, and if one heightened, deepened, and broadened the iceberg by a factor of fifteen, one began to see wider holes, and more extensively dished plates, with leaks yawning open at their seams; one began to understand what Ralph Hollis and Paul Tibbetts, Frederick Barrett and George Kemish saw . . .

IT WAS DRY in the boiler rooms aft of number four. In number two, Fireman George Kemish concluded that the red warning lights ordering "STOP," the "heavy thud and grinding tearing sound" and the slamming down of watertight doors meant that the ship had run aground off the banks of Newfoundland.

Up to that moment, the voyage had been somewhat of a picnic for Kemish. Being the finest and newest addition to the White Star fleet, the best of Southampton's seamen and engine room department men had been anxious to join her—"Oh, yes," he recalled for a young pen-pal named Walter, "the pick of Southampton went in her."

He was proud to be aboard, but whenever anyone called her the largest ship in the world, he was quick to point out that she was larger than her nearly identical twin sister, *Olympic*, by all of nine inches. She was, however, more luxurious. The A deck promenade was enclosed by thick windows, and on B deck, Edwardian staterooms rivaling the finest London and Paris hotel suites were expanded all the way up to the bulkheads, removing the twin's second promenade deck completely. Its only surviving vestiges were the private promenades of Lady Cardeza's and J. Bruce Ismay's suites (B-53 and B-54, on opposite sides of the second smokestack). Further aft, under the fourth smoke-stack, the *à la carte* restaurant was expanded to the port-side bulkhead, and the French Café Parisian took the starboard side, collectively removing what had, on the *Olympic*, been the second-class promenade deck.

The plan, George Kemish wrote, "was to have these two prestigious ships always at sea—one homeward bound (to Southampton), one outward bound (to New York).

"*Titanic* had six boiler rooms—each with five boilers abreast . . . two coal bunkers to each boiler room . . . and fifty-three firemen, twenty-two coal trimmers and five leading firemen on each four-hour watch. Being a new ship on her maiden voyage, everything was clean. She was a good [easy] job in the stokeholds; not what we were accus-tomed to in other, older ships—slogging our guts out and nearly roasted by the heat. Even so, the *Titanic* would have burned over three thousand tons of coal on each trip.

"Well, being what I have called 'a good job,' we just had to keep the furnaces full and not keep on working the fires with slice bars and rakes. We were sitting around on buck-ets. I had just sent a trimmer up to call the midnight watch when the thud and grinding came.

"We had a full head of steam, then, and we were doing about twenty-three knots per hour. We had an order to 'box up' all boilers and put on dampers to stop steam rising [in the pipes] and lifting safety valves. The trimmer came back from calling the 12–4 A.M. watch and said, 'Blimey! We've struck an iceberg!'

"We thought that a joke . . . a big joke."

Nearly four hundred feet forward of George Kemish and boiler room two, James Hyland found the joke neither big nor funny. In the forwardmost compartments, he had seen water and pebbles of crushed ice actually gushing through the hull, gushing through with enough force to raise the air pressure and pop his ears. Now, pacing the well deck, he noticed that the canvas coverings on the cargo hatches were billowing out from the rise of air displaced by the water entering below.

"This can't be a good sign," he told himself.

Down in boiler room four, Trimmer George Cavell found a stoker looking mournfully at the bowl of soup he had been warming on a steam pipe. The impact had over-turned his midnight meal. Cavell was reminded of the or-ders that came down from the bridge during the previous two days, one after another, to light more furnaces and put on more steam power. What he would never forget about that night was that they were "steaming ahead like hell" when they hit. His career would be all but terminated when he testified to Lord Mersey's examiners that the gauge, at the moment of impact, had shown 225 pounds per square inch on engines designed for a working steam pressure of 215 psi.

With the engines stopped, Cavell began clearing coal from the furnaces, hoping to keep the pressure from climb-ing any higher and causing permanent damage to the *Ti-tanic*'s valves and joints. Had he known what was happening just 150 feet forward in the mail room, he might have spared himself the trouble.

Mr. and Mrs. Norman Chambers had felt that stateroom E-7 was too hot, so they went to sleep with their porthole open. At 11:40 P.M., a large chunk of ice tumbled through the opening onto the bedroom floor. Their cabin was located near the forward part of the first smokestack's casing, opposite the crew's lavatory and the steps leading down to the mail room.[2]

Curious to learn what other mischief had been worked by the ice, they descended the stairs to F deck, and discovered, to their delight, that the mail room was *the* place to be visiting ten minutes after the collision. The water had chased two postal clerks from the stacking room on the orlop deck, then from the sorting room on G deck, and was now threatening to reach F deck. The Chamberses and the clerks joked about more than two hundred soaked mail bags on the decks below, and speculated about the contents of the letters they could see floating toward them.

Fourth Officer Boxhall came down, watched silently for a minute, cursed, then hurried away. Moments later, Mrs. Henry Sleeper Harper came down and instantly concluded, from what she saw, that it was foolish to wake Mr. Harper at a time like this. When Stewardess Ann Robinson arrived, she was reminded of a previous iceberg collision on the *Lake Champlain*. "Oh, no," she said, "not again." Next came the ship's carpenter. He simply shook his head and went away without any words at all.

Finally, Captain Smith joined them. He whispered the phrase, "Bloody hell," then left in a hurry. Even this response did not convince the Chamberses that they might be in danger.

To George Kemish, the *Titanic* seemed as steady as if she were in dry dock. He was sent forward from boiler

---

[2]Men in starboard staterooms below E-7 also complained of excessive heat. What these rooms had in common with E-7 was that they were located above Coal Bunker 10, which had been on fire throughout the voyage and probably contributed to the heating problems in those regions of the ship (boilers vent their heat away, coal bunkers do not). The excess heat, in its own turn, might have contributed to the passangers' habit of leaving portholes open in the worst possible location, at the worst possible time.

room two to make sure other workers were shutting down the fires and lowering the steam pressure. Because the watertight doors were closed, he had to climb up to E deck and follow Scotland Road along the port side, climbing down again on escape ladders over the tops of boilers. When he reached his quarters in the forecastle he found men from the 12–4 A.M. shift packing their bags and dragging their beds up to the recreation deck because their rooms were flooded. "Oh," he recalled years later, "we thought this was a huge joke and had a good laugh." Even when he saw the first lifeboats being lowered, the fireman could not bring himself to believe that he should be worried. Indeed, had Thomas Andrews not been aboard to assure Captain Smith that the *Titanic* could not possibly stay afloat, it would have been possible for all of the officers and crew to believe that the bow would sink only so far and then be halted from sinking any further. Had Andrews not taken Lord Pirrie's place at the last minute, the boats might not have been launched until much later and the loss of life would have been nearly total. As it was, by the time the first boat cast off at 12:40 A.M., an hour after the collision, the pace of the *Titanic*'s sinking did slow down; the bulkhead between boiler rooms five and six actually did seem to be holding the ship up. For a long time, the forecastle and the forward well deck remained poised above the water line. At 12:40, time seemed to have stopped and the *Titanic* seemed really to have sunk as far as she would go. If not for two or three minor but all too critical failures, she might actually have done so.

With all the compartments forward of boiler room five's bulkhead flooded to the waterline, almost to the floor of E deck, the rate of sinking was now dependent upon water spreading aft along corridors and spilling down stairwells, or finding new means of entry through the hull. Open port-

holes provided one of those means. The opening in Mr. and
Mrs. Chambers' bedroom was still above water, but if a
weight gain aft of boiler room five's forward bulkhead
were to pull that single porthole below the surface, the
flooding from cabin E-7 would add nearly 10 percent to the
twelve square feet of punctures made by the iceberg. And
that was the potential of a *single* porthole.

Yet in boiler room five, the flooding of the *Titanic*
seemed to be totally under control. When George Kemish
climbed down during his journey aft from the forecastle,
Frederick Barrett had already sent most of his stokers up to
their boat stations and the pumps seemed capable of handling the spray from a single puncture wound located two
feet aft of five's forward bulkhead.

About the same time Barrett decided everything was
under control, Charles Lightoller had ordered three men
down to the port side's E deck gangway door, hoping to
make the loading of lifeboats a little easier, from water
level, through the long companionway known as Scotland
Road. Lightoller's team managed to unlatch the heavy
steel door and push it open, and no one ever saw them
again. About 12:45 A.M., the water surged in through the
doorway and the ship began listing over toward the port
side, toward Scotland Road. In boiler room five, everything
was suddenly far from under control. The main transverse
bulkhead, an iron dam four stories tall and a quarter inch
thick, had, about the time of the Scotland Road flood,
buckled near the starboard hull, sprouted jets of water, and
two seconds later failed completely. Five minutes after
that, the sea was slopping over the lower rim of the open
porthole in cabin E-7.

The balance had shifted. With the dam in boiler room
five gone, the surface area now available for the entry of
water through the upper decks was at least equal to the
twelve square feet originally opened in the ship's side. E

deck forward was descending, and gradually quickening its pace. The flood from above, through forgotten portholes recalled too late by the Chamberses and the Thayers, through gangway doors, and soon enough through hatch covers, was shrinking the relative surface area of holes made by ice. The flood from above was about to double, then triple by comparison. The size and shape of iceberg wounds became academic, once the wall beneath the first smokestack fell.

IT WAS CLEAR that no one at the British or American inquiries wanted to approach what happened to the wall any closer than they wanted to approach what happened to the Third Class. Fireman Samuel Collins had been working in boiler rooms five and six, right alongside Frederick Barrett and Charles Hendrickson. In May, 1912, he mentioned in a letter to Mrs. Frank Goldsmith that he would soon "open the eyes of scores of people," but for his own sake he dare not write of it yet. A few days later, examiners Aspinall, Scanlan, and Edwards did not ask him a single question about what was already known to be the most critical structural failure of the night. After one question to confirm that he was working as a fireman at the time of the disaster, and a second question confirming that he had been aboard Miss Francatelli's and Lady Gordon's lifeboat, Mr. Aspinall said, "I am going to take you straight to that," and turned the examination into a fishing expedition for any words that might discredit the Gordons and their secretary.

Leading Fireman Charles Hendrickson testified that the lights kept going out in the boiler rooms, so he had gone aft to collect some lamps, and was trying to make his way down the sloping deck of Scotland Road about ten or fifteen minutes before the wall collapsed and Lightoller's gangway door let the sea in.

"I had a bit of trouble to get through the steerage passengers with those lamps," Hendrickson said. "They were in the working alleyway, going along with trunks and bags . . . Yes, a big bunch of them."

Oiler Fred Scott followed this same route at about the same time, but he claimed never to have seen the third-class passengers—"No," he insisted, "I never looked for any."

"Your evidence," said examiner Harbinson, "is that during the whole of this time you did not see from beginning to end a single third-class passenger?"

Scott replied, "There may have been some about there, but I never noticed them."

"You did not see them?"

"I never noticed any."

Hendrickson wondered how anyone could possibly have missed them. The crowd was still there when he climbed up from boiler room five and went aft for more lamps, but his testimony on this matter was quickly redirected toward alleged acts of cowardice by the Gordons and their secretary. Then, almost in passing, examiner Lewis mentioned a "common" coal fire in one of the bunkers—

("A very small affair," Ismay had said. "Fires in coal bunkers are quite common on ships. Nothing to worry about.")

—and Hendrickson's job, as a loyal White Star employee, was to uphold the Ismay view, but he did not.

"It is a common occurrence for fires to take place on boats?" the examiner asked.

"No," Hendrickson replied.

"It is not common?"

"No."

And then, apparently shaken and irritated, the examiner asked him how long he had been a White Star employee.

"About five years," came the reply, and he added that during those five years at sea he had never before seen a fire in a coal bunker.

"It has been suggested," said the examiner, "that fires in coal bunkers are quite a common occurrence," and Hendrickson insisted again that they were not. Nor was the fire in coal bunker ten "a very small affair." He testified that the fire had begun smoldering when the *Titanic* left Belfast on April 2, and was not yet under control when the ship departed Southampton a week later. It flared up fully on April 10, whereafter Hendrickson and a crew of ten toiled in round-the-clock shifts for more than three days to extinguish the coal.

The wall of steel plate that formed the bunker's rear wall—formed the starboard bulkhead separating boiler room five from boiler room six—glowed cherry red on the first day of "full flare." On the morning of the second day, April 11, it had brightened to orange, almost to yellow, almost to the color of steel emerging molten from a furnace. Captain Smith and Joseph Bell spoke of having the Marconi operators call ahead for assistance from the fire department if Hendrickson's crew was unable to put out the fire by the time the *Titanic* arrived in New York harbor.

"Did it take much time to get the fire down?" asked examiner Lewis.

"It took us right up to Saturday [April 13, evening shift, 4–8 P.M.] to get it out," said Hendrickson. "The fire was not out much before all the coal was out."

"The fire was not extinguished until you got the whole of the coal out?"

"No. I finished the bunker out myself, me and three or four men that were there . . . you could see where the bulkhead had been red-hot. All the paint and everything was off. It was dented a bit."

"Damaged?"

"Yes, warped."

"Was much notice taken of it?" the examiner asked. "Was any attempt made to do anything with it?"

"I just brushed it off and got some black oil and rubbed over it."

"To give it its ordinary appearance?"

"Yes," said Hendrickson, and the examiner seemed suddenly to realize that he had gotten off the "right" track, that the witness was leading him away from the prevailing "fatal-ice-tray theory," in which a 300-foot wound in the starboard side simply filled the first five watertight compartments (the first four cargo holds and boiler room six), dragging the *Titanic* down by the bow. About an hour after impact, in accordance with the ice-tray theory, water in boiler room six (the fifth compartment) began spilling over the bulkhead separating it from boiler room five (the sixth compartment). When boiler room five was full, it spilled over the bulkhead into boiler room four (the seventh compartment) and so on.

Charles Hendrickson's testimony became an ugly fact challenging an otherwise beautiful theory. Lewis reminded the witness (and the court), "You are not a professional expert and would not be able to express an opinion as to whether that had any effect on the collision," and examiner Cotter promptly broke in, changing the subject to . . . allegations of bribery against Sir Cosmo Duff Gordon.

Eighty-six years later, marine engineer Tom Dettweiler sent the robot *Magellan* through a rupture in the after part of the *Titanic*'s bow section, but he was unable to proceed any closer to the critical bulkhead than George Kemish's abandoned post in boiler room two. His way was blocked by equipment that stood surprisingly intact, in spite of the roof being downblasted into the room. He recalled hearing that after the *Titanic*'s band had been engulfed, after George Kemish found William Stead calmly reading in the smoking lounge, after the fireman leapt at, and missed, a rope dangling from the stern ("I reckon a parachute would have been handy in that drop," Kemish told Walter Lord), he heard metal breaking loudly against metal and had interpreted this as the sound of boilers shifting from their beds as the ship stood on its head. Kemish had pictured boilers tumbling down through bulkheads and piling up in the forward cargo holds, but Tom Dettweiler found the machines in boiler room two still lying in their beds, right where George Kemish last saw them.

The ship had been well built, the engineer concluded. It was not the *Titanic* that had gone wrong, it was the way men had treated her. She was a beautiful child, abused.

"'More power' was the order," Trimmer George Cavell had said; this for engines that were already operating almost a full atmosphere above the working steam pressure for which they had been certified. During the Saturday afternoon of April 13, George Kemish had heard a proposal to bring the *Titanic* up to twenty-three knots, some three knots above her scheduled cruising speed, as if someone were determined to bring her to the dock on Tuesday night . . . under cover of darkness . . .

Meanwhile, Hendrickson's fire had brought part of the main transverse bulkhead between boiler rooms five and six to a reddish-orange glow, meaning a minimum temperature of 1333 degrees Fahrenheit. The iron had originally been rolled and pressed, repeatedly, much in the manner of fine Damascus steel. The crystals lost their alignment once the metal became hot enough to be annealed, and with that loss of alignment, the iron also lost some of its flexibility. In this hot, almost molten state, the crew's attempts to extinguish the burning coals with cold water would have quenched the steel, making it harder, but more brittle.

When Thomas Andrews examined the still-glowing bulkhead on Saturday, and noticed that it was distorted slightly off center near the bottom, he announced that some of the steel would have to be replaced at the end of the maiden voyage. Normally, under a billion other sailing conditions, a weakened wall section near the lower starboard hull could be replaced before being called upon to do any work. Even if never replaced at all, probabilities and statistics dictated that the ship would grow old and be forgotten, with its beautiful woodwork passing from the scrap yard to the walls of London pubs and hotels, without the iron dam being called upon to hold back even a trickle.

But man and nature seemed to have conspired in perfect unity against Mr. Andrews' creation that night. It wasn't that the damage was too extreme for the ship to have possibly survived, it was that all events converged, in sequence, so chillingly close to the dividing line between life and death . . . If the *Titanic* had not missed by a margin of inches a collision with the *New York* while leaving the dock, she would have been held back for a damage report and missed the ice field . . . If the crewman on the *Californian* had picked up the headphones fifteen seconds earlier, or later . . . If the iceberg had been a little taller, or a little smaller . . .

If the granulation and pounding of ice along the starboard hull had stopped just a few feet forward, in boiler room six, that single damaged bulkhead between five and six should have survived the fire in the absence of hammering and additional warping, and held back the sea. Alternatively, had the bulkhead not been warped a first time by fire, and embrittled, and partly melted, it should have survived a direct broadside strike from a one- or two-ton ice boulder. But instead, as if by a dark miracle, by a chance of one in billions, fire and ice found each other. Frederick Barrett knew that they had met at the worst possible point: the fire hose–shaped spray he discovered in boiler room five (not in itself dangerous because it was easily contained with the 150-ton-per-hour pump in the boiler room) shot through the starboard hull two feet aft of the critical bulkhead, and the starboard shell plate had apparently been thrust inward, against this fire-damaged bulk-head, about a half inch. By a margin of only two feet . . . and a half inch . . .

And the cruel jokes of nature—the ironies, God's dark design—never did seem to know an end that night. About forty minutes after the wall fell in boiler room five, Dining Room Steward F. Dent Ray found Dr. Washington Dodge watching rather forlornly as one of the last boats was being lowered on the starboard side. Ray felt a terrible pang of guilt, for he had served the Dodge family on the sister ship *Olympic* and it was he who had convinced the doctor to switch booking and bring his family home on the even grander *Titanic*.

"Have you seen your wife and son off?" the steward asked, and the doctor nodded.

"Then you had better get into that boat yourself," Ray urged.

"No," the doctor said, "I must be a gent—"

No time for chivalry, Ray decided. He had heard men utter that phrase at least three times during the past half hour and it was wearing thin on him, so he stepped back behind Dodge and kicked him overboard into boat number thirteen.

Forty-five minutes later, when the steward looked up from the sea and watched the stern break away, he noticed a strange glow near the smoking room, where Thomas Andrews and William Stead had last been seen. From boat four, Oiler Thomas Ranger also thought some of the ship's lights had stayed on long after the last of the steam engines should have died. He distinctly recalled seeing a fiery red glow abreast of the fourth smokestack, shining through the windows of the smoking room.

Near the end, the broad fireplace aft in the smoking room had still been burning, only a few feet from Thomas Andrews. During the moments leading up to the break, the room had tilted forty-five degrees, and the fireplace must surely have spilled its contents across the carpeted floor. Had no one tried to save the ship by running pump hoses forward through the turbine room door, had the resultant opening in the bottom of the turbine room not let the sea in, and had the stern continued to float, fifteen hundred would-be survivors, thinking themselves lucky, would soon have realized, in the brightening glare, that they were standing on a half-ship meant to burn before it sank. The only saving grace was that the flames needed time to spread, and that the fire could not possibly have escaped notice by the steamer standing silently within reach: "the mystery ship." Ranger and Ray were convinced that she could not have stood more than eight miles away.

8

•

No Absolution

•

Passengers asked, "Why are you getting the lifeboats out?" I told them it was merely a precaution and that, at worst, they'd all be taken on board the ship everyone could clearly see only a few miles away. But here again we were up against it. That ship was the *Californian*, and though all her lights were plain to everyone aboard the *Titanic*, she seemed not to pay the slightest heed either to our wireless calls or to the distress signals we were firing every minute.

—SECOND OFFICER CHARLES LIGHTOLLER

Grave error on the part of Captain Smith: kept course in spite of ice warnings and severe drop in temperature from 5 P.M.

—CHIEF BAKER CHARLES JOUGHIN

And if ever a ship was thrown away, the *Titanic* was thrown away, that beautiful ship.

—ASSISTANT PURSER FRANK PRENTICE

After lunch, I was walking with my mother along [Scotland Road]. A wide door opened and I saw Captain Smith and his officer coming toward us in full regalia—lots of gold braid—and I knew him, as he looked so much like Edward III with beard and all. I asked what they were doing and was told they were inspecting the watertight compartments and doors. That was the last inspection, eh? Those doors were only about forty feet from our cabin. Later, after the collision, I left behind my lovely doll in the little net holder inside my bunk. Guess she is still there—petrified.

—SECOND-CLASS PASSENGER
MADELINE MELLINGER, AGE 13

MAJOR ARTHUR PEUCHEN'S wallet went overboard between 12:30 and 12:50 A.M. It probably formed the very first trace of the *Titanic*'s debris field, about an hour after the meeting with the iceberg. About an hour and one-half after the wallet arrived on the bottom, the *Titanic* ruptured and rained debris a half mile in every direction, and yet the major's wallet, with his business cards inside, and the streetcar tickets he had intended to use in Toronto, lay within the boundaries of the debris field.

Quartermaster George Rowe, watching from the afterbridge, noted that once the engines had stopped and the *Titanic* was adrift, she alternately swung her port, bow, and starboard sides north, in the direction of the mystery ship whose lights he could see. Oiler Walter Hurst reported that he could clearly see all of the other ship's lights, including its red riding light on the port side, while other witnesses occasionally saw its green starboard light. In the north, aboard the *Californian*, Stone and Gibson observed a large ship stopped in the south, firing rockets and displaying for them alternately its port and starboard riding lights, in full conformity with the motions George Rowe described for the *Titanic*.

Both the *Titanic* and the *Californian* must have been twisting in the Labrador Current as they lay stopped within sight of each other in an ice field.

Major Peuchen's wallet tells us that even as the *Titanic*

pivoted in the current, it did not drift very far during its last ninety minutes on the surface, suggesting that the two ships, each regarded by the crew of the other as a "mystery," maintained the same relative distance between the hours of midnight and 2:20 A.M.

As if to make the sinking of the *Titanic* more fully a Shakespearean tragedy, God, or the universe, or mere chance (call it what you will) placed a would-be savior on the horizon, so frustratingly near that after the first six distress rockets and several attempts to attract attention with the *Titanic*'s Morse lamp failed to rouse the stranger to action, Fourth Officer Joseph Boxhall threw something at Quartermaster Rowe's feet and declared, "If we had a cannon, I swear I'd put a shell in her side."

The stranger's lights seemed to wink on and off mysteriously, and at least twice the ship disappeared completely, only to reappear minutes later. Aboard the *Californian*, Seaman Ernest Gill noticed that the lights of "the visitor in the south" had disappeared around 1:00 A.M., when he went to bed. As the *Titanic*'s second rocket went up, he saw only the rocket, with "no sign of the steamer at the time." Ten minutes later, Second Officer Stone was able to distinguish deck lights and individual rows of portholes through binoculars. Ten minutes after that, he handed Gibson the binoculars, explaining that some of the rows appeared to be slanting down into the water.

From boat number two, Mrs. Walter Douglas observed the likely (indeed, inevitable) cause of the disappearing and reappearing lights. The *Titanic* did not simply run up against a lone iceberg prowling the North Atlantic. It had encountered an entire field of icebergs, more than ten miles wide (generally) and nearly seventy miles long.[1] Mrs.

---

[1]Wireless Operator Cyril F. Evans of the *Californian* had in fact barged in on the *Titanic*'s messages at 11:00 P.M. to warn that his ship was stopped and surrounded by ice. He was, at that moment, so close to the *Titanic*'s re-

Douglas could hear water lapping at the feet of several large icebergs, but she could see them only as shadows moving against fields of stars on the horizon, causing some to wink on, others to wink out, then to wink on again minutes later, as the shadows passed.

As above, so below.

As for stars, so for the lights of ships. In addition to sporadic power failures aboard the *Titanic* (including light outages reported by Fireman Charles Hendrickson), in addition to the pivoting motions of two ships, another random element was thrown into the confusions of the night: ice eclipses. These confusions would be seized upon by lawyers and other defenders of the *Californian* and its skipper as "inconsistencies" upon which a foundation could be built, placing Captain Stanley Lord almost as far away from the *Titanic* as the captain of the rescue ship *Carpathia*—which took three and one-half hours to reach the lifeboats at (variously) ten to seventeen knots.

And yet, Third Officer Groves of the *Californian* would testify that before Captain Lord went to sleep, he had shown his skipper the ship that came in from the southwest at 11:10 P.M. and stopped, he estimated, less than seven miles away at 11:40; and Lord had told him, "That will be the *Titanic* on her maiden voyage."

About 1:10 A.M., as the *Californian*'s second officer noticed that Mr. Gill's missing deck lights and portholes had reappeared, the *Californian* seemed so near to Captain Smith that he ordered the people in boat eight to row as fast as they could "to that steamer" and bring it back with all of its boats ready.

The Countess Rothes, in a letter written days after the

---

ceiver that the sputtering in Operator Jack Phillips' earphones came in above his threshold of pain, forcing him to throw the phones off. Still reeling, he snapped back: "Shut up, shut up! I am busy." Forty minutes later, the *Titanic* was deep within the ice field.

sinking, distinctly recalled Smith identifying the "mysterious lights" as a "steamer," and though they seemed to her eyes like a cluster of bright stars on the horizon, she decided that Captain Smith, if no one else, would have known the lights of a steamship when he saw them. What troubled her was that, by all available accounts, neither Smith nor Boxhall nor anyone else in charge had taken notice of the lights until the lifeboats were already being prepared for lowering and the boilers were already being shut down. She could not understand why the captain did not, immediately after impact, search the horizon for a nearby ship, for a fishing boat—for anything warm and still floating—and steam toward it.[2]

Helen Candee's group had also been ordered to row toward the lights, and they had managed to propel boat six three or four miles north, until a breeze came up, the waters rippled, the icebergs shifted, and the lights were hidden from view. Shortly before dawn, passenger Spencer V. Silverthorne watched the lights reappear (still in the north), just as the sea became threateningly choppy, just as the rescue ship *Carpathia* appeared in the south, firing rockets as she advanced. The stranger in the north was, as revealed by the approach of daylight, none other than the single smokestack, four-masted *Californian*. Both the "mystery ship" and the lifeboat were surrounded by dozens of ice-

---

[2]No one knows for sure that a search was not made, though no one who survived from the bridge (Boxhall and Hitchens) recalled hearing of it. According to Joseph Boxhall, the lights were "suddenly just there . . . straight ahead of the bow" around the time the first canvas cover was removed from the first lifeboat. If ice eclipsing had initially hidden the *Californian*, the search would have turned up nothing. Additionally, Murdoch had tried to "port around the iceberg," aiming the *Titanic*'s bow south. The *Californian*, in the north, was probably not visible, initially, unless one physically walked off the bridge and looked north along the stern. Thus, Boxhall did not notice the lights until the bow (and the bridge) had swung north, and suddenly they were "just there—straight ahead of the bow."

bergs, and as the light strengthened, the vessel started its engines and headed west, as if trying to hide itself from view in the thickest part of the ice field, as if intent on re-maining a phantom, forever eclipsed by ice.

From boat number eleven, Steward Charles Donald Mackay had seen the stranger's white mast light and red port-side riding light when he reached the water at 1:30 A.M. He rowed toward it until about 3:30 A.M., when a slight breeze sprang up and the visitor seemed to disap-pear.

In his affidavit to the British inquiry, Fifth Officer Harold Godfrey Lowe recalled that when he was helping to lower a lifeboat at 1:00 A.M., someone mentioned that there was a ship visible along the port bow. "I glanced in that di-rection," said Lowe, "and saw a steamer showing her red [port-side] light about five miles northward of us."

Lowe could still see the red riding light after he lowered himself to sea level in boat fourteen at 1:30 A.M. Sometime between 2:15 and 2:30, he herded five boats together, transferred most of his passengers from boat fourteen, and rowed back to the site of the sinking. He noticed, then, that the stranger had altered her position—pivoted, and was showing her green starboard light. At some point during the next hour, while the fifth officer's attention was focused on finding survivors in the water, "all the lights went out, and I did not see any more lights until I saw the lights of the *Carpathia*."

Quartermaster Walter Wynn told examiner Aspinall that after Sixth Officer Moody put him in command of boat nine and sent him down at 1:20 A.M., he saw the "mystery ship's" red port light and white mast light in the north. Cu-riously, the red light appeared first, then the taller mast light simply winked into view (or out of ice eclipse). He judged the steamer to be seven or eight miles away and, as he watched, both lights disappeared, followed by the reappearance of the mast light about fifteen minutes later, in the same direction.

At the British inquiry, Captain Lord tried to place the *Californian* at least thirty miles away from the *Titanic*— too far to have enabled him to be of any practical assistance, given a maximum cruising speed of fourteen knots.

Eyewitness accounts of the lights seen from the lifeboats, combined with the same mathematical realities that require the towers of the Golden Gate Bridge to compensate for the earth's curvature by leaning more than three feet out of parallel, provide clues to the true distance between the "mystery ships."

The *Californian*'s white mast lights stood more than a hundred feet above the water and, to a person standing in a lifeboat, would have been visible above the horizon ten to fifteen miles away. The red and green side lights were lower—no more than seventy feet above sea level—so they stood above the horizon out to a radius of only seven miles. If the passengers of a lifeboat saw the red or green riding lights, then their boat was located within a circle of seven-mile radius drawn about the ship, beyond which, the curvature of the earth would have bulged the ocean above eye level and eclipsed the lights.

Steward Mackay, Fifth Officer Lowe, and Quartermaster Wynn all saw the steamer's riding lights from sea level, and all judged the ship to have been within five to eight miles of the *Titanic* and its lifeboats.

The survivors often saw the same things differently, depending on their states of distress, their eyesight, their mind-sets.[3] In the case of the side lights, however, the

---

[3]Some people, of course, did not know *what* they saw. On May 9, 1912, Seaman John Poingdester told examiner Aspinall that he was very clear on having seen his ship break in half ("because she was short—the forward part disappeared and the after part uprighted itself as if nothing had happened, straight on the water again"), but he referred to the light he observed

British and American inquiries contain account after account describing the same thing. From collapsible D, Crewman William Lucas saw the red port riding light of another steamer. He judged it to be eight or nine miles away because it was "right on the horizon" when he was "down on the water . . ." Steward James Johnson rowed boat two toward the red port light and the white mast light of a steamer in the north. He thought it was eight to ten miles away, but it disappeared suddenly. Continuing north, he was halted by an iceberg directly ahead, rolling and making sloshing noises . . . Fourth Officer Boxhall identified the "night visitor" as "a four-masted steamer," only five miles away in the north, showing its red side light intermittently . . . Passenger Lawrence Beesley reported that Boxhall and Smith "could distinguish [from the boat deck] the masthead lights and a red port light." They hailed the ship with Morse lamp signals, "to which Boxhall saw no reply," said Beesley, "but Captain Smith and stewards affirmed they did. Third Officer [Herbert Pitman] saw the signals sent and her lights— from the lifeboat of which he was in charge [number five], and we in boat thirteen certainly saw it in the same position and rowed toward it for some time . . ." Steward Ed Wheelton observed, from boat eleven, a red side light, about five or ten miles away . . .

Taking these multiple, independently witnessed firsthand accounts seriously, the *Titanic* was within the seven-

from the lifeboat as "imaginary." Aspinall wondered aloud how one sees an imaginary light. "Well, there is such a thing as seeing imaginary lights," Poingdester explained. "Oh, is there?" said Aspinall. "Yes," said Poingdester. "This one was about four or five miles away." He added that, as ship's lookout, he saw imaginary lights all the time—"as soon as you see it, it has gone again," and Aspinall broke in, "I do not understand it. Did you imagine that you saw a light, or did you see a light that you imagined?" The lookout replied, "Well, one way or the other . . . I spoke to the women [in the lifeboat] about this light and said, 'We are all right. We shall be picked up in a minute; there is a ship coming.'"

mile radius drawn by the *Californian*'s side lights; beyond the three- to five-mile radius at which reports from the *Titanic*'s rockets would have been audible, beyond the five- to six-mile range at which signals from Morse lamps would have been clearly distinguishable from each ship's bridge, yet within the five- to eight-mile range that many of the *Titanic*'s observers had estimated.

Stanley Lord, of course, denied that the lights belonged to his ship, but the other overwhelming reality of that night was the chronology of events involving ice, lights, and rockets, as seen from the *Californian*.

Third Officer Charles Victor Groves recalled that at 8:00 P.M. on the evening of April 14, Captain Lord notified him that several wireless messages had warned of ice ahead, so the skipper decided to "double the lookout" by supplementing the sailor in the crow's nest with "an extra set of eyes, lower to the horizon," on the point bow. At 10:30 P.M., an hour and ten minutes before the *Titanic* struck ice, Groves saw several white patches moving into his path. He thought they were dolphins crossing the bows, but Captain Lord, standing beside him, knew otherwise and shouted for "Full speed astern!" When the ship came to a stop, Groves saw that he was surrounded by light field ice—mostly little "growlers" rising no more than a foot or two out of the water, but ahead, in the west, stars were being eclipsed by actual mountains, some of them more than a hundred feet tall. "Despite the clarity of the atmosphere," Groves recalled, "this ice was not sighted at a distance of more than four hundred yards nor was it seen by the lookouts before it was seen from the bridge."

Their path west hopelessly blocked until daylight, Captain Lord decided to "stay put for the night." He posted extra lookouts and ordered the boilers kept hot, just in case one of the larger bergs drifted near, threatened "to get into us," and made necessary a hasty retreat.

Forty minutes later, at 11:10 P.M., the forward mast light of a steamer appeared on the horizon, approaching from the east on a heading that would bring it five to ten miles south of the *Californian*—in the same heading as the *Titanic*.

At 11:25 P.M. the green riding light was visible on the ship's starboard side. The maximum distance at which the curvature of the earth permitted the riding lights of the *Titanic* to be seen from the height of the *Californian*'s bridge was sixteen miles, though the *Californian* might have been deeper within the *Titanic*'s "circle of green light" by the time Lord and Groves noticed it. The rise of the starboard riding light over the curve of the earth some fifteen minutes after the mast lights permits a rough estimate of the approaching ship's speed: between 5 and 7.5 miles in fifteen minutes, or twenty to thirty knots.

During the next fifteen minutes, the steamer approached within five to seven miles, according to Groves. If the visitor's starboard lamp were first seen at the maximum "green light" distance (from bridge altitude) of sixteen miles and stopped, say, ten miles away, it would have covered roughly six miles during the fifteen minutes between 11:25 and 11:40 P.M. Groves probably brought the lower limit of the steamer's final stopping distance (five to seven miles) two miles too near, but slight errors of observation and timing (up to three miles and/or two minutes) bracket the ship's velocity between twenty and twenty-six knots—almost twice the speed of all but a handful of the newest ships in 1912. The last order George Kemish heard, before the alarm sounded, was to bring the *Titanic* up to twenty-three knots.

As Groves watched, the stranger—which had been steaming steadily toward the west "in a blaze of deck lights"—seemed to change orientation and come to a stop at 11:40, just as the *Titanic* did, at 11:40 P.M. Interestingly, Groves was mystified by the sudden shutting out of many

lights at this time, followed by the ship's reappearance in a
new orientation, as if the stranger were facing him stern-
on. Forty-three years later, when he wrote to historian Walter Lord, the mystery was still unsolved, and had begun to
trouble him.[4] And yet the "putting out of lights" which
turned out to be transitory, and which ultimately made no
sense at all to Groves, was in fact the only thing that did
make sense, from a certain point of view.

If the *Titanic* had been located south of the *Californian*,
and the iceberg brushed by on the *Titanic*'s starboard side,
then the three peaks (or "icemasts") observed by passengers would have blocked whole rows of portholes, and
many deck lights, from the *Californian*'s view during the
half minute the *Titanic* took to cross the berg's far side.
What Third Officer Charles Groves described, without
knowing it, was the moment of impact—the saddest ice
eclipse of all—and he would never have witnessed this
particular eclipse were he not standing on a ship located a
few miles north of the *Titanic* when the Atlantic's hemorrhage into boiler rooms and cargo holds began.

Aboard the *Titanic*, in a stateroom on the port side of C
deck, Jack Thayer felt the floor sway slightly, and realized
that the ship had veered to port as though gently pushed. A
few moments later he felt the engines slow and stop, and
there was not a sound except the breeze coming through

---

[4]Charles Victor Groves was certain that he had seen at least some of the *Titanic*'s brilliant deck lights go out. Unlike his former commander, he had no
doubt that the ship in the south was the *Titanic*. Groves was not, at first,
troubled by the sudden dousing of lights, for as he explained in his July 17,
1955 letter to Walter Lord, "I had been for some time a junior officer in the
Far Eastern trade where it was our custom to put the deck lights out at midnight to encourage the passengers to turn in and I concluded that the *Titanic*
had put her lights out for the same purpose." What troubled him were eyewitness accounts that the lights of *Titanic*'s upper decks had never gone out,
not even for a second, until the very end. On this point, he had never heard
a contrary view.

his half-open porthole. A minute later the breeze, produced by the *Titanic*'s inertia through still air, also came to a stop.

"Very shortly the engines started up again," Thayer recalled, "slowly, not with the bright vibration to which we were accustomed, but as though they were tired."

Passenger Lawrence Beesley thought "the ship had now resumed her course, moving very slowly through the water with a little white line of foam on each side. I think we were all glad to see this: it felt better than standing still." Then he saw an officer climb atop boat sixteen and throw off the cover, and he became aware of a slight but undoubted tilt toward the bow. "After a few minutes, the engines again stopped."

From the *Californian*, Groves watched the "mystery ship" start up again, proceed slowly for a few minutes veering to port, and then stop again with its stern facing north—just as the *Titanic* did. At midnight he handed the night watch over to Second Officer Herbert Stone and his apprentice, James Gibson, who tried to call the stranger with a Morse lamp. At 12:10 Gibson thought he saw a flicker in reply, but the ship seemed just far enough away for the dots and dashes to be indistinguishable as actual words. He concluded, however, that the ship had indeed tried to Morse him—just as the *Titanic* did.[5]

At 12:45 A.M. the stranger began firing white rockets—just as the *Titanic* did.

Stone and Gibson counted eight rockets—the same number the *Titanic* fired.

---

[5]History will never know why Gibson believed the stranger had nothing important to say. What can be known is that his attempt to use the Morse lamp is an indication of how close he assumed the mystery ship to be. Every sailor knew that Morse lights were only useful within a radius of five or six miles. That Captain Smith also ordered the use of the *Titanic*'s Morse lamp indicates that he, too, believed his ship was either within this radius, or close to it.

Stone noted at the British inquiry that one of the last three rockets appeared to be much brighter than the others—and from the *Titanic*, Quartermaster George Rowe recalled that the sixth or seventh rocket had flared out much brighter than the others.

About 1:20 A.M., the ship fired its last rocket. Stone and Gibson noticed that the stranger had skewed its rows of portholes at an odd angle: some dipping very low on the horizon while others, including the stern light, were apparently being raised. Examining the ship through binoculars, Gibson remarked, "She looks rather to have a big side out of the water." Then she began dousing her lights, more and more of them, until she doused them altogether around 2:20, her stern light being the last to go—all just as the *Titanic* did.

At 3:05, a visitor steaming up from the south at seventeen knots fired the first of three rockets. Stone and Gibson saw all three, and quickly identified them as coming from some ship other than the one that had fired the first eight. The new ship was further away, and it approached from the south—just as the *Carpathia* did.[6]

---

[6]The *Carpathia* received the *Titanic*'s SOS at 12:30 A.M., approximately 15 minutes before the bulkhead between boiler rooms five and six collapsed and Quartermaster Rowe fired the first rocket. By 12:35, Captain Rostron was steaming north at a top speed of 17 knots. The *Titanic*'s rockets, as reported by Quartermaster Rowe (and by Stone and Gibson in reports on their mystery ship), did not climb much higher than her forward mast light. The last rocket was fired about 1:20 and should have been visible, over the curve of the earth, from the bridge of a ship at a radius of 20–25 miles. Rostron of the *Carpathia* reported seeing no rockets, confirming that he was still over the horizon, more than 20 or 25 miles away at 1:20 A.M. An hour and fifteen minutes later, at 2:35, Captain Rostron saw one of the green Roman candles Fourth Officer Boxhall had been lighting at intervals in boat two, about the same time the first iceberg loomed ahead and course had to be altered. The same rules of distance that applied to sightings of the *Californian*'s side lights from the lifeboats applied to sighting a flare in a lifeboat from the *Carpathia*'s bridge. Assuming that the flare was held over Boxhall's head,

At 3:35 A.M., Captain Rostron of the *Carpathia* estimated that "we were almost up to the position and had the giant liner been afloat, we should have seen her." Stone and Gibson watched the ship come up and stop, and turned the watch over to Chief Officer Stewart at 4:00 A.M.

At 6:20 A.M., Second Officer James Bisset of the *Carpathia* noticed that the four-masted steamer with one smokestack—which had been within sight since at least 3:30 A.M.—started its engines and left the ice field's eastern rim, where it had been floating idly since first sighted. It headed inexplicably westward—*into* the ice. Bisset watched it disappear behind a large berg, reappear behind some shallow pack ice, disappear again, reappear, still heading west—just as Spencer Silverthorne said the *Californian* did.

On the other side of the ice field, Captain Moore of the *Mount Temple* was trying to guide his ship east through the ice, to the place from which the *Titanic* had signaled distress. It was 6:30 A.M. In daylight, he was able to determine that the *Carpathia* was six miles east of him, on the opposite side of the ice field, and that the *Californian* was on a heading that would bring it through the field's western rim six miles to his north.

Ten minutes later the *Californian*'s wireless operator, Cyril Evans, received a call from the *Virginian*, requesting information. He tapped back, "Can now see *Carpathia* taking passengers aboard from small boats." At 6:50 A.M., a

---

the *Carpathia* must have been eight miles away from boat twelve at 2:35 A.M., fifteen minutes after the *Titanic* sank. From the upturned keel of collapsible B, Jack Thayer observed the *Carpathia*'s masthead light approaching from the south at this same time, again indicating that the ship had come within 8–15 miles. A half hour later, the *Carpathia* fired the first of three rockets, each rising about as high as the *Titanic*'s rockets. Stone and Gibson saw all three, meaning that at 3:05 A.M., the *Carpathia*, though further south than the *Titanic*'s lifeboats, was already within 20–25 miles of the *Californian*, perhaps within as few as 15 miles.

clearing through the ice allowed Groves to see, by aid of binoculars, that the *Carpathia*'s flag was at half mast. He estimated that the *Carpathia* was about five miles to his south.

Captain Lord's "official" log would claim that his ship started steaming "toward" the *Titanic* site at 6:00 A.M. and did not reach the *Carpathia* until 8:30 A.M.; yet two hours before the *Californian* "officially" arrived, her crew was close enough to distinguish lifeboats, passengers, and flags.[7]

In his report to the American inquiry, Captain Lord emphasized that he was slow to reach the *Carpathia* and the scene of the sinking, once he started his engines, because he found his path blocked by ice. He failed to mention that there was no reasonable need for him to maneuver westward through the ice field, following a strangely circuitous route that sent him ten miles south along the field's west rim, then east through the field a *second* time, bringing him into view, as if for the first time, almost two miles south of the *Carpathia*—as if to suggest that he had approached, like the *Frankfurt* and the *Mount Temple* (whose skippers were able to corroborate the *Californian*'s path), from the southwest. Citing a maximum cruising speed of fourteen knots, and accounting for caution when he saw ice, Captain Lord (as if to suggest that he had steamed in a straight line toward the *Carpathia*) told the American examiners, in April, 1912, that a two and one-half-hour travel time to the *Titanic* would have put him at least twenty miles from the disaster.

---

[7]The "official" log was, as revealed by Captain Lord's and Third Officer Groves' testimony before Lord Mersey, a "replacement" for a "scrap log." Under examination, they admitted that the "scrap log," or original log, was copied and "discarded . . . overboard." The official log made no mention whatsoever of rockets, or of anything else out of the ordinary during the night the *Titanic* went down.

A month later, he pushed his ship thirty miles away for British examiners, and a month after that, he had stretched it to forty.

Eyewitness accounts (some from the very ship whose crew had much to lose if it were proved that they could have saved 1,500 lives), combined with the unbreakable rules of planetary curvature, place the *Californian* within seven miles of the *Titanic*, a distance equal to the length of Manhattan Island.

In terms of travel time, it would have taken the *Californian* just under a half hour to reach the *Titanic*, seven miles away, at fourteen knots. Allowing for caution, owing to the possibility of encountering ice in the dark, Lord could have reached the *Titanic* in forty minutes at ten knots. According to Third Officer Charles Groves, the ship was prepared to get under way almost immediately, should an iceberg drift too near the *Californian* as she lay to about a hundred feet east of the main field.

If the *Californian* had responded to the first rocket at 12:45 and was coming up to speed (ten knots) ten minutes later, she would have arrived on the scene at 1:37 and found the liner with her forward well deck still above water, the lifeboats still lowering, and the bulkhead between boiler rooms four and five still holding back the Atlantic.

Even if Stone and Gibson had waited until after the ship fired all eight rockets, waited until they noticed, through binoculars, at about 1:20 A.M., that rows of portholes were angling down into the sea before waking their captain and insisting that he take action, they would have arrived (given a ten-minute start-up time) at 2:10 A.M.—in time to have pulled hundreds of people from the water before hypothermia overcame them.

CAPTAIN STANLEY LORD found a loyal supporter in J. Bruce Ismay—naturally. At the British inquiry, the managing director of the White Star Line—alone among the *Titanic*'s witnesses—testified under oath that the vessel whose lights he had seen could not possibly have been the *Californian*. If that was his conclusion, the court asked, could he guarantee that it was not born of the peculiar coincidence that the Leyland Liner *Californian* was, like the *Titanic*, owned by his company? Ismay had no answer to that.

The question might never have been asked, had Captain Lord kept a low profile when he arrived in Boston, and refrained from giving press conferences in which he praised his own good judgment to drift without power when he saw ice, and sniped at poor Captain Smith—too far away to be helped—for rushing into the field at full speed.

"He probably thought posterity would look kindly, even proudly upon him," Walter Lord said of Captain Stanley Lord. "But it was there, in Boston, that he succeeded in hanging himself. Posterity would call him despicable."

Walter Lord, who as a boy became so intrigued by the *Titanic* (and by the Alamo, and by everything else historic) that he coaxed his parents into crossing on the liner's twin sister *Olympic* in 1926, had always scoured the nation's libraries for newspaper interviews dating back to the spring of 1912. He found Captain Stanley Lord's April 19 interview for the Boston *Evening Globe* shortly before Bob Ballard's team found the *Titanic*. The skipper spoke of dodging huge icebergs and plowing through fields of sheet ice; he spoke of the "mighty good seamanship" required to pilot a freighter under such conditions; he spoke of having started his engines as soon as he received news of the *Titanic* at 5:30 A.M.; he spoke of making every effort to reach the scene as quickly as possible, taking fully three hours to close the gap, from thirty miles to zero.

He said nothing about rockets.

And the press said nothing further about Stanley Lord, on April 20, 21, or 22.

Officers Stone and Groves, Apprentice Gibson, Engineer's Assistant Ernest Gill, and Carpenter Will McGregor were not so silent, as they visited relatives and Boston pubs while the *Californian* lay peacefully in port. Fueled by anger over their captain's boasts, their tongues loosened by stout and grief and shame, they began talking about seeing the *Titanic*'s lights and her rockets. Rumors of the *Californian*'s "death watch" spread out of Captain Lord's control along Pub Row, until inevitably, a reporter tracked one of its sources back to the ship's carpenter.

Walter Lord found the first mention of rockets seen from the *Californian* in the April 23 edition of the Clinton *Daily Item*. A tearful Will McGregor told of rockets seen by Stone and Gibson, of how they had been reported to the captain, "but he failed to pay attention to the signals, excepting to tell the watch to keep his eye on the boat. At this time, the two boats were about ten miles apart."

A day later, Captain Lord gave an interview to the *Post*, in which he stated that there was no merit to tales that the crew of the *Californian* had seen "rockets or other signals of distress." He did, however, give a new estimate on the *Titanic*'s distance: twenty miles.

On April 25, an agent for J. Bruce Ismay declared Carpenter McGregor's story "perfectly absurd," emphasizing that none of the crew had seen any signals of distress or any unusual lights on the night of Sunday, April 14.[8]

Captain Lord chimed in by calling the tale of rockets seen on April 14, "a lie . . . bosh . . . poppycock!" Second Officer Stone supported his commander's version of events, denying that he had seen anything. For the Boston *Herald*, he "*emphatically* denied that he had notified Cap-

---

[8]Later, the lie would be retracted with a "letter of the word" defense, in which it would be noted that the rockets and the unusual tilt of the porthole rows had not been noticed until after midnight, "on the morning of Monday, April 15," and hence the agent's denial was "not really a lie."

tain Lord of any rockets, as he had seen none, nor had any been reported to him."

Lord, Stone, Gill, and Groves were summoned a day later to the inquiry, whereupon, under cross examination, they told a very different tale about rockets and lights seen during the night, and in their defense tried to conjure up a third "mystery ship" between the *Californian* and the *Titanic*, in order to double or triple the *Californian*'s distance from the *Titanic* to at least twenty miles.

The paper trail reveals, beyond serious dispute, that Captain Lord and the Leyland Line were quite willing to lie on this subject. Were they present and able to be questioned today, they would arrive with the distinction of having already painted themselves into the unenviable corner of denying their own denials.

"ODD THEORIES ABOUT third mystery ships do nothing to exonerate the *Californian*," said Walter Lord, during the planning stage of yet another expedition to the *Titanic*. "I will never understand why, given the information he was receiving, the captain did not wake up his wireless operator who was sleeping only a few feet away from the chart room, while rockets were flying up on the horizon."

"And the suggestion of a third ship out there, a smaller ship," I asked, "firing rockets?"

"Captain Lord tried to say it was, 'a tramp steamer like ourselves,'" said Walter.

"I don't understand how that was supposed to excuse him. Was he trying to suggest that if it was a less important ship than the *Titanic*, then it was all right if they stood by and did nothing? Even if there were *five* ships firing rockets—"

"Well, some of the *Californian*'s defenders claim that there were at least two."

"Yes, but all one needs to ask is, what would Captain Rostron of the *Carpathia* have done?"

"Exactly," said Walter. "Rostron would have turned his ship around and headed for the position, or he would at least have had his wireless operator check to see if it was truly a distress call."

"It makes no sense, sitting in an ice field watching rockets go up all night—rockets could have meant only one thing in an ice field: have struck ice . . . sinking . . ."

"No, it made no sense," said Walter. "The captain told me that he was lying on a couch in the chart room, fully clothed. By his own admission he had to walk across the room to answer calls from the bridge, where his men were counting off more rockets as the night progressed. Captain Lord had never been in ice at night before. If he headed toward the rockets, he might easily have ended up in the same condition as the ship firing the rockets. I think he saw a ship that he sensed was in trouble and he just did not want to see it. Given that mind-set, the *Californian* needed more forceful minds [more forceful junior officers] on watch that night."

"Yes," I agreed. "As George Tulloch has pointed out, no one on the watch ever claimed to have told Captain Lord, 'Sir, I think it's a passenger liner, sinking. Do something!' "

"There's some question as to whether Stone, Gibson, and Groves were the ideal men to be in that position—all too afraid to challenge a reluctant captain."

EXCERPT FROM A LETTER TO WALTER LORD FROM WHITE STAR LINE EMPLOYEE BRIAN MANNING, MARCH 29, 1956:

I met [Second Officer Herbert Stone] during World War I. It was a well-known fact and quoted by him to his friends that Captain Lord of the *Californian* was an insufferable SOB. That after Stone had tried to get him to come up on the bridge, he turned to the apprentice [Gibson] and said, "Well, let the bastard sleep."

Unlike Herbert Stone, Charles Victor Groves never did excuse himself for not being more forceful with his captain. He could not forgive himself for getting in line when the system told him he should, could not forgive himself for failing to deviate, and for shutting up when authority told him to do so.

On April 23, 1957, the forty-fifth anniversary of Carpenter McGregor's breakdown in the presence of a reporter, Groves wrote to Walter Lord, blaming himself for not listening a little longer to the Marconi apparatus, for not doublechecking that it was wound up to full power, "at which time the ether was being rent by calls of distress." Speaking of himself in the third person, he concluded, "The fate of those [fifteen] hundred lost souls hinged on the fact that Mr. Groves failed . . ."

Groves remembered seeing the so-called mystery ship veer to port after "dousing its lights," and he recalled that by the time Captain Lord returned to the bridge, at about 11:50 P.M., it had moved almost a half mile south and appeared to be showing only its stern lights.

Given merely a foreshortened view of her lights, the skipper judged that it could not possibly be the same ship he had identified for Groves as the *Titanic* a half hour earlier. This ship was smaller, Lord said, "not a passenger ship."

Groves, who thought the ship had swerved "to escape some ice," replied, "It *is*, Sir. When she stopped she put all her lights out."

The captain, whom Groves described as "an austere type,

utterly devoid of humour and even more reserved than is usual with those who occupy similar positions," announced that he was retiring to the map room and instructed Groves to call "if that ship makes a move or if anything else heaves into sight." The ship remained stationary, and Groves said nothing more to his captain and lived to rue it the rest of his days.

"No absolution . . .

"At midnight," he wrote (again, speaking of himself in the third person), "Mr. Groves was relieved by Mr. Stone [and Apprentice Gibson], to whom the captain's orders were passed. The apprentice was a bright lad, keen on his profession and one who showed every sign that he would make headway in it. Herbert Stone, the second officer, was a stolid, unimaginative type and possessed little self-confidence."

As for Captain Lord, Groves said, "Many times the question of his sobriety on that occasion has been raised but it cannot be too strongly asserted that he was a most temperate man and that alcohol played no part in the matter."

As for himself, Groves wished only that he could somehow communicate, back across time, with the young Third Officer Groves. Not a night of his life had passed without that wish, not since the day he heard witnesses speak of how the officers of the *Titanic* had pointed out to them the lights of a vessel stopped only a few miles away, and reassured passengers with promises that this ship—his ship—would soon come to their assistance.

"No absolution . . . All that middle watch, *Californian* remained stationary, for news of the rockets being seen did not stir her captain into action and Mr. Stone lacked the necessary initiative to insist upon his coming to the bridge—and it did not occur to him to call the chief officer when he realized the apathy of the captain."

There was no doubt in Groves' mind that Stone had

known there was some sort of trouble aboard the vessel from which distress signals were being fired—not necessarily that the vessel was sinking, but that something was definitely wrong. "But he failed to convince his captain," Groves wrote, and wondered, "Was Mr. Stone afraid that if he was too insistent he would arouse the wrath of his superior? And why," Groves added, "did Captain Lord make no efficient steps to render assistance until 6 o'clock? Did he consider problematical damage to his own ship was of more importance than the saving of lives?"

By the time Groves wrote to Walter Lord, someone had told him that much of what he witnessed from the *Californian* had been prophesized in a book rumored to have been placed in the *Titanic*'s library, "somewhat as a grim joke."

Its author, Morgan Robertson, had penned what in those days were known as "penny dreadfuls," and his writing—even without its occasional lapses into racist babble—was indeed a painful read. In 1898, he began a series of tales about machines that did not exist in his time, tales about a great human change arising from a global war fought in the air and under the sea. He was, in essence, writing science fiction, and he agreed with Verne and Wells (and with John Jacob Astor, who had written a novel about spaceflight) that men might one day go to the moon, adding that the first man to walk on the other side of the sky would have a distinctly American name: Armstrong.

His predictions were wrong at least as often as they were right (for example, the internment of Japanese Americans in camps was the provocation for, rather than a response to the Empire's attack on American naval bases in Manila and Hawaii on a December morning), but he did write about a giant passenger ship named the *Titan*.

Robertson's fictional ship was virtually the same length and tonnage displacement as the *Titanic*, still thirteen years from being designed and built when he put pen to paper.

His fictional ship had an identical twin sister named the *Gigantic*. The real ship's identical sister, under construction when the *Titanic* left Southampton, underwent a name change after the sinking: to *Britannic* from *Gigantic*. The fictional sister was stricken by a mine or torpedo on the starboard bow, and raised her stern into the air, dripping and gleaming in brilliant daylight before she plunged down—just as the real sister did, during World War I.

Robertson's *Titan* and the real life *Titanic* were powered by three giant propellers to cruising speeds of twenty-five knots. Both carried about twenty-two hundred people, and the fact that their lifeboats had a capacity for only half that number was of small concern, because both giants were said to be "unsinkable."

On a cold April night, Robertson's ship struck an iceberg on the starboard side and went down by the bow—just as the real ship did, more than a decade after Robertson concocted the story.

By the time Walter Lord heard from Groves of the *Californian*, he was sufficiently intrigued to have noted some of the odd parallels between Robertson's fiction and the *Titanic*'s reality in the prologue of *A Night to Remember*, but he was always quick to point out some of the glaring departures from reality—such as Robertson's melodrama about two passengers who never made it to the *Titan*'s lifeboats, yet managed to pull themselves safely atop floating ice . . . only to face slow death because no ship saw them and came to their rescue.

To Groves, this was hardly a departure, as he recalled for the historian how the same captain who had reclassified the foreshortened *Titanic* as a small ship next assured him that "those figures" he saw through the binoculars were not "people on the ice," and then expressed not the slightest curiosity in them.

The *Carpathia* had asked the *Californian* to search the

vicinity for further possible survivors, then steamed west toward a channel in the ice field with seven hundred of the *Titanic*'s passengers and crew aboard.

"This was nine o'clock," according to Groves. "Less than twenty minutes later, [the *Carpathia*] disappeared from view, hidden by icebergs."

An hour later, following what Groves characterized as the most cursory of investigations, Captain Lord ordered the *Californian* westward to Boston. For all anyone knew, the Grand Stairway (which, if reasonably intact, should have been standing a full story out of the water) was adrift nearby, with people moving unseen upon it, eclipsed like the *Carpathia* behind any of fifty tall icebergs.

"The sea was covered by a large number of deck chairs, planks, and light wreckage," Groves told Walter Lord, and then, speaking still of himself in the third person, "Scanning the sea with his binoculars the third officer noticed a large ice floe a mile or so distant on which he saw figures moving and, drawing Captain Lord's attention to it, remarked that they might be human beings. [The third officer] was told that they were seals. *Californian* now made one complete turn to starboard followed by one to port and then resumed her passage to Boston . . ."

COLLAPSIBLE D WAS ordered to row toward the lights—for what reason, Steward John Hardy did not know. At 2:05 A.M., as he cut loose from the davits, he still had "full confidence that the ship would float," even after the sea came pouring in a waist-high waterfall over the metal wall forward on the port-side promenade deck, even after Hugh Woolner leapt at D through the open gunwale, even after he looked back and saw water pouring in through the same door Woolner had just exited—"rising so rapidly that had [Mr. Woolner] waited another minute [he] should have been pinned between the deck and its roof."

A half hour earlier, First Officer Will Murdoch had said, "I believe she's gone, Hardy," and still the steward thought the watertight compartments would hold the ship afloat.

"All this is going to cost someone a pretty penny to fix up," Hardy said to Woolner. The young, sopping wet millionaire guessed that Hardy was the last man anywhere on, or in, or around the *Titanic* to be harboring a belief in "the unsinkable ship." He guessed so, but to judge from other things heard that night, he would not have bet good money on it.

Fireman William Taylor told the American inquiry that the majority of the crew "did not realize that she would sink."

"Was that ship regarded by the crew as an unsinkable ship?" asked examiner Newlands.

"So they thought," said Taylor.

"How do you know?"

"Because they were all skylarking and joking about it."

The examiner went silent for a very long time before asking, "After the accident they were joking about it?"

"Yes, sir."

"If they had realized that there was serious danger," said Newlands, "there would have been a terrible scene there, would there not?"

"Yes, sir. Everybody would have been rushing for their lives," and he explained that when he was ordered to assist boat fifteen at 1:30 A.M., he thought the boats were being lowered only as a precaution against an emergency that had not yet, and probably never would, develop.

Eight decks below Taylor, in the boiler rooms, George Kemish saw the ship's carpenters constantly taking soundings. "They might have known," he recalled for Walter Lord, "but no one else (except Skipper Smith) that things were going to happen."

Given the twenty-twenty hindsight of decades, Fireman

Kemish understood that Carpenter J. Hutchinson must have felt there was not a moment to lose, while at the same time knowing that no one could afford a rush on the lifeboats, a panic. During the first five minutes after impact, Boxhall went down to F deck forward and found no sign of damage. "A close call," he had judged, and returned to the bridge—where, a few minutes later, he met the carpenter rushing up from E deck, pale and out of breath.

"What's wrong?" Boxhall asked.

"She's taking water fast!"

"Where?"

"Everywhere—"

"Nobody ever thought the ship was going down," Mrs. J. Stuart White explained to the American inquiry. From her vantage point on the starboard side, up to the moment an officer calmly ushered her into boat eight at 1:10 A.M., she recalled, "I do not think there was a person—a man, on the [Titanic] who thought the ship was going down. They speak of the bravery of the men. I do not think there was any particular bravery because none of the men thought it was going down. If they had thought the ship was going down, they would not have friveled as they did about it."

Captain E. J. Smith had suspected even before he went below with Hutchinson and Andrews that people were going to die. By the time he returned to the bridge, it was beyond doubt. He also knew there were 2,200 people aboard, and that the lifeboats could hold only half that number.

"Space for 1,100 people in the lifeboats," Senator William Smith emphasized, at the conclusion of the American inquiry. More than anything else that happened on the Titanic, more than the fact that the liner had been speeding toward an iccfield in the dark, it was the four hundred empty seats in the lifeboats that troubled Senator Smith. *How could the captain have kept back the news that his ship was sinking and watched those first lifeboats go down on the davits with almost nobody in them?* the senator wondered. He had heard a survivor explain, "Well, with the band playing cheery ragtime music, it reminded me of a bloomin' picnic."

That sounded like an apt summation of the night, William Smith decided. The boiler rooms and the cargo holds were flooding and the lifeboats were going away half empty . . . *and the band played on* . . . "I don't know why," Senator Smith told the Congressional investigators. "I don't know why Captain Smith, after forty-three years at sea, just went drunk with negligence and recklessness that night."

MORE THAN EIGHT decades later, as he planned a robot reconnaissance of Captain Smith's stateroom, explorer George Tulloch pointed to something I had written during the Ballard expeditions to the *Titanic*. He read a passage to me in which I had summed up the skipper's behavior that night by his decision to go down with the ship, calling it "a good career move."

"Evidently," George said, "you, and Walter, and Ballard—and almost everyone else who has approached this subject—has bought into Senator Smith's assessment of Captain Smith. And I was just wondering: If you were E. J. Smith's little girl growing up (or his grandchild), don't you think it would bother you that all the argument has been over Captain Stanley Lord's actions, and that your father just took the pipe?"[9]

---

[9]Almost from the moment he landed in Boston, Captain Stanley Lord had the backing of Ismay's Leland Line and the Mercantile Marine. The "responsibility" to keep the argument alive and angry seems to have been passed down multigenerationally, and has occasionally led even on scientific expeditions to such threats as, "Eight hundred miles from New York, only the sharks can hear you scream."

(Drunk with negligence and recklessness that night . . .)

George let that sink in for a moment, while he tried to enhance a fuzzy image on the computer screen, showing a crack aft of the *Titanic*'s bridge, through which a rusticle-encroached bathtub could barely be discerned. "Well, Charles, I don't think that's the way to finish this guy's career," he continued, making a motion with his hands that removed all color from the recording and improved the contrast on our peek into Smith's quarters, revealing dangling wires, broken pipes, and part of a bed frame. "I don't think it's right that our Congress should summarize this man's life with that kind of indictment. They said very clearly, 'We find him guilty.' And I, as a historian, don't believe that's an accurate portrayal of the event."

I wondered. "It's often said that when a plane crashes and the pilots are killed, the investigators will almost invariably blame it on the dead pilots."

"Exactly," said George. "And the question about all those half-empty lifeboats is, if you were E. J. Smith, and it was twelve o'clock and Mr. Andrews was telling you, now, 'We've got an hour and one-half afloat, Captain,' and the unthinkable question is, *What do you do to save the greatest number of people*?

"Do you make sure that each boat is packed completely?

"Maybe . . . but I think the answer clearly has to be that Smith made a brilliant decision. He said, 'Don't tell anybody anything' because he knew, *if we tell, we'll have panic and we'll have murder right here on the deck, probably before the first boat is down on the falls.*"

"You mean," I said, "better to have the first few boats go down half empty than to have them all overcrowded on the davits and broken and sunk."

"That's the way I see it. Smith instructed his officers to start out with the loading of the boats as if it were a lark. It was he, I would guess, who sent the band out onto the deck. And he told his crew to say, when the women moaned and complained, 'Ah, it's just an exercise. You'll probably be back before breakfast—just a precaution.' He also told them, 'I want seamen in each of those lifeboats and I want them to come back and pick up more passengers as the ship settles lower.' "

"And those seamen all went out, and paddled away, and never came back."

"So, 705 people, out of the approximately eleven hundred that should have been in the lifeboats, made it. Another four hundred would have made it if Quartermaster Hitchens and the rest of those in charge of the lifeboats had followed their captain's orders and stayed near the ship to take on more passengers when the danger became apparent. The 705 who made it got away in relatively orderly fashion, without murder and mayhem on the decks all night long. And *that* you can thank Captain Smith for—because I'd like to see how you would handle it in the middle of the North Atlantic if it were your job."

WALTER LORD WAS puzzled by what he called "Captain Smith's missing hour."

For much of the time period between 12:10 and 1:10 A.M., very few survivors' accounts included sightings of the *Titanic*'s skipper. It was as if, at long intervals, he simply disappeared.

"During that critical first half hour," said Walter, "he seemed to be in a daze—at times actually forgetting which ship he was on." It was during this period (somewhere between 11:40 and 11:50 P.M.) that Beesley and Thayer recalled the engines starting up again and the ship steering slowly south, as far as a half mile. George Tulloch suspected that the captain was simply putting the machinery back into gear and driving forward, trying to glean from the ship's navigational behavior clues to how badly she was hurt, much as someone might drive slowly forward and test a car's steering after hitting an exceptionally deep pothole. The idea made sense: Even before Boxhall and Hutchinson finished their inspection, the forepeak and the mail room began to flood with many tons of water, and Smith must have felt some strange handling and listing, and realized the true seriousness of the damage. After three or four minutes, he shut the engines down.

"Soon," Walter said, "Thomas Andrews gave him the news, and that's when *he* began to shut down."

After steering southwest and ordering the forward boilers vented and cooled, Smith left the bridge. The next people to see him were Mr. and Mrs. Chambers, between 11:50 P.M. and 12:00 A.M. He joined them at the flooding mail room, watched for a little while, and hurried away.

About midnight he appeared on the bridge again, but vanished from the upper decks by 12:15 A.M., where the last person known to have seen him during the next half hour was Marconi Operator Harold Bride. According to Bride, the captain appeared, at that time, to be coming out of his daze. He acted very "in charge" during his visit to the Marconi shack, and even took pause to laugh at one of Bride's jokes.[10]

Between 12:15 and 12:20 A.M., Steward Charles Donald Mackay saw Smith below deck, heading from the working stairway toward the engine rooms, where Chief Engineers Bell and Frost were keeping the generators alive. He met the captain again, below deck, about ten minutes later.

Quartermaster George Rowe found him near the bridge

---

[10]History never did record the joke. Little is known except that the *Titanic*'s two Marconi operators responded to the coming horror with what had to be the longest and strangest fit of gallows humor the North Atlantic had ever seen—including a message to the *Olympic*: "Looks like it will be fish for breakfast for us tomorrow . . . or vice versa." It did not end until Bride beat a fellow crewman to death at about 2:10 A.M.

at 12:45 A.M., and he was present twenty-five minutes later when the Countess Rothes departed in boat eight. Smith sightings became spotty after that, until he appeared again in the Marconi shack and almost simultaneously on the bridge, near the end, acting very captainly.

"Here is what I think happened," said Walter Lord. "We do not encounter him, during this *missing time*, in survivors' accounts because those accounts come almost entirely from the boat deck, where of course most of those who survived were congregating. We know almost nothing of what was happening deep within the ship and it seems to me that this is where Captain Smith happened to be during his disappearances."

Tom Dettweiler agreed. As science officer for Jacques Cousteau and Bob Ballard, he had survived several desperate situations at sea. "And at such times," he recalled, "with the engines dead and the ship in total darkness during a storm, I have seen that the captain often goes below and enters the (normally 'verboten') territories of the engine room, making sure all that can be done has been done.

"Likely, Smith was receiving advice and advising on jury-rigged pumping systems, which probably contributed to keeping the forepart of the ship above water forty-five minutes longer than Thomas Andrews had predicted. Given all the other errors of the night, this might have made the difference between the boiler room four bulkhead collapsing at 2:10 A.M., when most of the boats were away, or at 1:25 A.M., when boats A, B, C, D, 1, 2, 4, 11, 13, 14, 15, and 16—twelve out of twenty—were still aboard."

MRS. ARTHUR RYERSON wondered how it had come down to launching lifeboats at all. Had E. J. Smith truly been the man with his hand on the helm during that voyage, she did not believe the *Titanic* would ever have ignored pleas for help from another ship in distress. It would all have ended differently that night, with the *Titanic* on a rescue mission, instead of keeping an appointment with the iceberg at 11:40 P.M. Mrs. Ryerson would not have become a widow and her son would not have been fatherless if it had ended that way, but it did not. Ismay had seen to that.

EXCERPT FROM MRS. ARTHUR RYERSON'S AFFIDAVIT FOR ATTORNEYS REPRESENTING THE THIRD CLASS, APRIL 18, 1913:

They have asked for my testimony in regard to my conversation with Ismay on board the *Titanic*. And I feel there is no reason now to decide to want to hide it if it is any help in the steerage claims. This is the first time I have been asked directly to give this, which seems quieter and less public to give it now than [for you] to mail me a subpoena which will involve an appearance in court.

As far as I can now recall . . . I was on deck [with Mrs. Thayer] in the afternoon of April 14 between 5 and 6 o'clock. And Mr. Ismay came up and inquired if our staterooms were comfortable and the service satisfactory. And then [he] thrust a Marconigram at me, saying we were in among the icebergs. Something was said about speed and he said that the ship had not been going fast but that they were to start up extra boilers that afternoon. The telegraph also spoke of the *Deutschland*—a ship out of coal [and out of control] and asking for a tow. When I asked him what they were going to do about this, he said they had no time for such matters. Our ship wanted to do her best

and something was said about getting in Tuesday
night . . . Mr Ismay's manner was that of one in authority and the owner of the ship and that what he
said was law.

If this can be of service to anyone I do not wish to
be silent or seem to be protecting him.

On that last day, six ice warnings were received, and
Ismay testified that at least one of them was taken from the
bridge by Captain Smith and handed personally to him. He
still had it in his pocket when he ran into Mrs. Ryerson and
Mrs. Thayer, two of the wealthiest and most socially
prominent ladies aboard. He seemed to find the news of
icebergs ahead "titillating."[11]

Mrs. Thayer remembered Ismay showing the Marconigram as if specifically to remind her "who he was." She recalled that the ice warning was from the *Baltic*, and Ismay
had uttered something about reaching that position about
9:00 P.M.

"It's a damning recollection," said Walter Lord. "Thayer
should have been friendly to Ismay, because the families
were close. Mrs. Thayer said she became very serious, and
told Ismay, 'With all this ice ahead, I guess you'll be slowing down,' and Ismay replied, 'No, we'll be going all the
faster to get by it. Put the trouble behind us as quickly as
possible, that's what I always say.' "

---

[11]During the final forty-eight hours, a total of nine ice warnings were received. The most haunting of them came on April 13 at 6:00 P.M. when the
Titanic passed within sight of the partly crippled steamer *Rappahannock*.
Traveling whence the *Rappahannock* had come, the *Titanic* received word
via Moss lamp that the London-bound steamer had damaged its rudder and
bow in heavy field ice and bergs. The *Titanic*'s bridge flashed a brief ac-
knowledgment and continued to hold the ship on course.

What must Smith have been thinking, she wondered, as Ismay waxed courageous and decided to charge FULL AHEAD through the ice?

EXCERPT FROM SECOND CABIN PASSEN-GER EDWINA TROUTT'S RECOLLECTIONS FOR BILL MACQUITTY AND WALTER LORD, NOVEMBER 11, 1958:

I was on deck when [the departing *Titanic*'s] collision with the *New York* was narrowly avoided. A sailor standing nearby was the first to suggest the impending disaster with the remark: "There goes old Captain Smith again trying for a third time unlucky. He's already had two collisions!"

During a pre-expedition discussion with George Tulloch, we reviewed the near-collision with the *New York*. "In 1911," George reminded me, "the Royal Navy cruiser *Hawke* was struck by the *Olympic*, with Captain Smith in charge. Now, Charles, haven't you been told historically that Smith was a hot rod?"

"Yes," I said.

"And when the *Titanic* left the pier and headed out to sea, and missed colliding with the *New York*—haven't you been told that Captain Smith was hot-rodding?"

"Or that he just did not know how to handle these new ships; they were getting too big for Captain Smith."

"Right," George said, sadly. "Captain Smith—right?" And then, after a pause, he gave me another reminder: the *Hawke* and *New York* incidents took place as Smith was taking the ships out of port—same captain, same port-side pilot. "And who was really—really and officially—in charge in both situations?"

"The pilot . . ."

"In both situations, the pilot was in command of the ships because they were in his waters," George said. "Captain Smith was, under those conditions, the pilot's armchair assistant. And yet Smith, by reversing the engines as the *New York* snapped its mooring lines and drifted toward the *Titanic*, saved his ship from a collision on the way out.

"He was the one who, when a crisis loomed, took over for the pilot. So Captain Smith was neither a hot rod nor drunk with negligence."

I was not quite sure of that myself. "Twenty-three knots in the dark?" I shook my head. "Toward an ice field he knew lay ahead? I'm sorry, George, but the guy was clearly outrunning his headlights." And George asked me if I could really say who had his foot "on the gas pedal," and why. He reminded me that when the captain sat with Ismay and the Thayers at the dinner table on the evening of April 14, Smith again discussed the Marconigram ice warnings.[12]

"Don't you think that was a suggestion they ought to be slowing down?" George said. "It really gets difficult to figure out what the hell was going on there. By his own testimony, Ismay acknowledged that he had the gas pedal. He spoke of Chief Engineer Bell coming to his room all the time, and of telling Bell how many boilers to light. 'I told him how many revolutions I wanted,' said Ismay. Isn't that the same as speed?"

---

[12]Walter Lord comments, "George Tulloch brings up a valid point; there was some unusual behavior here. Captain Smith sat at the Thayers' table (with Ismay) on the way across. I never understood why he did that. It was his duty, almost, to sit at the captain's table and entertain the most prestigious of his passengers. But he did not. Mr. and Mrs. Thayer and the Ryersons were there when Smith discussed, again, speed and ice warnings."

"Yes," I said.

"Now, why would he be doing that if he wasn't the captain?" George asked.

According to Mrs. Ryerson, it had been decided by Sunday, April 14, that the ship would arrive in New York Tuesday night—almost a day early. The early arrival would have been a good headline for the managing director, demonstrating that his ship really was capable of superior performance, but it was a headline made possible by the lighting of extra boilers early in the voyage, an opportunity, George Tulloch suspected, arising from the higher energy through-put of what was, initially, an act of desperation.

The coal bunker fire might have worked more mischief than helping a life-saving bulkhead to fail; it created out of necessity a rate of speed that, once permanently adopted, became a prescription for disaster.

Leading Fireman Charles Hendrickson testified that the fire had burned for more than a week, ultimately requiring a dozen men working "round-the-clock" to put it out. He had heard both Chief Engineer Bell and Captain Smith speaking, on April 11 and on Friday, April 12, of increasing the ship's speed for a Tuesday night arrival, with the New York City fire department ready to assist.

"By the morning of April 13," George said, "both Smith and Ismay knew that they either arrived in New York and got the fire out—preferably Tuesday night, under cover of darkness, before the press could take any clear, daytime photos of the fire department's activities—or else the White Star Line's biggest effort was a disgrace."

He could imagine the Astors and the Cardezas: "You mean, you put me on that ship and you knew it was on fire before we left? I'll never sail this line again!"

"How would you like it," George asked, "if British Airways flew you on an aircraft with a burning engine, and it had been burning before you left? Would you fly that airline again?"

"So, even if no disaster had resulted from the fire itself—"

"The disaster was publicity, Charles, not fire. The fire wasn't—hopefully—going to get out of the boiler room. But if people found out about it . . . Well, as one of the firemen [J. Daly] said, they were instructed to make sure the passengers *did not* find out about it."

"And then, with the time they gained in their rush to New York . . ."

"Yeah," said George, "I guess they saw a chance to arrive early and turn a horrible management decision into a triumph. By all accounts, Ismay was determined to make the *Titanic*'s maiden voyage into a legend."

"And like King Midas, he got what he wished for. But Smith—do you really think he wasn't so arrogant after all? Do you really think he was afraid of the ice, seriously concerned about it?"

George became stern, almost angry. "Why else do you suppose he kept mentioning it to Ismay? Kept showing him Marconigrams—in front of people? It wasn't just the Ryersons and the Thayers—Lady Duff Gordon saw it, too."

But why, I wondered, did Smith behave toward his managing director as Groves of the *Californian* had behaved toward his captain? George had raised several possibilities, including the fact that Smith was retiring immediately after the voyage and, if he offended Ismay, could become a pariah in his own social circle—which was, in Edwardian times, a fate often more frightening than death. And, of course, Smith did not know, as we do, that the *Titanic* has sunk. It was still, to him, on the morning of April 14, 1912, something that might never happen.

"Groves and Smith," I said at last. "If either of them had taken the initiative. Either of them! Why did they just—"

"Why did your friends on the *Challenger* take the ship

up when they could plainly see that the ship and the launch tower were covered with ice?"

I had no answer. When I had seen video footage of icicles hanging from the tower that morning, I ended up missing the actual launch, because I knew they would never launch. *Knew* it.

"I'll tell you why," George said. "It was the chain of command. I think it is very clear that being honest in this world and questioning authority is a dangerous occupation. I think in the case of the *Titanic* it was as true then, in the age of the steam engine, as it is now, in the age of space-flight."

Make the voyage into a legend, George had lamented. He seemed to have a good grasp of the behaviors involved, and the extent to which egos and "everyday office politics" held command over human affairs. Years earlier, on a panel assembled to consider the possibility of crewed, interplanetary voyages, a man I had never met before, who had remained strangely silent throughout the proceedings, seemed to have gained the power of speech only when it came time to decide what to order for lunch. After twenty minutes, he was still debating the relative merits of a tuna sandwich over peanut butter and jelly (and vice versa) loudly and at length, with himself. A man whose specialty was Martian and Jovian weather patterns muttered something about "rectal-cranial inversions," and many laughed at "the funny little man," until a colleague called "the weather man" aside and explained that, as near as he could tell, the last time the funny man had made a clear decision about anything, he had firmed his resolve with the words, "Roger, you are go, *Challenger* . . ."

George was shaking his head. "History is full of good, competent men who in a moment of weakness did not follow their instincts, who did not take the hard road, who did not challenge their bosses when they saw a horrible decision handed down from above. And I guess sometimes it's easy to cross your fingers and hope nothing will go wrong, and usually it does not. Usually, no one gets hurt, whereas if you blow the whistle or refuse an order and you expect somebody to thank you, they're not going to. Maybe you'll save lives, maybe not; but you'll certainly get punished for stepping out of line. And yet Captain Smith did go up against Ismay on the day of the accident, and did try to slow him down."

"But it wasn't enough."

"Minus the gift of hindsight," George asked, "is it right to expect more than what he gave you? If he knew for a fact that fifteen hundred people were going to die, I'm sure he would have gladly confined Ismay to quarters and taken his lumps later. He was not a coward, and he certainly did not die like one. After the impact, he made every effort to keep the ship afloat as long as possible, and to get everyone off. Everyone except himself. And of course Ismay made *his* management decision. He found a lifeboat. And J. P. Morgan made *his* management decision."

"Morgan?" I asked. "Morgan didn't even sail on the *Titanic*!"

"Of course not. He canceled at the last minute. So did the other owners, Vanderbilt, on the 9th of April. And Lord Pirrie—he sent Thomas Andrews in his place. Now, what is your explanation of that?"

"Well," I ventured, "Lord Pirrie had been laid up in bed with a flu virus during the previous week, and—"

"Right," George said. "So had J. P. Morgan. So had almost anyone who was in a management position and who had thought about sailing on the maiden voyage—*and knew about the coal bunker fire*. They picked the ship up for sea trials on April 2, and when it arrived in Southampton the fire was already growing out of control. I can't state as a fact that this is why they took themselves off the passenger list, but Morgan took his art collection off as well—his art that had already been loaded for shipment to New York. I guess his art was sick, too."

George had allowed me to hold (in gloved hands) the aluminum megaphone from the debris field, very likely the same megaphone with which Smith had tried to call the lifeboats back. George would be putting it on display soon. "When school children come to see this," he said, "I don't want them going home and thinking that this man killed fifteen hundred people. That's not what happened here. What happened here is the age-old story of power. What happened here is simply this: The man who is looking out the cockpit window, and who knows better, can't do something because the chain of command is just too distorted. And Ismay can't do much because he's afraid of Morgan. And Morgan can't do much because he's afraid of publicity—"

"Then it's not much different from Michael Smith sitting at the helm of the *Challenger*," I said. "NASA management knew that the president was scheduled to give his State of the Union Address that night. Below Smith, on the mission specialist deck, waited America's first teacher-astronaut. The 'teacher in space' program had been *created* by President Reagan, and he was sure to mention the orbiting classroom in his speech, so it was a publicity coup that was not to be missed . . . and if there happened to be ice on the rocket, then ignore the ice . . . just this once . . . ignore the ice . . ."

"So Michael Smith found himself in the same position as Captain Edward J. Smith," said George. "Management issued a command to 'Get this ship off the pier, because they expect us in New York.' So, therefore, you're right: Neither man was in the chain of command, really. They did the best they could with a very tough situation, and what they have given us is a very clear example of 'Don't do what management or authority tells you to do if you're looking out that cockpit window and you know it doesn't feel right.'"

"Put another way: Before you relinquish your common sense to a group of people in control, you'd better jolly well understand that people can behave far more badly in a group than they can alone."

"With far worse results," George added. "That's when havoc strikes: when people are unwilling to question authority, to take the difficult path and instead they follow their leaders, even when it feels wrong."

"Germany in 1936 . . ."

George nodded. "Be willing to take the hard road. *That's* the lesson I want the children to bring home from the *Titanic*. Not that God can kill you with an iceberg if you cross the ocean. What they should be learning is that we must never follow people into anything we believe may lead to evil."

9

Dead Calm

I've seen worse.

> —EDWINA TROUTT, *TITANIC* SURVIVOR, DURING
> A STORMY CARIBBEAN CRUISE, IN RESPONSE TO A
> FELLOW PASSENGER'S QUERY, "ARE YOU WORRIED?"

A LENGTH OF clothesline tied in a noose. That is how it ended for *Titanic*'s Lookout Frederick Fleet, with a decision to hang himself from a post in his garden on the tenth day of January, 1965.

His obituary alleged that he had died as he had lived: in the shadow of the iceberg.

"Is there any more likes to have a go at me?" Fleet had shouted at examiners Findlay and Harrison, in response to questions about women left aboard the *Titanic* and how one manages not to see an iceberg until his ship has almost crashed upon it.

"Do you want to ask him anything more?" said the commissioner.

"Oh, no," said Harrison, and Fleet hollered, "A good job, too!"

BROOKHAVEN NATIONAL LABORATORY physicist Jim Powell had calculated, based upon the number of large, ship-destroying icebergs described by Captain Rostron of the

269

Carpathia, that the *Titanic* could have run through an average part of the ice field up to a hundred times without suf-
fering damage from anything bigger than a marginally
dangerous "growler," or a broad flat plain of pack ice.

Frederick Fleet reported to the commission that when
the sun came up the next morning he could see, out to the
horizon, about fifty large icebergs, some of them over two
hundred and fifty feet tall.[1] He spoke of an oversight at the
port in Southampton that had left the crow's nest lookouts
without binoculars and, though he had been told by the
bridge at 10:00 P.M. to keep a sharp lookout for icebergs,
he explained that in order to do so, one needed to scan the
horizon through binoculars—"constantly."

He was certain that the larger bergs would have been
seen as multiple little nubs against the star-lit horizon
while they were still miles away and the ship could be
called to a stop before it actually reached the field. There
was a pair of binoculars on the *Titanic*'s bridge, but the officer in charge had told Fleet they were not for the lookouts.

"Were you told," asked examiner Scanlan, "that there
were [no binoculars] intended for the lookout?"

"Yes," Fleet replied.

"Then you had to accept that as the provision of the
ship?"

"That is it."

"If you had complained," the examiner pressed, "would
you have got yourself into trouble with your superior officers?"

"No," Fleet said. "I should have been told the same, I
suppose."

Scanlan asked him directly why, if it was necessary for
him to have binoculars, he did not challenge his superior

---

[1]Fleet's iceberg count was corroborated by Rostron of the *Carpathia*.

officers by saying, "I am told to keep a sharp lookout for ice and I have no binoculars."

Fleet had no answer.

THE EXTRA BINOCULARS were found, eventually—but like everything else about that night, too late to be of any assistance. Somewhere aboard *Titanic*, there existed an adequate supply. George Tulloch began finding them in the debris field eighty-two years later.

"BUT EVEN WITHOUT binoculars," Jim Cameron pointed out, "the odds are always in favor of the first large iceberg you see passing hundreds of feet away on your port or starboard side, or you'll see a couple of little growlers passing below and reflecting the ship's lights—they're at least a hundred times more numerous than actual icebergs, and when you see them you know you are approaching an ice field and that it is time to stop.

"Who would ever have believed that the first sign of ice would be a giant berg aimed right at the bow?" and then, unaware of the echo from Bill MacQuitty, he said, "It makes you think about fate."

IF FLEET AND Rowe's estimate that the pinnacles stood just above the forecastle—"about as high as the boat deck"—was accurate, then the *Titanic*'s meeting with the iceberg was a little less likely than Powell and Cameron had supposed, and a little more fateful, and a little meaner as well.

Captain Rostron had measured icebergs standing up to two hundred and fifty feet above the water. One of those giants could easily have been seen from the *Titanic*'s crow's nest a mile away, or more, eclipsing the stars—even without the aid of binoculars. The iceberg Frederick Fleet saw stood only eighty-five feet high; it was just large enough to inflict lethal wounds, just small enough not to be seen above the horizon until it lay within a radius smaller than the *Titanic*'s length.

"The first seconds of the disaster are rather difficult to sort out," said Walter Lord. "We have, from a mere handful of survivors' accounts, a series of rapidly changing orders being sent down from the bridge, but there is little agreement on the sequence of the orders, save that they included, very early on, STOP ENGINES. The matter is further complicated by a tendency for events that must have encompassed all of two or three seconds to be stretched almost into the realm of minutes when recalled."

Nowhere did the elasticity of time in a moment of distress seem to create more confusion than in the testimony of Quartermaster Hitchens, who claimed that during the interval between Frederick Fleet's ringing of the crow's nest bell and the impact with the iceberg, he had noticed, while turning the ship's wheel as hard as he could, that the *Titanic*'s compass veered fully two points to port.[2]

Taking "Hitchens' number" at face value, investigators ran the *Titanic*'s sister ship *Olympic* up to twenty-two and one-half knots and observed how long she took to turn two points to port with the helm HARD OVER. The answer came in at thirty-seven seconds, and that became the official accounting of the time elapsed between Fleet's sighting of the iceberg and the collision.

"But it's hardly so simple as taking Hitchens' number as gospel," said Walter. "When you really sit down and read the accounts of witness after witness, paying close attention to the sequence of events, you begin to get a sense that it was considerably less than thirty-seven seconds. And before we even get to the sequence itself, you have to wonder if Hitchens really did have his eyes fixed on the instru-

---

[2] A point can mean any of 32 compass directions, 11 degrees, 15 minutes apart. Therefore, the *Titanic*, according to Hitchens, had swerved 22 degrees between the sounding of the bells and the collision.

ments at both instants: the ringing of the bell and the crash. He *shouldn't* have been looking at the compass while Murdoch ordered him to turn the wheel with all his might and the berg began to loom out of the dark. No one knew there was even going to *be* a crash until it happened."

The first indication that anything out of the ordinary was about to occur was when three bells sounded from the crow's nest, followed only a second or two later by the ringing of the telephone on the bridge.

Sixth Officer James Moody lifted the receiver and said, "What did you see?" and Fleet replied, "Iceberg right ahead!"

That should have been enough for Moody, but he had to repeat it: "Thank you. Iceberg right ahead. Thank you," and then he announced it to the bridge.

Murdoch, who had been standing on the starboard wing bridge, was already rushing in and shouting an order to Hitchens, possibly having sighted the iceberg simultaneously with Fleet.

Murdoch next pulled the engine room switch to STOP and pulled down the lever that closed the watertight doors. The two switches were located side by side; and Hitchens was still turning the wheel hard over and Murdoch was still pulling the watertight door switch when the crash came. A moment later, Captain Smith came striding onto the bridge.

Fireman George Beuchamp was standing within ten feet of Mr. Barrett, in boiler room six's number ten coal bunker beneath the first smokestack, when the impact came, "just like the roar of thunder," and immediately after the shock, he heard the telegraph ringing STOP. Fred Barrett thought the STOP order came just before the crash, but he was certain that the crash came before the dampers could be shut, meaning that there was almost no time at all between the alarm and the impact.

Trimmer Patrick Dillon noticed a lag of at least two seconds between the ringing of the engine room telegraph and "a slight shock," apparently reverberating up from the keel. He was standing in boiler room two, between the second and third smokestacks. The lag time, relative to what Beuchamp and Barrett saw and felt beneath the first smokestack, is consistent with telegraph messages racing, at lightspeed, an iceberg that was moving between Barrett and Dillon at only thirty-eight feet per second. Still . . . the interval between the signal and the crash was, even from Dillon's perspective, exceedingly small.

In the forecastle, Able Seaman Joseph Scarrott heard the three bells and felt the jar. To him, at least five minutes seemed to have passed between the two events, yet he rushed out to the forward well deck in time to see the iceberg passing behind the bridge: "I saw a large quantity of ice on the starboard side on the forewell deck, and I went and looked over the rail and I saw an iceberg. It seemed the ship was acting on her helm and we had swung clear of the berg—her starboard quarter was going as if to make a circle around it."

Walter Lord had always believed Scarrott accurately reported to the examiners what he thought he saw, but there was no way that five minutes had passed between Fleet's sighting of the berg and its impact against the starboard bow. Given this implausibility, the likelihood that a ship the size of the *Titanic* could have responded to a turn of the wheel with such apparent agility seemed, to the historian, equally implausible. "A motorboat—yes," said Walter. "A 46,000-ton liner—not possible."

I was not so sure about the implausibility of a rapid turn. Scarrott's timing of events—the iceberg still very near the bow, and the ship already changing direction—might have been more real than his perception of seconds and minutes suggested.

Having survived two plane crashes, two spectacular tornadoes at close range, a temperamental volcano, and the odd "unscheduled energetic disassembly," I knew from experience that when the brain shifts into maximum overdrive, snatching up every available sight and sound and spreading them out on the floor of the skull to find a way out, seconds are stretched to their most fascinating limits and time itself becomes so strangely elastic and beautiful that if you knew in advance that you were about to walk away unscathed, you would actually look forward to the adventure.[3]

This illusion of time dilation gives rise to a clever ruse, used by lawyers to attack the credibility of witnesses once the cause of the dilation effect reaches the courtroom. The attorney will typically ask, "Well, when you saw the defendant's car racing through the intersection, how long did it take to hit you?" And the victim replies, "Oh, about fifteen seconds," whereupon the attorney smiles indulgently and says, "Count off fifteen seconds, please."

Working from the likelihood that Scarrott had recalled accurately the motion of the deck beneath his feet at the moment he saw the iceberg, and that only his sense of time (between bells and bangs) had been distorted, I went again to letters and inquiry proceedings to see if testimony tended to refute or corroborate the able seaman's impression that the ship had somehow responded to danger with the apparent agility of a motorboat.

---

[3]When I was twelve years old and an approaching tornado lifted off the ground and passed directly overhead, carrying away several small trees, I was absolutely amazed to discover that there was time to sightsee, despite the fact that the actual passover could only have lasted two or three seconds. I have had a strange love of tornadoes ever since. Similarly, some who survived the *Titanic* seem to have become "action-adventure junkies"—which explains, perhaps, how fashion reporter Edith Russell chose to join soldiers in the trenches during World War I, where she became one of the world's first war correspondents. Others brought with them the lesson "never sweat the small stuff"—which Walter Lord believes explains how a disproportionately high number of *Titanic* survivors lived beyond the age of 100.

Jack Thayer was about to step into bed at the moment of impact, and suddenly he noticed that he seemed to sway slightly. "I immediately realized," he wrote in a memoir for his family, "that the ship had veered to port as though she had been gently pushed."

"She started to go to port while I was at the telephone," Frederick Fleet reported.

"Is that right?" Sir Robert Findlay asked. "The ship was going round to port while you were still on the telephone?"

"Yes," said Fleet.

Second Officer Lightoller told the examiners, "Practically at the same time that [Fleet] struck the bell, I noticed the ship's head moving under the helm."

Lightoller's conclusion was that the ship had started responding to the helm even as Moody, still on the phone, repeated to Fleet, "Iceberg right ahead," even as Murdoch shouted for Hitchens to turn the wheel, even before Hitchens had actually turned the wheel . . . The *Titanic*, it seemed, was responding to the helm before the helm responded . . . it seemed so, but it could not possibly have been so.

The only reasonable explanation, if these accounts bore currency, was that the ship did not alter course in response to the helm, but in response to the iceberg. This would mean that the *Titanic* struck, and was being shoved gently to port, a very short time after the iceberg was sighted.

"Perhaps a shorter time than you think," Walter Lord emphasized. "It could not have been thirty-seven seconds of watching and waiting for the ship to turn away from the iceberg. It really does seem that once the three bells rang from the crow's nest, she was already hitting it—almost right away."

Between the ringing of the crow's nest bell and the impact, Captain Smith, whose quarters were adjacent to the map room and the bridge, had jumped out of bed and joined

Murdoch on the bridge. Considering the ice warnings discussed at the Thayers' table, Smith's first words to Murdoch—"What did we hit?"—struck Walter as rather amusing ("What else did he think they hit?"); but more importantly, it was impossible for the historian to believe that Smith would have required thirty-seven seconds to put on his slippers and reach the bridge—which was only a step through the door.

Fourth Officer Boxhall told examiner Asquite that a few minutes before the accident occurred, he had left the bridge for a cup of coffee, and was walking along the starboard boat deck, near Ismay's boat and the first smokestack, when he heard the three-bell warning. Quickening his pace toward the bridge, he saw Murdoch run from the starboard wing bridge and heard him order Hitchens to turn the wheel. He heard the engine room telegraph ring, and he had not quite reached the bridge by the time he felt the shock.

"How soon after you heard the bells did you feel the shock?" asked the examiner.

"Only a moment or two after," said Boxhall, emphasizing that he was almost on the bridge when the *Titanic* struck.

The first thing he noticed, when he actually reached the bridge, was that the engine telegraphs indicated FULL SPEED ASTERN.

"Was that immediately after the impact?" Asquite asked.

"Yes," said Boxhall. "And I saw Mr. Murdoch closing the [watertight] doors, then—pulling the lever."

"And did the captain then come out onto the bridge?"

"The captain was alongside me when I turned around."

"*There's* our critical time factor!" said Walter Lord. "Hitchens saw Boxhall come in, and Captain Smith was already out and the impact had already occurred by the time Boxhall reached the bridge. Boxhall was walking near boat

A when he heard the three bells, followed shortly but still before he could get to the bridge, by the crash."

We then mapped the distance out in Walter's living room: about forty feet (and probably less than forty feet) between the bells and the crash. Even with a recent leg injury, I was able to cover the distance in fewer than twenty seconds. Later (after the leg had healed), our re-enactment of Boxhall's walk came in under eight seconds.[4]

At twenty-two and one-half knots, the *Titanic* was moving at thirty-eight feet per second. Boxhall's walk suggests that the berg was sighted less than 380 feet away (at ten seconds), and probably within as few as 300 feet (at eight seconds).[5]

How, then, did Lookouts Frederick Fleet and Reginald Lee miss seeing the iceberg until it was within one-third the *Titanic*'s length?

"The Fates were all against us," Charles Lightoller said. He told Lord Mersey's investigators that at 11:00 P.M. on the night of the accident there were not even traces of a long wavelength swell on the sea—the first time he had ever seen such extreme calm in the North Atlantic. Even after the impact, the *Titanic* felt as steady and solid as an

---

[4]The next person to enter the bridge, about five or six seconds after Boxhall but in time to hear Murdoch reporting to Captain Smith that he had closed the watertight doors, and to actually see Murdoch working the lever, was Quartermaster Alfred Olliver. A competent observer (providing yet another description of the stern's breakaway), he reported to the American inquiry that, while still running along the boat deck from the compass tower, a grinding sound had reached him from far forward (from the forepeak, probably about five seconds before the iceberg passed the bridge), and the berg itself passed by on his right side, "just abaft of the bridge when I saw it." Its pointed top was "about the height of the boat deck . . . The top did not touch the [ship], but it was almost alongside of [the hull]—I saw only the tip of it, and it was not white, as I expected to see an iceberg. It was kind of a dark-blue hue."

[5]A knot is equal to one nautical mile per hour. A nautical mile is 6,076.12 feet long, as opposed to a statute or land mile 5,280 feet in length. In nauti-

island, and it did not occur to the second officer until much later that this stubborn illusion of calm and safety had created the perfect formula for calamity. Normally, ocean swells, even those with half-mile wavelengths and heights of only three or four inches, create a static glow at the base of an iceberg, making it visible more than a half mile away.

Under such unusual conditions, in the absence of both swells and moonlight, the first hint of danger ahead would have been a dark shape moving against the stars, causing them to wink out. The horizon that night was a vivid black line against starlight, and everything below that dividing line, including the ice, was also black.

Had the iceberg stood as tall as some of the giants reported by Captain Rostron, it would have towered over the crow's nest and begun eclipsing stars more than two miles ahead of Fleet and Lee. Anything shorter than ninety feet was visible from the crow's nest only as black silhouetted against black, until, barely more than three hundred feet away, its tip rose above the horizon. The iceberg the *Titanic* struck stood about eighty-five feet tall, and no one will ever know how many icebergs of equal or lesser height passed beyond a three hundred-foot radius of the crow's nest prior to 11:40 P.M., on both port and starboard, neither observed nor observable.

It is often said that even a clock that is not running will be right twice each day. The one thing Lord of the *Californian* got right was, once he received warnings of ice ahead, to place extra lookouts *below* the crow's nest, giving them a vantage point from which an eighty-five-foot berg would protrude above the horizon and begin eclipsing stars at a substantially greater radius. This gave his ship something the *Titanic* did not have: maximum response time.

---

cal velocity, the *Titanic* was moving at 38 feet per second (not the 33 feet per second derived from statute miles). This confusing system of measurement, called the "British system" was long ago abandoned by the British (in favor of metric) and persists only in America.

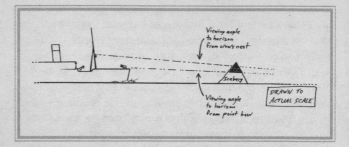

The timing of such events as "Boxhall's walk" suggests that the iceberg was not sighted until it was well within the *Titanic*'s own length, and renders academic all arguments about the ship's rudder size or Murdoch's "wrong turn"—there was simply no time to react. According to eyewitness accounts, the iceberg's peak stood level with the boat deck, making it just short enough not to be seen from the crow's nest until it loomed in front of Fleet and Lee like a giant flyswatter. Other bergs in the ice field stood 250 feet high, and would have been visible miles away as dark nubs on the horizon had the lookouts not been denied binoculars. Alternatively, had Captain Smith, like Captain Lord of the *Californian*, placed additional lookouts at a lower viewing angle on the point bow, a boat-deck-high berg would have stood above them, would have risen more than a third of a mile away against the starry horizon, and would have provided nearly a minute's response time.

Historian George Behe, in his 1997 book, *Titanic: Safety, Speed and Sacrifice*, uncovered a survivor's account that not only supported Captin Lord's strategy of stationing lookouts at the lowest possible viewing angle, but also suggested that under the *Californian* protocol, the *Titanic*'s lookouts should have seen ice in time to avoid catastrophe even without the aid of binoculars.

At approximately 11:00 P.M., more than half an hour before impact, third class passenger Neshan Krekorian actually saw icebergs passing by. He shared quarters with five other Armenian emigrants who, troubled by cabin heating problems, had opened the portholes—which made the room too cold for Krekorian, and kept him awake. When he rolled out of bed to close the portholes, he saw "icebergs in the water of a comparatively large size." The cabin was located in the bow, four decks (and forty feet) below the level of the forecastle, fully nine decks (and ninety feet) below Fleet and Lee in the crow's nest. The room's lights were out at the time, meaning that Krekorian's eyes were, like the eyes of the crow's nest lookouts, night adapted. Even so, he described the bergs as "hardly perceptible"—shadowy, due to their apparent distance from the ship. On April 25, 1912, he told the Hamilton Ontario *Spectator*, "About 10:30 P.M. [I] laid down on my bunk to retire for the night. After I had been there for a while I noticed that our quarters were getting colder. I got up and looked to see if any of the portholes were open and I found that two of them were. As I was closing them I noticed many icebergs in the water of a comparatively large size. I thought little about them, however, despite the fact that they were the first I had ever seen, as they were hardly perceptible from the distance they were from the boat. I then went back to my bunk, and the next thing that I remember was when I felt the vessel jar from stem to stern."

And so it came to pass that the only survivor who was positioned low enough to see the danger did not understand its significance and, after deciding that the first icebergs he had ever seen were merely interesting, went back to bed without telling anyone.

Had Captain Smith followed Stanley Lord's example and posted extra lookouts on the *Titanic*'s forecastle, they would have stood fifty feet lower than Fleet and Lee. Under this condition, a berg standing eighty-five feet tall could be seen creeping above the horizon, against the stars, at least a quarter mile away. Thus would the *Titanic* have gained thirty seconds of response time and, by everything Walter Lord and I had learned, only two or three seconds (or feet) of maneuvering space could easily have determined whether or not the fire-embrittled bulkhead between boiler rooms five and six fell before help could arrive.[6]

But the *Titanic* had no more than ten seconds—total. Boxhall testified that he had heard Murdoch explain to Smith, "I hard-a-starboarded and reversed the engines, and I was going to hard-a-port around it, but she was too close. I couldn't do any more." Lord Mersey's examiners, concluding that Murdoch had far more than ten seconds, suggested that the first officer could indeed have done more had he thought more quickly. Rather than attempt to steer away from the berg, it was suggested that he should simply have done nothing, and let the ship strike the ice head-on. With only the first two or three watertight compartments of the forecastle taking the brunt of the impact, and rupturing, the *Titanic* should, in theory, have continued to float.[7]

Boxhall's observations, and Fleet's, and Scarrott's suggest otherwise. Although Murdoch was the officer in command of the bridge when havoc struck, and though he probably carried a horrible guilt with him to the grave, there was essentially nothing left for him to do by the time the bell rang. The iceberg was sighted so late that in order for him to strike head-on, he would have had to steer, and there was no time for steering, no time for choices.

Evidently, the *Titanic* and the iceberg met in precisely

---

[6]Had the berg inflicted only fractionally less damage, the *Titanic*, though foundering, should still have been afloat when the first rescue ships arrived: the *Carpathia* and the *Californian*. Had the bridge been given just a few seconds more, history might have seen Captain Lord knighted alongside Captain Rostron.

[7]In actual practice, the "armchair second-guessers" were forgetting that most of an iceberg's mass lies beneath the sea surface, producing an unseen, random typography as indicated, perhaps, by flooding from beneath the *Titanic*'s floor plates, as witnessed in boiler room four. As an example of how far the subsurface typography can extend, during the 1950s Seaman Albert Petry was aboard the U.S. Coast Guard ice breaker *Half Moon* when it approached a "small" iceberg, standing about eighty-five feet above the

the configuration toward which they were headed at the moment Frederick Fleet saw the first star wink out on the horizon. And Fleet would always remember the curious detachment with which Moody had responded to his call: "Thank you. Iceberg right ahead. Thank you."

During the interval between his ringing of the bell and Moody's last "thank you," Fleet watched the silhouette swallow dozens of stars. Within only two or three seconds, it had come near enough—

(*What did you see?*)

—to catch the rays of the ship's mast light and deck lights and throw them back at him. Two seconds more and it was almost eighty feet nearer, looming larger and brighter, spreading and glistening in a billion points of backscattered light.

Then, as if guided by the hand of God, just as the berg seemed certain to strike the starboard bow and as Fleet, still on the phone, braced himself for a crash, the ship seemed to answer her helm and swing to port at the last possible instant.

Fleet craned his neck over the nest's starboard rail and during the next second and one-half he watched the ice glide the length of the well deck and disappear behind the bridge.

"Missed," said Lee.

"Yes," Fleet agreed. "A very close shave."

"I mean, a *mist*," Lee said, almost at a hysterical pitch.

---

sea. Nine hundred feet off (which he had assumed to be a safe distance), Petry's sonar revealed that the *Half Moon* was over one of the berg's undersea ledges. He called, "Back out of this!" knowing that if the berg chose that moment to flip over, his ship could disappear without even a "Mayday." In actual practice, the second-guessers had no way of knowing that the *Titanic* was traveling at approximately the same speed with which its bow section struck the sea floor, and might actually have received similar damage from a head-on collision with ice, sinking even before the first lifeboat could be launched.

"Did you see it? That's why we didn't see the ice until we were right at it—a mist came up just before the ice."

"There was no mist," Fleet said.

"A haze," Lee insisted. "It came up suddenly—just for a few seconds, and it blocked the ice from view."

Fleet looked aft again and saw officers peering over the starboard wing bridge, along the side of the ship. The stars were clear all the way to the knife-edge of the horizon. Lee was right about one thing: In the morning, Smith and Murdoch would demand an answer from them, explaining how they had managed to miss seeing an entire mountain of ice until it was almost too close to be avoided, almost close enough to scrape off the *Titanic*'s paint.

There went any chance of promotion, Fleet warned himself. *Any* chance—forever. And on the heels of that cheery thought came the realization that he might be lucky to keep his job at all, especially if his mate kept jabbering about a phantom haze, so plainly a lie that no one else anywhere on the *Titanic* would have seen it.

"Good plan, Lee," Fleet said at last, and he looked up at the dome of stars and asked himself, *God almighty, how can this night possibly get any worse?*

Afterword: Their Fates

Thomas Andrews was standing aft in the smoking room when the *Titanic* broke in two and the fourth smokestack canted toward him. Though his body was never found, objects from the room, including stained glass windows and patterned floor corking, are scattered within a 500-foot radius of the stern. Agustus Weikman (the ship's barber and a boat A survivor) reported meeting Mr. Andrews shortly before midnight in the bow section of third class. According to Weikman, the designer was, along with the baker, one of the few who gave any thought to the steerage passengers. Finding the decks below the forecastle crowded with husbands and wives, Andrews delayed his return to the bridge and passed the word that everyone must evacuate immediately to the top deck. Irish immigrant Dan Buckley was among those passengers ordered to the well deck by Andrews. They were the lucky ones. Minutes later, many of those still in the bow were sheperded by sailors and stewards up Scotland Road to E deck aft and locked in. THS historian Paul J. Quinn has noted that most of the Andrews evacuees were able to climb from the forward well deck to the boat deck.

Emily Badman had left everything she was bringing with her, to start a new life in America, in two suitcases under her bunk. In 1912, sending a Marconigram message was considered to be an exotic luxury, and could easily cost the average wage earner a week's salary—*per word*. Consequently, while first-class passenger George Rheims could afford to send entire sentences from the *Carpathia*—"Meet me dock with $200 underwear cap big coat. Am well but feet slightly frozen—" Emily, using all the money she had in the world, was able to pay Cottam and Bride for the transmission of only two words to anxious relatives in England: "Quite safe." Rarely in history have so few words meant so much.

"*The BIG Piece*," recovered from the *Titanic*'s debris field in 1998, stands three stories tall and, based upon Harland and Wolff naval architect David Livingston's analysis of hull plate and porthole patterns prior to raising, was identified as coming from the area of cabins C-86 to C-88, two decks above Chief Baker Charles Joughin's bunk on the port side. After the hull section was placed facedown on the deck of the recovery ship, Dr. Livingston noticed a special web plate attached to one of the ribs and, using detailed Harland and Wolff plating plans, concluded that the "*The BIG Piece*" could also have come from cabins C-79 to C-81 on the starboard side (all apparently unoccupied during the voyage). As for the detailed plans of the *Titanic*, long said to have existed as one original copy that went down with Thomas Andrews' stateroom A-36, and therefore never available to the American and British inquiries, it turns out that there was concern, back in 1912, about lawyers using the plans "to concoct some sort of structural defect case" if actual blueprints could be found. Hence, Ismay and Morgan blamed Andrews for bringing the plans out to sea and sinking them with him. In reality, they remained sealed in a shipyard vault until the expedition of 1996.

The recovery of artifacts from the *Titanic*, and their display in museums, is at this point in history (when it is easy to forget that one day the expeditions themselves will be the substance of history and archaeology), a controversial subject. For my own part, I have to say that had we never recovered live rusticles (which, just for a start, are teaching us how our immune systems were evolved), several potentially life-saving medicines would not now be under development. Nor would we even know that the rusticles are "alive," with the result that our universe would be a little less knowable, a little less fascinating, and a little less beautiful.

As for explorer/salvor George Tulloch, my most lasting impression of his operation goes back to the 1996 expedition, when I wanted to recover three objects on and near the stern. Three pieces of thin, rippled metal seemed to have preserved additional clues bearing on the downblast hypothesis, but George had announced that he would be raising only about twenty new objects—only as many as he knew his curators could handle—and he was sticking by that decision. I admired the decision, despite the fact that it made my own research a little more difficult.

I still cannot bring myself to touch items of clothing, either at the *Titanic* or at Washington, D.C.'s Holocaust Memorial Museum. We humans are visual and tactile creatures, which explains why objects have the power to carry us back across time, and to touch our souls. I have held the clarinet Howard Irwin brought aboard the *Titanic*, and at the Holocaust Museum, I have touched the violin that Henry Rosner played at parties given by Oskar Shindler for the Nazis he pretended to befriend. *Titanic* and *Treblinka* both lie in that gray area between oral history and archaeology, when survivors can still contribute details. Both places provide signposts for the future: "Help us not to kill people this way again, and again." In museum displays can be seen an actual part of a barracks . . . an actual piece of hull . . . children's toys . . . victims' cards and personal letters . . . and people can be heard to say, "The shoes—I can't forget the shoes."

Helen Churchill Candee was both liked and disliked when she sailed on the *Titanic*, owing to the popularity of her recent book, *How Women May Earn a Living*, in which she presented practical advice on "how to get along very well in life without a man." She wrote this book after a marriage-turned-prison-sentence, and the resulting vicious divorce that left her penniless with two small children whom she supported by becoming a journalist. Her message of independence for the working woman was so well received that it became one of the century's first international best sellers, allowing Helen to cross the Atlantic in a first-class cabin. Two years after the *Titanic*, she joined the Red Cross in Italy, during the start of World War I. A decade after that, she was living in Beijing, where she became involved in the Chinese Civil War on the side of the Nationalists against the Communists, sending periodic dispatches from the front lines to the *New York Times*. Helen Candee was nearly seventy years old at this time. After being decorated by the King of Cambodia for her book about the lost city of Angkor, she eventually returned to her summer home in Maine, where she died in 1949 at the age of ninety.

Fireman Samuel Collins, who told Mrs. Frank Goldsmith that he intended to "open the eyes of scores of people" at the British inquiry, continued to correspond with Mrs. Goldsmith, who survived with only her son. According to young Frankie, "Sam Collins was a grand person, who had notions for a while of becoming my stepfather." It did not work out as Frankie had hoped, but Mr. Collins had given his mother a crewman's tunic button—which she made into a hat pin and wore for as long as they were fashionable.

Frankie was ten at the time of the sinking. He remembered his father saying, "So long, Frankie, see you later," as Frankie was about to be lowered into collapsible C. Aboard the *Carpathia*, Mrs. Goldsmith left Frankie under the "watchful" eye of Sam Collins, who had shown her son the huge stoking rooms on the *Titanic* and to whom Frankie had taken an immediate liking. Mrs. Goldsmith asked Mr. Collins to keep Frankie's mind occupied "on this ship full of mourners," to divert him as often and as much as possible from thoughts of his father's whereabouts. It would take the boy a half year to stop expecting, every day, that Daddy would walk through the door, keeping his promise, "See you later." Even as an adult, he sometimes felt as if Daddy might suddenly step up behind him.

Bound for New York, Sam Collins made Frankie an honorary member of *Carpathia*'s crew, on the condition that he survived the rite of passage: to drink a Bombay Oyster in a single gulp (the "oyster" was a mixture of raw egg, vinegar, and water).

Until his death at age eighty, Frankie still considered himself part of the *Carpathia*'s crew. On April 15, 1983, the U.S. Coast Guard, in addition to its annual commemorative wreath, scattered Frankie's ashes over the site where father and son had last seen each other, seventy-one years before. "See you later" became a promise kept.

Coal Trimmer Thomas Patrick Dillon, who assisted in the reopening of the watertight doors in the reciprocating engine room, and finally with the launching of boat four, later reported "some strange encounters" during the *Titanic*'s final minutes.

At 2:00 A.M., he found a steward still standing at his post deep inside the ship, serving free whiskey to passers-by. "Go on, lads!" the steward cried. "Drink up. She is going down."

"Don't mind if I do," Dillon replied. He and several other engine room workers joined with people from the third-class cabins and filled their glasses. "We got our share," Dillon said later.

He returned with his friends to the aft poop deck, just ahead of 2:10 A.M. One man had a strip of cigarette paper, another some tobacco. They made a single cigarette and passed it around, waiting for the end. Dillon was standing next to his friend, an oiler named Johnny Bannon, when the bulkhead in boiler room four collapsed and the bow began to plunge. There was no commotion on the port-side poop deck at all, he told the examiners. "They simply waited for death . . . I went down with the ship and was sucked down about two fathoms. Then I shoved myself off, and I seemed to get lifted up. When I came up again I saw the after part of the ship come up. Then she went down again and was finished."

At this point, there *was* panic—hundreds of people shouting and climbing on top of each other, trying in vain to get out of the water. Dillon swam away from the crowd, and though he would always remember their screams, he could recall nothing shouted articulately except for a man crying out, "Mother, mother." Being a Roman Catholic, Dillon took this to be a prayer, and joined in, as he swam, with prayers of his own: "Our Father" and "Hail Mary."

He then came across his friend Johnny Bannon, floating on an ornate slab of wood that, seen only in starlight, resembled a grating. There was room on the panel only for one to keep his upper body out of the freezing water, in the relatively safer freezing air.

"Cheer-o, Johnny," said Dillon, and Bannon replied, "I'm all right, Paddy."

Dillon said good-bye and swam off in the direction of a bright star. Johnny had said he thought he saw a flashlight under the star, and after a few minutes, Thomas Dillon came upon boat four. He wanted to go back for Johnny, but hypothermia had done its work. "Paddy" lapsed into unconsciousness as they dragged him into number four, and he lay until sunrise on the bottom of the boat, with a seaman and a passenger dead on top of him.

The Duff Gordons lived, for a while, in obscurity. Sir Cosmo never did recover from claims that he was a coward, but Lady Gordon was not content to remain in the shadows. As a fashion designer, she reported for *Harper's Bazaar*, inventing the word "chic," introducing slits in skirts for ease of movement. She also introduced the idea of presenting new collections on mannequins in store windows and, after hearing Helen Candee's account of Kent and the locket, invented pockets for women. Of herself, Lady Gordon wrote, "I have always had too much imagination . . . I do not think that, on the whole, it is good for a woman to have temperament. It is much better for her to be a vegetable, and certainly much safer."

Colonel Archibald Gracie, though rescued by collapsible B, was fatally wounded during the sinking of the *Titanic*; but he had one more book to write, and was determined not to die until he completed the manuscript. He retreated with his wife and daughter to Boeuchers Cottage in Long Beach, New York, and, throughout the summer of 1912, wrote *The Truth about the Titanic*, corresponding with survivors until early fall and compiling their accounts in exhaustive detail. He turned the manuscript in before Thanksgiving, and died a few days later.

The Grand Stairway, all five stories of it, apparently broke free and floated out through the *Titanic*'s crystal dome. There is some evidence (including the beam Jim Cameron's robot revealed in Lady Cardeza's stateroom) that the wooden tower underwent at least partial disintegration, but in order to lift out every trace of the crystal dome's glass and steel, a section at least two stories tall must have departed intact.

Because ships coming to the *Titanic*'s rescue were searching for lifeboats, and because all lifeboats were quickly accounted for, no one seems to have searched for what was probably the largest floating remnant of the liner. If it had drifted amongst the surrounding icebergs and pack ice, where ships were least likely to venture, any who climbed atop the wreckage on the morning of April 15, 1912, would have gone undiscovered, and in the absence of the sort of inter-ice search procedures that would have been initiated had even one of the lifeboats gone astray and been listed as missing, they would have frozen to death by nightfall.

In his testimony before Lord Mersey's commission, Able Seaman Joseph Scarrott said that when he went back to the wreck site with boat fourteen, he encountered, amongst bodies, what he believed to be a relatively small portion of the stairway. "Mr. Lowe decided to transfer the passengers that we had [into the other lifeboats], and go in the direction of the cries and see if we could save anybody else . . . When we got to where the cries were, we were amongst hundreds, I should say, of dead bodies floating in lifebelts, and the wreckage and bodies seemed to be all hanging in a cluster . . . we got two [people out of the water] as we pushed our way towards the wreckage, and as we got towards the center we saw one man there—I have since found out he was a [ship's] storekeeper. He was on top of a staircase; it seemed to be a large piece of wreckage anyhow which had come from some part of the ship. It was wood anyhow. It looked like a staircase. He was kneeling there as if he were praying, and at that same time he was calling for help. When we saw him we were about [fifteen yards] away—I'm sorry to say there were more bodies than there was wreckage—and it took us a good half hour to get that distance to that man through the bodies. We could not row the boat, we had to push them out of the way and force our boat up to this man. But we did not get close enough to get him right off—only just within reach of an oar. We put out an oar on the forepart of [our] boat and he got hold of it, and he managed to hold on, and we [walked him off his island] into the boat."

About a week after the sinking, the German liner *Bremen* passed through ice, wreckage, and a cluster of previously undiscovered bodies, only a few miles south of the position given for the *Titanic*'s sinking. "There was [a woman], fully dressed, with her arms tight around the body of a shaggy dog that looked like a St. Bernard," wrote passenger Joanna Stunke. "The bodies of three men in a group, all clinging to one steamer chair, floated by—we could see the white life preservers of many more dotting the sea all the way to the iceberg . . . The scene moved everyone on board to the point of tears, even the officers making no secret of their emotion."

Two days later, the steamer *Minia* arrived to recover the bodies. On May 5, 1912, First Officer James Adams wrote to a friend, "We are now on our way to Halifax after a job somewhat out of the usual." His ship had recovered, along with bodies, planks of carved oak believed ever since to have come from the after-first-class stairway, but far more likely to be representative of the Grand Stairway itself. They had found, among the scattered deck chairs and planks, millionaire Charles Hayes, who at dinner, on that last night, had inexplicably raised his glass and proclaimed "that the time has come for the greatest and most appalling of all disasters at sea."

The *Minia*'s carpenter recovered more than two hundred pounds of wood, some of it displaying the distinctive carved-leaf pattern of the first-class stairways. He fashioned much of the wood into commemorative tables and chess boards, and brought other pieces to the cemetery for the *Titanic*'s dead in Halifax. The planks are displayed in a memorial library nearby.

"Most of the [bodies we found] were members of the ship's crew," wrote Adams. "I have no doubt there are many more still afloat, but they are getting . . . widely scattered now . . . We covered an area of about sixty miles square . . . The temperature of the water was 34 degrees Fahrenheit, so the bodies were well preserved but they are gradually nearing the Gulf Stream where the water is nearly 60 degrees, and when they get there they will soon decompose. It was a terrible disaster, but only . . . what may happen again so long as there is a demand for passengers and mails to be rushed across the Atlantic in the shortest possible time."

Mrs. Henry B. Harris said she cried for two years after losing Henry, until her tear ducts "dried up" and she never cried again. In 1929, she finally decided that she could try her luck at sea again without fearing disaster, and while in Egypt she received a cable telling her to come home at once because the stock market had crashed, a depression was setting in, and her business manager was in a state of collapse.

When Walter Lord met her, she was living in a small room in 1977 Broadway in Manhattan (at Fifty-third Street), where she "brewed the best tea and had the cheeriest disposition of anyone in the whole city." She became Walter's personal favorite of the *Titanic*'s survivors, telling him that she often "wished I didn't know now what I didn't know then," but also driving home the message that most of the big annoyances that bother us in life are really of just trifling importance. Compared to losing a man so loving that "he spoiled me for any other man in the world," even the Great Depression, which eventually left her homeless, was "just one of life's challenges . . . you simply live through it, and adapt to it, and try to grow stronger and more sensible through it."

But a part of her was still down there on the abyssal plains, with the as-yet-undiscovered wreckage, and when a woman once asked her if it was true that she had been saved from the *Titanic*, she replied, "No."

"Since then I have often wondered," she wrote in a notebook. "I have tried through the years to make it a night to forget; otherwise I would not have had the will to live."

Oiler Walter Hurst was called to the British inquiry but was never asked to testify—"I'm sure," he wrote in a 1955 letter to Walter Lord, "because I spoke of the [lifeboats] leaving half empty." He added that the White Star Line had paid the crew only up to 2:20 A.M., April 15, docking him the cost of his sea kit. "Had it not been for the generosity of The Seamen's Mission in New York," he wrote, "I would have come home half naked—as my clothes were put to dry in the *Carpathia*'s engine room and got lost."

J. Bruce Ismay lost his position as managing director of the White Star Line, and became a pariah in Edwardian society. Put another way (by Ashley, age four), "He was bad and he got a big time-out."

Chief Baker Charles Joughin developed a legendary "tolerance" for alcohol after his adventure aboard the *Titanic*. When Walter Lord spoke with him in 1955, he said of himself, "Retired now at seventy-seven. Very comfortable and not even harkening for a sight of salt water."

Captain J. J. Anderson, who as a young seaman had sailed with Joughin on an American ship during the prohibition period, recalled, "Joughin still worshipped at the shrine of Bacchus when I knew him and while the ship's bottled goods were not available he made up for lack by having a small still in an unused locker, as I well remember for I helped him run off a few batches myself." He added that Joughin, who believed that whiskey had saved him from freezing to death after he swam away from the *Titanic*, was nevertheless rattled by a deep chill when he arrived aboard the *Carpathia*. Rather than have the ship's surgeon look him over, he sought out the ship's bakery and convinced the staff there to thaw him out in the best way he knew. As Joughin expressed it, "They popped me in an oven like one of me own pies!"

Fireman George Kemish noted that his pay was five pounds per month at the time of the *Titanic*'s sinking (roughly $450 adjusted for year 2000 dollars). "A promise from the White Star Line of a job for life," he wrote in a letter dated June 19, 1955, from Southampton, England, "but I have never had anything from them. I have had long unemployment at times, and some very hard times, at present. I work as a fitter's mate—when I can get work. [But] never mind. I suppose I am lucky to be here at all."

Second Officer Charles Herbert Lightoller performed bravely if not competently on the night the *Titanic* went down. It seems likely that he helped the ship to sink more quickly by ordering a gangway door opened in the port bow, thus converting Scotland Road into a canal running toward E deck aft. Still in his thirties, Lightoller was a reasonably young man in 1912, not unlike Winston Churchill, whose exploits early in the century were equally ludicrous. By the time World War II broke out, Lightoller had become a man of such superior skill and seamanship that, using only a sixty-foot boat (which arrived in England shrapneled and machine-gunned practically to splinters), he was able to rescue 130 men from the Nazi occupation of Dunkirk.

Captain Stanley Lord remains an enigma. By all accounts, trying to arouse curiosity in this man was like beating a dead horse (no get up and go). He was, however, eventually promoted. Evidently, in the Ismay line, one could fail upward. Stanley Lord did attempt through legal means to challenge historian Walter Lord's conclusion that the would-be rescue ship *Californian* had been agonizingly near to the foundering *Titanic*. Captain Lord's own, firsthand attempt to refute the evidence was winnowed down ultimately to a single point: On the last page of chapter nine, in the first edition of *A Night to Remember*, the captain insisted that it was to be made crystal clear in all future editions that he slept fully clothed in his uniform, not in pajamas and not partially clothed, while the *Titanic* sank nearby.

Michel Navatril, though only four years old in 1912, retained vivid recollections of the entire voyage, right down to such details as the fried eggs he had eaten one morning as the ocean passed by the dining saloon window. When he and his brother were reunited with their mother, the *New York Evening Journal* protested that the boys should have been adopted by a wealthy American family, rather than returned to a hopeless future with their poor Italian mother. Michel's younger brother became an architect but received lingering and ultimately fatal wounds when he joined the French Resistance against Nazi occupation during World War II. Michel obtained his Ph.D. in 1952 and taught philosophy at the University of Montpellier.

I remember him telling us in 1996 that his father would soon return to sing him to sleep one last time, at the hour of his death—sing for him the old folk song Michel remembered from earliest childhood: "If I could make a perfect day for you, I'd give you a morning golden and new . . ." Michel sang the song for us in French and a couple of years later, a friend dragged me to what I had resigned myself to as a "silly" movie about an old man who sings to a little pig named Babe. When I heard the tune, without having any idea at the moment why, I burst into tears. And still, I find it difficult to watch the scene in which Mr. Hogget sings Babe back to health, and to keep my eyes dry.

In February 2001, Michel fell into a deep and everlasting sleep; and it is easy to believe that Daddy came to sing for him, one last time.

Louise "Kink" Pope was, like Michel Navatril, four years old in 1912. She had essentially no recollection of the disaster, but her humor and her zest for life made her my personal favorite among *Titanic* survivors I have known. We had numerous discussions about the equipment Jim Powell and I had designed for raising large, fragile objects (including the *Titanic*) from the sea floor. Of course, no actual funding was in effect, and "Lou" seemed to take great pleasure in shouting, across a crowded room, double entendres about why I had not yet managed to "get it up" for her. (Well, I *think* she was talking about the *Titanic*.) At the May 1992 Titanic International Convention she was still able to outpace me, and I was thoroughly convinced that by 1993 she would become the first survivor to actually visit the *Titanic* in a submersible. As always, we talked about the possibility of raising the *Titanic*, and she wrote on my menu, "Charlie, if you don't get it up soon I won't get to see it." We both had a good laugh; the joke seemed never to wear thin. What I did not know—what even the pace of her walk did not betray—was that she was already far advanced into lung cancer, and had only a few weeks to live.

I miss you, Lou.

* * *

Assistant Purser Frank Prentice, in an undated account prior to the first Ballard expedition, said he always dreamed of seeing the *Titanic* found and raised: "She's in one of the deepest parts of the ocean, but if they ever get it up, I'd like to see her come through the water again." His eyes filled with tears as he said this. "I've had a lot of [harrowing sea] experiences during my life," he continued. "Two World Wars. Badly shattered right arm. Another wound in the leg. And all anyone wants to know about is the *Titanic*."

Steward Frederick Dent Ray, who, overcome by guilt for having convinced Washington Dodge to sail on the *Titanic*, consequently kicked him overboard into one of the last lifeboats, was feeling apologetic for the kick when he met Dr. Dodge aboard the *Carpathia*. Ray then had in his pocket a menu ("put there when clearing the dinner table and should have been put in the receptacle for garbage over the side, but remained to become a museum piece") and two silver salt spoons. The doctor insisted on dividing between them the small amount of currency that had survived in his pocket. Ray recalled, "as he had been so generous, I could make some little return in offering them [the menu and the spoons] to him as a memento." He always wondered if Dr. Dodge had kept them, and was glad to have the mystery solved when Walter Lord published a photograph of the menu in *A Night to Remember*.

"I am sorry that I can't find a memento for *you*," the ever-polite Ray wrote to Walter Lord in 1956, "but you have 'A Night to Remember.' What do you want better than that?" He went on to explain that he had never meant to walk off the ship with the items; they came to be in his pocket because in clearing the table, depositing the menu in the garbage dump bag, and the spoons in the sideboard drawer, would have meant walking the length of the room. Before he could finish the table, the iceberg intervened.

* * *

George Rheims, who undeniably made one of the *Titanic*'s most harrowing escapes to boat A, was wrongly labeled "the man who got off dressed as a woman." His niece, Mrs. D. H. Patterson Knight, noted that the label became so pervasive as to result in her uncle's name being listed, at Norfolk's Maritime Museum as, among those saved—*Mrs.* George Rheims. The story, naturally, had a rather depressing effect on the rift Mr. Rheims was trying to mend with his in-laws at the time the *Titanic* sank. George Rheims' wife had eloped with him, marrying against her family's wishes. Her mother and her brother were beginning to soften their position in April, 1912, and when the new Mrs. Rheims heard that her brother, Joe Loring, was planning a New York sailing at the same time as George, she convinced him to sail with her husband aboard the *Titanic*, to plead the newlyweds' cause with the family.

According to Mrs. Knight, George Rheims had told her when she was a young girl, "He and my father [Joe Loring] had gone on deck after dinner; it was very cold, and my father went to his stateroom and came back with a coat. It was then that they saw the berg. My father remarked that he wouldn't survive two seconds in that cold water, and said good-bye, and the last George saw of him was as he stepped into the companionway."

Mrs. Knight's grandparents became even more bitter: Not only had their son-in-law eloped with—*stolen*—their daughter, not only had this unworthy pair subsequently coaxed their son into sailing on the *Titanic*, but as the newspapers told it, George had let poor Joe go to his death while managing to save his own skin by aid of a hidden talent for cross-dressing at short notice.

"My grandfather refused to see either of them again," said Knight. "But my grandmother accepted them after [Grandpa] died."

* * *

Marjorie Newell Robb and the Third Class seemed galaxies apart, but Marjorie became "diseased with grief" the moment the stern disappeared, and diseased with "survivor's guilt" when she understood what she had seen happening to people in the third-class cabins. For seventy-four years she rarely spoke about the *Titanic.* Then, in 1986, she saw the video Bob Ballard had shot, and heard the explorer speaking about how it had felt to be in a submarine on the decks of the *Titanic.* Simultaneously, Marjorie and at least two other survivors mouthed the same words at their television sets: "*On* the *Titanic?* You were only near the *Titanic.* I was *on* the *Titanic.*"

Weeks later, Marjorie made a pilgrimage to a cemetery in Litchfield, England. She stood under the memorial that served as a marker for Captain Edward J. Smith, and as she stood on that spot, she heard music, "as though it came from near and far, both at once," and she was certain she had heard it on the boat deck, that cold April night . . . an Irving Berlin tune . . . "*One o'clock in the morning I get lonesome . . .* "

She began talking to people, then, talking about how she remembered some of the lowermost lights going off, then on again; but much of the night they just seemed to go off, and to stay off, along the decks she knew to be Third Class forward and Third Class aft.[1]

---

[1]Lily Potter, a passenger in boat seven (which departed about 12:50 A.M.), corroborated Marjorie's account: "At first the windows and portholes of all the decks were alight, but it was not long before the lower deck lights were extinguished suddenly." Third-class Steward Leo James Hyland noted that from boat eleven (which departed about 1:25 A.M.) he could see rows of porthole lights going out in his part of the ship, he presumed because water had reached the fuse boxes. Interestingly, witnesses on the *Californian* also noticed (probably for various reasons including ice eclipses) "some strange light activity" and tried to convince themselves that the *Titanic* was really a small tramp steamer, on account of its doused lights.

Looking back, Marjorie realized that "being privileged had everything in the world to do with being alive. There was always something really odd about first-class passengers. They had different ways. They never looked over to Third Class, not even at the worst moments. They were apart. Those in the third-class area had the lights turned off on them. In Third Class you had *no* light, but in First Class you had all the light you wanted. Money talked. In the darkness, the passengers in Third Class could not find their way out. They couldn't see anything at all. The women and the children were trapped in the dark. They were screaming. It was the single most callous, inhumane act. The image of the gallant officers saving all the women and children—it is a falsehood. A complete falsehood."

Six years after breaking her silence, Marjorie Newell Robb died—in 1992, at the age of 104.

Every April, the U.S. Coast Guard flies over the site of the *Titanic*'s sinking and drops a wreath of red and white carnations. That year, they released a second wreath. It held a container bearing (and scattering) Marjorie's ashes. It was her last wish that she be returned to the *Titanic*. Two and one half miles below, the sea reduced her ashes to a very dilute broth, and the currents mixed her atoms impartially with those of little Frankie Goldsmith from the third class cabins.

Morgan Robertson claimed, after the *Titanic* sank, that his visions of the future came from a "muse," an impish little creature who visited him regularly. By 1913, the "muse" had stopped coming and he began drinking heavily, telling friends that he planned to "live fast, die young, and leave behind a good-looking corpse." As "prophesized," he lived fast and died young, but his corpse, displaying the ravages of alcoholism, was not very good-looking.

* * *

Captain Arthur Rostron, when he spoke to Captain Barr of the *Coronia* (one of the rescue ships that warned the *Titanic* of icebergs) about his race through the dark at the helm of the *Carpathia*, recalled, "When day broke and I saw the ice I had steamed through during the night, I shuddered, and could only think that some other hand than mine was on that helm during the night."

In a letter dated February 7, 1956, Arnold Robert recalled for Walter Lord, "In March 1918, I sailed off to war on the *Mauretania*, making her first trip to Europe with American troops. As the ship left New York harbor, the captain gathered all the American officers in the library and began, 'Gentlemen, I am not anticipating trouble, but in the event of an emergency, I shall expect every one of you to do his utmost.' The speaker was Captain Arthur H. Rostron."

Rusticles have begun to teach us that when we look down at our hands, we must begin to consider that what we believe to be our cells might actually have originated as collections of bacteria (with the admission of "useful" protozoans into the club as they became available, some millions of years later), and that our cells might not truly be ours at all. Continuing research reveals that the rusticle immune system, though primitive, is very effective at combating rapidly dividing, invasive cells "unwelcome" in the consortium, leading now toward the development of new medicines to combat antibiotic-resistant bacteria and cancer. By acting as a gathering place (or culture medium) for these organisms, the *Titanic* might, nearly a century after striking the iceberg—and in a way that shipbuilder Thomas Andrews could never have anticipated—save many more lives than she claimed. I sometimes wish I could reach back across time and tell this to Mr. Andrews. In the end, he saw only that his creation was tearing itself apart and becoming a killer—never guessing that from this terrible end, nearly a hundred years later, might come tens of thousands, perhaps even millions of new beginnings. Some of my more spiritual friends (among them a Jesuit) have said, "It's okay, Charles. He probably knows."

Editor William T. Stead, who was last seen in the *Titanic*'s first-class smoking room, had published a fictional tale in the Christmas edition of the 1892 *Review of Reviews*, in which he depicted the real-life Captain Edward J. Smith pulling half-frozen people out of the water in the aftermath of a collision with an iceberg. Some eyewitnesses did in fact claim to have seen Captain Smith in the water trying to rescue people after the ship went down, although the most credible testimony (while the ship was still well lighted) suggests that he met his end on the bridge. Oiler Walter Hurst recalled that when he reached the overturned collapsible B, Lightoller handed him an oar and told him to row clear of the swimmers before their float became overcrowded. "But I could do nothing about it," he told Walter Lord. "There was one man quite near us. He had the voice of authority. Kept cheering us with, 'Good boy! Good lads!' I reached an oar out to help him but he was too far gone. As it touched him, he turned about like a cork and was silent." There was no doubt in Hurst's mind that the man was Captain Smith. Less credible accounts have William Stead and Captain Smith walking together outside a men's club in Boston some three or four months after the sinking, both with vacant expressions on their faces. Smith sightings continued for decades beyond what would have ordinarily been his life span, proving that these sorts of urban myths were nothing new by the time Elvis died.

*   *   *

Edwina Troutt, who approached every catastrophe in her life, subsequent to the *Titanic*, with the words, "I've seen worse," died at the age of 100, only a few months before the *Titanic* was discovered. When asked by a reporter for her secret to longevity, she replied, "I drink plenty of whiskey and keep late hours."

George Tulloch (along with the rest of R.M.S. Titanic Incorporated's management) was removed by a "hostile takeover" on November 26, 1999. Owing to the fact that SOST was, at that time, one of Wall Street's most under-valued stocks, an estimated investment of $2 million earned a small consortium of shareholders 51 percent own-ership and also gave them legal possession of recovered ar-tifacts valued at a quarter billion dollars. With the Ballard and the Tulloch eras receding into history, the ultimate fate of the *Titanic* becomes a story for another time.

The Zooplankton Crisis, when first recognized during the *Titanic* 1996 expedition of the *Ocean Voyager* (a rebuilt and renamed ice breaker, originally christened *Pandora II*), represented an approximately fourfold increase in the amount of deep-ocean "sea snow" (organic debris consist-ing primarily of the dead bodies of copepods and other mi-croscopic animals).

The primary cause of a massive bloom of animal plank-ton in the upper half mile of the ocean, much of it falling to the bottom uneaten after dying of natural causes (i.e., "old age"), appears to be the removal of 90 percent of the North Atlantic fish population. With 90 percent of the zooplank-ton's natural predators gone, a plankton bloom seems the likely if not inevitable outcome.

The zooplankton feed primarily on one-celled plants (called phytoplankton). As for the North Atlantic, so for the South Atlantic, and the South China Sea, and the Mediterranean, and the Pacific. For two years following the 1996 expedition, the proposal that overfishing might set in motion a biological chain reaction that could lead to overgrazing of phytoplankton around the world was ignored as "rubbish . . . the stuff of science fiction." Warnings that it was the phytoplankton—those top few inches of the ocean surface, and not the Amazon rain forest that removed carbon dioxide from the atmosphere, and that the "greenhouse effect" may be real, but not for the reasons anyone believed (and that it may be coming sooner than anyone believed, bringing with it shifting trade winds and more energetic hurricanes and tornadoes than we have ever seen before), were ignored as "too speculative" and "lacking clear scientific proof."

Then, in the summer of 1998, an ocean surveillance satellite detected the first tentative clues of phytoplankton declines in the Atlantic, Pacific, and Indian Oceans, and under the North Pacific, the deep-ocean snowstorm itself was found to be in decline (by more than 50 percent) in apparent association with higher sea-surface temperatures.

That very same summer, the *Ocean Voyager* went back to the *Titanic* with forty aboard and a lifeboat capacity for twenty-five . . . while unusual shifts of the jet stream and trade winds produced a forecast that some of the season's hurricanes were bound to shoot north, toward the Grand Banks and the *Ocean Voyager*, and they were growing more energetic than in previous years.

And monitoring equipment designed to record changes in the deep-ocean "snow"—to assess whether or not there existed "clear scientific proof"—stayed unfunded and ashore because there was no room for, or serious interest in, the study of biological chain reactions and possible connections to global warming.

And carbon dioxide increased its content in the earth's atmosphere by more than 2 percent in only three years.

And the temperature of the earth was ratcheted up ever so slightly.

And the polar ice caps shrank a little bit faster.

And hurricanes grew noticeably stronger.

And the band played on . . .

Titanic Expedition List

1985 Woods Hole Oceanographic Institute/Infremer, French-American expedition: discovery of the *Titanic* made by the research vessel *Knorr* using the robot *Argo*.

1986 Woods Hole Oceanographic Institute/National Geographic, American expedition: first landings on the *Titanic* using the submersible *Alvin*. First photographic reconnaissance of debris field and stern section. First robotic penetration of *Titanic*'s interior using the robot *Jason Jr.*

1987 Infremer, French-American expedition: first recovery of artifacts from debris field using the submersible *Nautile*.

1991 Soviet Navy/IMAX, Russian-American expedition: high-resolution filming expedition using submersibles *Mir I* and *Mir II*. First attempt to collect and identify strange invertebrate fauna living near the *Titanic*.

1993 Infremer, French-American expedition: further recovery of artifacts; first exploration of mail room, crew quarters, cargo hold, and Marconi shack using the robot *Robin*.

1994 Infremer, French-American expedition: recovery of diaries and other paper items preserved in sealed (but rapidly decaying) containers in the debris field.

1995 Lightstorm/Soviet Navy, American-Russian expedition: filming for aiding of authentic set construction and shooting of actual interior footage used in James Cameron's *Titanic*. Most notable engineering accomplishment: conversion of a "prop" into a tiny robotic camera that, launched from the submersible *Mir I*, penetrated deeper into the ship's interior and (at a fraction of the cost) functioned far better than any robot the U.S. or Soviet navies had designed.

1996 Infremer, French-American expedition: first recovery of live rusticles on the *Titanic*'s hull plates (affectionately dubbed by Roy Cullimore as "The Rusticle Park Expedition"). First cruise ships arrive at site, bringing tourists to observe a scientific expedition in progress. First test of TV images converted to sound waves for live broadcast through 2.5 miles of water.

1998 Infremer, French-American expedition: first test of high-resolution, live global broadcast capability using the robot *Magellan* and a fiber-optic link. First successful raising of a three-story-tall hull section from the sea floor.

1998 Soviet Navy: first expedition to bring paying tourists on overnight "camping trips" to the *Titanic*'s boat deck, aboard the submersibles *Mir I* and *Mir II*.

1999   Soviet Navy: *Mir I* and *Mir II*. Ten dives, some with paying passengers. The fare for "campers" was $35,000.

2000   Russian-American expedition: recovery of 860 artifacts from *Titanic* debris field by restructured RMS Titanic Inc.

2001   Soviet Navy: *Mir I* and *Mir II* with deep-penetrating robots; photography of previously unexplored rooms, including close-up views of fish and crabs sheltering amongst the broken but still gleaming tiles of the *Titanic*'s swimming pool and Turkish baths.

Future expeditions planned by James Cameron are aimed primarily at scientific research. James Cameron and his brother Mike are designing a new generation of smaller, cheaper, deeper-penetrating robots. Before his 1999 removal from the board of R.M.S. Titanic Inc., George Tulloch had expressed a desire to bring only scientists to the *Titanic*, with little or no media "circus" activity (which wreaked havoc on the 1985 and 1996 expeditions). By 1996, the most notable difference between expeditions of the 1980s and the 1990s was that during the Ballard expeditions one could sail into the middle of the ocean and be so completely cut off from the world that an entire continent could disappear and an expedition ship might never know of it until a passing vessel relayed the news or the right satellite rose above the horizon. Ten years later, it was impossible ever to know such peace again. The world was, from pole to pole, an uninterrupted membrane of satellite-aided human thought. It was possible to lose an entire morning of research to answering e-mail queries. Even lawyers were able to reach over the horizon, and send unwelcome faxes.

Before satellite television became available at sea, after-dinner entertainment was largely limited to videotape. For trivia enthusiasts, the most popular movies during the (American) Ballard expeditions were *Ghost Busters, Beverly Hills Cop, Star Trek III, The Emerald Forest*, and *Rear Window*. The most frequently watched films during the (French) Tulloch expeditions were *Aliens, 2001*, and *Terminator II*.

Postscript

Roy's Epiphany

When I coined the term *immunogenetics* in the 1980s, it was only science fiction. Now it is mainstream science: Simply find a "useful" substance (i.e., a new wonder drug) produced by one organism or another, locate the gene that produces the substance, plug it into another organism that can replicate it in large quantities and, if you have done your homework, you might earn yourself a biological Xerox machine with a patent on it.

My own immune system had led me in this direction. By the time I sailed with Roy Cullimore in 1996, geneticists and physicians understood that the aberrant gene complex that rendered me vulnerable to certain viruses against which the rest of humanity was born immune also served as one of nature's strongest prophylactics against cancer. People who carry (and express) the *a.s.* genes have unusually high levels of various immune-system signaling compounds running in their veins, among them interleukin 2 and interleukin 12. By the summer of 1996, scientists had already tricked *E. coli* bacteria into producing these same substances, and were already using them to successfully treat certain cancers. The problem, I explained to Roy, was that bacteria mutated too quickly (when regarded in human time frames)—which required new, human-enzyme-producing bacteria to be created daily. This was not only expensive but potentially dangerous because, as wiser men than I had said, life had a way . . . of finding a way. And so a Florida cornfield's fructose production declined ever so slightly on account of human-insulin-producing bacteria that had undoubtedly escaped from a laboratory. In the Carolinas, a tobacco plant that glowed at night was traced back to an experiment involving the transfer of lightning-bug genes to a plant-infecting microbe.

I told Roy that glowing or even sugar-deficient plants were not likely to threaten anyone—"but if you play this game a thousand, or a hundred thousand times over, you begin to play dice with the biosphere."

"I hope we don't create a molecular *Titanic*," Roy said grimly.

And I agreed that there simply had to be a better way than to take risks with bacteria. I had with me a letter describing a recent experiment in which multiple copies of a gene responsible for the production of a specific human enzyme were injected into cow embryos, where they had been incorporated, perfectly functional and seemingly with no effort at all, into the cow's developing milk glands. In a process far easier than anyone had anticipated, a desired substance might literally be bottled in the milk of a cow or a goat. The ease with which this might be accomplished hinted to me of the high level of bio-computation that must lie hidden in our DNA.[1]

---

[1]Several clues, including the incredible rapidity with which an Ebola virus had broken out of the jungle and adapted to its human hosts (killing most of the first generation of those infected, yet inexplicably becoming benign in the fourth generation of those infected even before the first generation was disabled and dying, before natural selection could account for the change) hinted that DNA could, on some as yet poorly understood level, behave like a well-written computer program that responds to feedback from its surroundings by something very much like the projection (and selection) of probability curves. Impossible; and yet it began to look as if computer scientists, as their programs increased in complexity, were unknowingly replicating what nature had accomplished hundreds of millions of years ago. At

I then told Roy about a family in Italy who lived on a high-fat diet yet had perfectly clean arteries; about people who seemed to age 30 to 50 percent slower than the rest of us; about how certain genes might eventually be bought from such individuals on a royalty-paying basis and bottled in the milk of cloned goats.

"Goats," I explained, "if they ever get out of the lab, have no chance of becoming a spreading infection." (I added, "This at once eliminates both the bacterial hazard and the problem of permanent 'gene therapy' in humans.")

My solution to the problem of playing dice with bacteria seemed to horrify Roy more than the original problem.

And yet, two and one half miles beneath our feet, a whole new set of genes, producing a whole new set of "desirable substances," was waiting for us.

There is an old expression in the pharmaceutical industry about where to look for a new drug, which goes as follows: "If you're prospecting for a new antibiotic or a new anticancer agent, go where no one has gone before and look for something primitive, blobby, brown, and ugly—the blobbier and the uglier, the better."

The *Titanic*'s rusticles fit the bill perfectly: Blobby, brown, and primitive, they had never seemed to anyone except Roy and me worthy of the word "beautiful." As a living example of how multicellular life began, the premise that the rusticle's immune system (in the absence of spe-

---

the bottom of all this, the human genome began to resemble, more and more, a very elaborate CD-ROM or DVD program. For decades, geneticists and evolutionary biologists had been thinking of DNA as the hardware, but I'm afraid we've had it backward all along: It's really the software. This has led to an idea that makes me very unpopular, as of late, with some of my colleagues. A major difference between a DVD program and a program for someone's genome is that each human program is unique. Smash a copy of *Citizen Kane*, and there are a million more copies left in the world. Smash the program that is you, and there are no more—and herein lies the unpopular part: If DNA is the software, then the program for every human being, cialized hunter-killer cells) would rely upon chemical defenses was both simple and obvious. With such grace would they ward off invading cells that did not contribute to the consortium. With such grace did they begin to fall into that mythical land of "intellectual property."

Later, at Roy's laboratory in Regina, though at least some of the rusticle's cells must have failed to survive the raising, drying, and subsequent rehydration (thus complicating our research), the remainder of the consortium was able to generate chemicals with antimicrobial properties—antibiotics—and apparently several different "flavors" of them. Additionally, we knew that scrapings from a bacterial mat in a New Mexico cave had yielded a new anti-cancer agent. "As above, so below," I suggested. What was unique about the rusticles, what separated them from a bacterial mat or a penicillin mold was that their chemicals were the synthesis of a whole group of bacteria, fungi, and apparently even archaea working together to protect their consortial "homeland." And they did so prodigiously. Even the water that flowed out of the rusticles, when Roy examined it for microbial activity, qualified in its own right as an antibiotic.

And then, a question: to patent or not to patent?

---

written in DNA and ready to be performed by protein, exists in the first diploid cell of the yet to be born. To say that the human program exists from the moment of conception has gained me a reputation for piety, but I am stubbornly agnostic and when I agree with the pious it seems only a coincidence born of cold science . . . the same sort of cold science that left me, by an unexpected turn of events, in possession of a half dozen frozen human embryos and a legal option only to leave them frozen or to destroy them. How could I ever do the latter, given what science teaches me? Or what my heart teaches me? When I am at play with my children—my adored sacred children—I know that it is only by the luck of the draw that it is not Kyle or Kelly who sleeps in a pool of liquid nitrogen tonight. It's only technology, we try to say. It's only science. And when most of us were born, many of our dilemmas were only science fiction.

"People who love and perhaps even worship technology often forget humanity," I had said. "The *Titanic* never lets you forget." Had the first rusticles been raised from anywhere except the *Titanic*, Roy and I might simply have written a patent covering all possible claims arising from the rusticle immune system, passed it to a lawyer who would translate it into legal jargon, and line up research money and grants.

"But this patent is different from any of the others you or I have written," Roy wrote to me, late in the fall of 1999. "Here is the very considerable potential to fight disease, perhaps even to fight cancer. And is it nobler in the minds of scientists to grasp at a property as a 'cash cow' for instant research moneys and long-term royalties? Or is it better to simply notice the phenomenon, report it, and walk away?"

Over the telephone, Roy sounded very tired, almost defeated. During the three years following the expedition, some of our colleagues had expressed such jaundiced opinions about the very idea of a consortial lifeform—"the 3.5-billion-year-old living fossil"—that they recommended against the publication of our findings in several scientific journals, even though a fossil displaying all the major anatomical features of the *Titanic*'s rusticles was subsequently found by Australian paleontologists, in rocks dating back 3.5 billion years ago. Arthur C. Clarke tried to comfort us with his observation of the four stages through which any new idea must pass these days: (1) You're crazy! (2) You may be right, so what? (3) We knew it was a good idea all along. (4) I thought of it first!

Roy sounded too tired to appreciate the joke, and I, too, was beginning to feel tired. We had already weathered legal battles with distant relatives. (They suddenly saw dollar signs in the *Titanic*. Sweet dollar signs.) Distractions from legal eagles had actually delayed some of our early research. Indeed, we were at least a year behind schedule, and we both understood that if the rusticles ever did yield up new medicines, they might come a year too late for people who weren't even sick yet. This realization weighed heavier on us with each passing week.[2]

On October 26, 1999, Roy wrote: "I'm afraid we have not seen the end of legal jackals. Of greed. In the past, I have witnessed the arrogance, worried about the ignorance, and all I could see was a pack of lawyers waiting to feed at the trough . . . You know what they will do with the rusticle drugs, if they work (and this is still a great 'if,' requiring further research). They will isolate individual substances without looking at the whole (and it may be that the rusticle secretions work best as a complex). The plan is to attach a methane to one corner of each useful molecule—their way of stamping a patent on it. And as they develop and market each new medicine, will they give any thought to making it affordable to those who cannot stand up on their own?

"This patent, I will not complete. Instead, it has been thrown in the waste bin without even being submitted. No,

---

[2]Thus far, the American legal system has spent millions of dollars on such matters as ruling "officially" that Bob Ballard and Woods Hole Oceanographic Institute did not discover the *Titanic*. The judge involved refused even to acknowledge that the 1985 and 1986 expeditions ever took place, nor did he consider that *National Geographic* had produced a documentary featuring the Ballard expeditions. In another court, precedent was being set for charging any journalist or scientist who credited the discovery to Ballard with "plagiarizing" the discovery for oneself. On June 23, 1998, a Norfolk district judge issued an injunction indefinitely prohibiting "all the world from entering a 168-square [nautical] mile area of the high seas encompassing the *Titanic* for any reason." As this area was still a major international shipping lane, the ruling was overturned on appeal. Meanwhile, the court ordered U.S. marshals to "arrest" the *Titanic* itself, but the U.S. Navy did not assist. All of this seems very confusing, at least to a mind so "uneducated" in law and so simple as mine. What I do know is that Gilbert and Sullivan would have loved it.

Charles, at my time of life I do not need the squalid crush
of greed. I do not want a patent that would be abused. For
all you and I now know, I have walked away not from a
gold mine of adulation and praise but from a hornet's nest
of greed. People may read this and say, 'He's crazy! I'm
going to steal that idea and become rich.' But then again
some may begin to see that we, as a society, will only ma-
ture when we stop playing the role of God and begin to
harmonize with the complex world of nature that surrounds us. If we don't, then that same complex world will
surely drown us in the seas of ignorance."

I did not know quite how to answer his faxes. I knew
that some people might indeed say Roy was crazy, but I
knew also that I could not fault his argument and that I was
feeling much the same way myself (and for some reason, I
kept thinking at this time of Thomas Andrews, wondering
what he would be thinking were he able to look on). I decided finally that Roy and I had started this together, and if
we were not going to finish it together, we would end together and pass the baton to someone else.[3] To move ahead
without him would have felt like taking credit for work that
was at least half Roy's; and to put it simply, it felt wrong.
So I threw in my hat with Roy, and he replied, "It could be
said that seeing the Royal Mail Steamer *Titanic* changed
me forever. That ship, so big, so bold, so fast, so certain,
now lies crumpled on the sea floor. Of all that we have
done, of the sciences thought and the dreams held, it is the
R.M.S. *Titanic* that is now the teacher, and are we prepared
to learn? We have to learn from the silence of the deeps and
recognize that the disaster that befell the *Titanic* could be
repeated again through that lethal cocktail of arrogance

---

[3]You needn't go to the *Titanic* for rusticles. Any iron-rich object lying more
than two miles below the sea will serve as a good culture medium. We have
seen them sprouting out of the top of Gus Grissom's capsule, and on the
hull of the WWII submarine I-52.

and ignorance with just the right dash of greed over ice. Science will go on and the arts will flourish if society matures to prevent such a disaster from happening on an infinitely larger scale."

Most people, even archaeologists, fail to notice that there is no shortage of dead ships and dead cities to be explored. The majority of these sites memorialize sane voices that were ignored or intimidated into silence by know-it-alls who demonstrated time and again that we, as a species, are capable of colossal stupidity. Those of us who dream of throwing open the doors to the genetic frontier, or to the frontiers of space, might pay heed to Roy's warning.

Acknowledgments, Notes, and Selected Sources

As with every book I have ever written, or ever will write, my first thanks go to Mom, Dad, Adelle Dobie, Barbara and Dennis Harris—five very special teachers and guides who helped me to beat the odds. ("Autistic" was one of the words commonly used to describe me in those days.) When experts predicted that the "ride the shockwave," school-hating little boy who loved Darwin and Beethoven and failed the I.Q. test would never be able to read books (much less to write them), my five teachers encouraged me to regard the predictions as a challenge. As I entered my teenage years, two other extraordinary teachers (Agnes Saunders and Ed McGunnigle of the Nassau County 4-H Club) emphasized the same lesson: Don't take proclamations from highest authority as unassailable facts. It turned into a valuable lesson, more than a decade later, when experts claimed that I would never again walk. So I stiffened my spine (literally) and learned to run.

The *Titanic* herself has become, in a strange and unpredictable way, another of my teachers. Anyone who has read my previous book on this subject will recall how she, and her survivors, helped me to understand and accept loss (and it is the ability to accept loss and to move on, according to some of my longest-lived acquaintants, that best explains their extreme longevity). And still at night, always late at night, she awakens my sense of mystery, and chills my bones. And the coincidences—they know no end. As the spring of 1996 passed and I prepared for a return to the *Titanic*, I was planning to meet the next French-American expedition in the Azores after a brief stop in France to re-examine some rusticle-damaged metal. The plan began to unravel in early July when my wife told me she was in love with someone else and wanted a divorce. At the time, I could not imagine many things worse in the entire world happening to me. I remember walking down to the beach and wondering how the night could possibly get any darker. I then scrubbed my plan—TWA One to France (the same path I always took to France): Flight 800.

About two weeks later, I was standing on the beach with my little girl when the plane in which I should have been seated passed overhead and, as it neared the horizon, exploded.

How could the night possibly get any darker? I had asked, never guessing, during my pity party for one, that what served for the moment as the defining tragedy of my life was in fact saving me from a rather broader definition of tragedy.

So, I dusted myself off and went to the *Titanic*. And, as always, she had lessons to teach.[1] What many might expect to be the most disappointing lesson of each new expedition is actually one of archaeology's great excitements. We are continually proving our previous conclusions wrong—a case in point being the Grand Stairway. The first robot reconnaissance in 1985 showed what appeared to be deck-wood intact, and all the wood of the *Titanic* was therefore assumed to be "in pristine condition." The 1986 expedition

---

[1] After I returned from the *Titanic*, former Apollo engineer and Grumman President (Ret.) George Skurla asked me if I would take a closer look at the reconstructed wreck of Flight 800. The synchronicity never ends.

revealed that only the tarry caulking remained between vanished strips of deckwood, and the missing Grand Stairway was believed similarly to have undergone a slow, stately disassembly by bacteria and wood-boring mollusks. All other organic material (paper, bone, and olives) was presumed to have disappeared with the stairway, leaving behind only an iron shell. Subsequent expeditions have changed these views dramatically, and are shedding new light on the British and American inquiries.

It happened that while our views were changing and while this book was being written, I was also revising the latest edition of *Her Name, Titanic*, and found myself tempted to correct old interpretations (now proved wrong) dating back to the first two Ballard expeditions. What stopped me from changing anything other than typographical errors or factual inaccuracies in time transitions from the expeditions to the night of the sinking (flashbacks were changed in accordance with new revelations in documents provided by survivors' descendants), was the photograph of Tom Dettweiler and Haraldur Sidurdsson in the *Argo* control van. At one time, that deep-ocean robot control room had seemed to me like a slice cut out of the twenty-first century and flicked backward into the 1980s, but it looked utterly primitive more than a decade later. I realized for the first time that the Ballard expeditions had themselves become historic, and that to "correct" our 1985 and 1986 interpretations would be to remove the story of the first expeditions, somewhat like a diary rewritten, from its true historic context.

At the time of the first expeditions to the world's first deep-ocean archaeological site, we knew more about ancient Roman and Egyptian shipwrecks than we did about the *Titanic* (unlike Roman and Egyptian vessels, the *Titanic* was not accessible in muddy river bottoms, or in royal tombs, and not even a set of proper deck plans was

available to us). The scenes in that first book, though rich
in archival details of survivors' experiences and firsthand
accounts of the discovery and early exploration of the *Titanic*, were necessarily vague on structural details of the
wreck. She was, initially, a misty shape looming out of the
dark. Only later, as we continued to probe and map the debris with submersibles and robots, did the *Titanic*'s features come into focus. In hindsight, I feel that the very
absence of details as we started out in 1985 was exciting
because people who have been reading this odyssey from
its beginnings have been able to participate vicariously in
the process of watching the *Titanic* acquire shape and color.

I therefore elected (rather than to go back and overly re-
vise scenes in *Her Name, Titanic*) to show, in this book,
how our interpretations have changed (and are still changing)—which should provide a real sense of how scientific
understanding is, in fact, an evolving process. My guess is
that I will go on to prove at least 20 percent of what I have
said in this book wrong in my final volume of this trilogy
(planned for 2010–2012). The problem is, I don't know yet
which 20 percent of what I've told you is wrong.

For eyewitness accounts of what was happening on and
around the *Titanic* the night she went down, I have relied
first and foremost upon the lengthy COMMUNICATIONS
FILE made available by Walter Lord, and upon the letters,
diaries, and oral histories made available by the families of
survivors. The Lord/Pellegrino files are presently being reproduced for the National Maritime Museum in London
(where Lord's originals will eventually reside; the Pellegrino originals, including expedition logs and the memoirs
of Helen Churchill Candee, will be housed in Long Island
University's John Steinbeck Project archive). Reproduc-
tion is also planned for the Titanic Historical Society, Titanic International, and for widest possible use, release via
the internet. (www.CharlesPellegrino.com. The first E-

book on this site, *In Their Own Words, Titanic*, has been created as a funding source for Parkinsons disease research.) Some of this material has already been made available—along with the 1912 American and British inquiries and a virtual tour of the ship's reconstructed rooms—in *James Cameron's Titanic Explorer* (Fox Interactive, three CD-ROM set; Lightstorm/Circumstance, 1998).

When I finished the first book in this series, I had said it would probably be the last book written while survivors were still with us and could contribute details. On that, too, I turned out to be wrong. This book has benefited tremendously from the recollections and opinions of Michel Navatril, Jr., Marjorie Newell Robb, Frank Aks, Eva Hart, Millvina Dean, and Louise Pope. I am also grateful for copies of contemporary letters and documents brought forth by the *"Titanic* families," including the estate of Thomas Andrews. Such documents are now reproduced on a regular basis in *The Titanic Commutator* and *Voyage*, published respectively by The Titanic Historical Society and Titanic International.

The Titanic Historical Society and Titanic International have expressed essential differences of opinion over the recovery of artifacts from the wreck site—so essential that the two organizations get along almost as well as Ahab and Moby. I belong to both and, though I tend to consider myself socially inept, I have somehow managed to become one of only two people in all the world (the other is Tom Dettweiler) who sails with members of the various warring factions without getting involved in the politics and becoming "he who sleeps with the fishes."

The undeniable fact of this whole continuing adventure is that if readers want to keep abreast of new discoveries and insights (as well as new leads into the literature), it is necessary to subscribe to journals on both sides of the canyon. You cannot learn about bioarchaeology from the

Titanic Historical Society (which has the better historians) and you won't learn all the history from Titanic International (which has all the biologists and archaeologists). For memberships: THS, P.O. Box 51053, 208 Main Street, Indian Orchard, MA 01151-0053, U.S.A.; TI, P.O. Box 7007, Freehold, N.J. 07728-7007, U.S.A.

The Titanic Historical Society also provides an invaluable service by keeping in print such rare firsthand accounts as Jack Thayer's *Sinking of the S.S. Titanic*, Frank Goldsmith's *Echoes in the Night*, and the complete text of the British and American inquiries (for trivia enthusiasts: the American inquiry was held in Manhattan's old Waldorf Astoria, now the site of the Empire State Building). Among the more notable books by members are Vera and John Gillespie's *The Titanic Man—Carlos F. Hurd* (THS. 1998: how the world first received eyewitness accounts of the disaster from a reporter aboard the *Carpathia*), Bob Ballard's updated *Discovery of the Titanic* (Warner, 1998), *Ken Marschall's Art of the Titanic* (Hyperion, 1998), and Paul J. Quinn's *Titanic at Two* (Fantail Press, Saco, Maine, 1997: the *Titanic*'s final twenty minutes, from a researcher who really did his homework and made an exhaustive study of the British and American inquiries). Notable books by TI members include: Susan Wels' *Titanic* (Time Life, 1997: notes from the French-American expeditions) and Judith Geller's *Titanic—Women and Children First* (W. W. Norton, 1998: This story of *Titanic*'s women is a treasure chest of previously unpublished accounts). Walter Lord, a member of both THS and TI, wrote the book that resurrected *Titanic*'s memory in 1955 and elevated it to a social icon. His 1986 sequel, *The Night Lives On* is, along with the others mentioned here, a good lead into the extensive literature on this unsinkable subject. For an introduction to the legal battles over the *Titanic*, see D.G. Conacannon, Esq., in the

Jan/Feb 2000 issue of *Underwater Magazine—Association of Diving Contractors International.*

For recollections of survivors's stories told to him during the filming of *A Night to Remember* (including the incredible account of Alfred White), I am very grateful to Bill MacQuitty, who saved, amongst other treasures, a letter from Alfred White to the brother-in-law of his friend Mr. Parr, who died in the turbine room.

For wide-ranging conversations spanning several years and most of the subjects encountered in this book, thanks are also due to: Father Bob McGuire and Rabbi Zuscha Freedman (both salt of the earth), Jim Powell (Brookhaven National Laboratory), Cyril Ponnamperuma, Sir Arthur C. Clarke (University of Moratura, Sri Lanka), Jesse A. Stoff (Solstice), Bill Schutt (American Museum of Natural History/LIU: friend to vampire bats, he identified mammalian bones from the soup tureen concretion), Edward I. Coher (a natural resource, LIU), Sandra Schumway (LIU: friend to the dinoflagellate from hell), Joshua Lederberg (Rockefeller University), Edward O. Wilson (Pellegrino University Professor at Harvard), Stephen Jay Gould (friend to snails and worms), Henrietta Mann (St. Mary's University, Halifax), Roy Cullimore (Droycon Bioconcepts and friend to bacterial sludge), Tom Dettweiler (Nauticos Corp), Fred Haise, George Skurla (Northrop/Grumman), General Tom Stafford (USAF/NASA), Scott Carpenter (NASA/U.S. Navy Deep Submergence), James Cameron (Lightstorm: friend to deep-ocean robots and Terminators), Jack Dawson (NASA/JPL: friend to the Mars Global Surveyor), THE Don Peterson, William N. Lange, Bob Ballard, Cindy van Dover, Ralph Hollis, David Sanders, John Salsig, Paul Tibbets (Woods Hole Oceanographic Institute), Ken Marschall (THS), Ed Bishop, Doug McLean (Smith Barney), William Garzke (Gibbs and Cox), Tony Jordan

(MIA), Vera Gillespie, Tom Vaccina, Dorothy Luftig, Susan Paxton, Mark Newman (Sonar), Lenny P. (here's looking at you, squid), George Tulloch, Matt Tulloch, Arnie Geller, Captain Paul Henry Narnageolet, Rhonda Wozmiak, Stephane Pennec, Ken and Karl Olson, Sharon Rutman, Jack Eaton, and Alex Lindsay (RMS Titanic, Inc.). Special thanks to Mary Lee Young, who wishes I would get off this subject already and move on to Mars. (Or is that move *to* Mars?)

Finally, I am indebted to my slave drivers (I mean, to my agent and my editors)—Russ Galen, Zach Schisgal, Jennifer Brehl, and John Douglas—and, yes, guys, I'll be back when I have a better story to tell. The "gray lady" has a way of drawing me back even when I resolve to stay away. How can I not weaken again? The tale of the *Titanic* has all the wondrous horror of a Greek tragedy penned by God with Shakespeare as his muse. And it will never be fully told.

Index

Page numbers in *italics* refer to illustrations